TRIGGER TIME

By Mick Flynn

Bullet Magnet
Trigger Time

TRIGGER TIME

MICK FLYNN CGC MC

with Will Pearson

PHOENIX

A PHOENIX PAPERBACK

First published in Great Britain in 2011
by Orion Books
This paperback edition published in 2012
by Phoenix,
an imprint of Orion Books Ltd,
Orion House, 5 Upper St Martin's Lane,
London WC2H 9EA

An Hachette UK company

1 3 5 7 9 10 8 6 4 2

ISBN 978-0-7538-2815-1

Typeset by Input Data Services Ltd,
Bridgwater, Somerset

Printed and bound by CPI Group (UK) Ltd,
Croydon, CR0 4YY

Contents

LIST OF ILLUSTRATIONS

MAPS

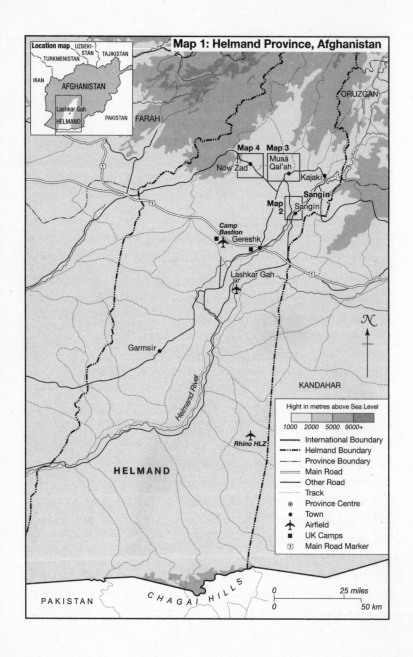

Map 1: Helmand Province, Afghanistan

Location map

UZBEKI-STAN
TURKMENISTAN
TAJIKISTAN
IRAN
AFGHANISTAN
Lashkar Gah
HELMAND
PAKISTAN

ORUZGAN

FARAH

Map 4   Map 3
Now Zad   Musá
Qal'ah   Kajaki

Sangin
Map
2   Sangin

Camp
Bastion
Gereshk

Lashkar Gah

Garmsir

Helmand River

KANDAHAR

Hight in metres above Sea Level
1000 2000 5000 9000+

Rhino HLZ

HELMAND

International Boundary
Helmand Boundary
Province Boundary
Main Road
Other Road
Track
⊙ Province Centre
● Town
✈ Airfield
■ UK Camps
① Main Road Marker

PAKISTAN   CHAGAI HILLS

0   25 miles
0   50 km

N

PROLOGUE

Sometimes in war, you get the chance to get even.

The Taliban had just killed one of my best men. But the way things were shaping up, we'd shortly be able to strike back. Dusk was falling. We were in a reach of land near a loop of the River Helmand, about 20 kilometres north of Forward Operating Base Dwyer, Garmsir district. My senior NCO, Corporal of Horse [CoH] Ben Woollaston had just spotted five men slinking through the tall reeds on the farther bank. They were about 250 metres away, heading for the hamlet that lay a little to the north of a Bedouin encampment. As the group turned in through the big metal gates of a compound, Ben saw that one of them had an AK47 assault rifle badly concealed under his clothing. We knew they were going to attack us, our i/com radio intercept scanners had picked them up saying so. Under the British Army rules of engagement then in force, Ben could have opened fire on the insurgents if he'd seen they were armed before they'd reached the gates. As it was, he'd missed the chance to do so by a second. We sat in the darkness, weapons cocked, staring through the night-sights, and waiting for the enemy to make their move.

We didn't have to wait long. A weird whooshing sound shattered the dead silence. In the same breath, a volley of rocket-propelled grenades speared in at us from the compounds and the reeds lining the river. Travelling at just under 300 metres per second, the RPG-7 warheads fizzed through the warm air, the propellant trailing bright streaks of orange-yellow flame. Two arrowed in at the Jackals. They missed, narrowly, to either side. The third rocket grenade arced skyward, reached the top of its parabola, stalled and began falling back to earth. Then it exploded. Shards of shrapnel spat into the barren terrain all around us, but again we were lucky – no one got hit.

Muzzle flashes rippled from the enemy lines. Another rocket shot past, missing Toddy's Jackal by a whisker. There was no need to give the order: every single member of the troop was already returning fire – except for me. Major Davies was in my usual commander's seat, which meant that he had control of the Jackal's front-mounted 7.62mm general purpose machine gun [GPMG]. The boss was blazing away at the Taliban, firing short, aimed bursts of three or four rounds at a time. Couldn't have done it better myself. And I wanted to be doing it. I got on the radio and sent a contact report to battle group HQ. Deceptively slow, the long, curling gobbets of orange tracer floated out from the muzzle of the Gimpy and thumped into the enemy firing points. I wanted my machine gun back – but I wasn't going to get it.

I grabbed my SA-80 from its stowage position in the door. It was fitted with a UGL [underslung 40mm grenade launcher] and opened fire. I put down a few bursts of 5.56mm, then I pulled up the UGL's sights, tilted the weapon and fired. The grenade made a pop as it launched up into the night sky, then a massive bang as it exploded among the reeds. But there was so much fire going down at the enemy positions, it was impossible to know where my own round had landed.

A new salvo of RPGs whistled past and detonated in the blackness beyond. Two feet above and behind me, Trooper Salmon was hammering away on the 40mm grenade machine gun [GMG]. The rounds were exiting just above my left ear. If I'd stood up, I'd have lost my head. Six inches to my left, the boss was still trying to melt the Gimpy's barrel. Deafened, I waited until he was reloading. Then I leaned and shouted: 'I've sent a contact report – and slow down your rate of fire!'

Major Davies looked across at me. I could see the adrenaline rush in his eyes, which were twice their normal size and staring wide.

The Taliban weren't hanging back when it came to putting down rounds: I heard AK47 bullets whang off the nearest Jackal's side armour. All our crews were firing back with everything they had – .50 cal heavy machine guns, GMGs, SA-80s, GPMGs. Watching fall of shot, I saw Junior Salmon find his range with the GMG, landing a steady stream of 40mm grenades inside one enemy compound after another. Then someone else – either Cox's or Woollaston's gunner – hit three Taliban fighters with a well-aimed burst of GPMG. I saw the men fly backwards and crumple to earth.

Toddy's .50 cal gunner was also on the money: a burst from his weapon exploded in a stand of reeds, spraying lethal packets of red-hot shrapnel out to all sides. The tinder-dry stalks caught at once and began to smoulder. We had to be hurting the Taliban, but the RPGs kept right on coming: another warhead flashed past, exploding to our rear at its maximum fused range. Then a new enemy weapon joined the party, a PKM light machine gun; the deep-throated rattle as it pumped out shells at a rate of more than ten rounds per second unmistakable.

The contact fell into a rhythm of fire and counter-fire. Both sides were putting down a murderous weight of ordnance; but our own fire was better aimed and it was beginning to tell. Toddy's gunner ploughed a new burst of .50 calibre into the reeds. A bright tongue of orange reached up from the heart of the smoke. Then the whole reed bed exploded into a brilliant wall of fire. Sparks and curls of flame spiralled skyward and the sharp tang of burning vegetation carried on the night air. We could see the silhouettes of enemy fighters, flitting through the reeds as they withdrew. We intensified our fire – we had a score to settle. Smoked out, a nest of enemy fighters burst from their hiding place like startled woodcocks, turned and ran up the slope to their rear. Outlined in lethal silhouette against the flames, they stood out plain as targets at a funfair. A dozen weapon systems zoned in on them, knocking the fugitives flat in their tracks. Strike another four Taliban. It wasn't going to bring Magpie back, or in any way make up for his loss – but they'd probably been part of the war band that had killed him. With any luck, we'd nailed the bastard who'd planted the IED.

CHAPTER ONE

Camp Bastion, Afghanistan, June 2006

When we first got there, few of us realized how brutal the Afghan campaign was going to be – or how long it was going to last. A handful of British units had found out the hard way, but for those of us in D Squadron, Household Cavalry [HCR] recently arrived in Camp Bastion, the lack of action was deafening. We'd been hanging around with our safety catches firmly set at 'On' for the best part of two months. And we were starting to get a bit twitchy.

Sitting outside the accommodation pods after scoff one evening, Corporal of Horse Julian 'JC' Moses turned to me and said: 'This is boring. We need to get some trigger time.' I knew exactly how JC felt: the squadron needed to stop messing around with its armoured vehicles and get them out on the ground. The Scimitar came equipped with a very accurate 30mm Rarden cannon and a co-axial 7.62mm GPMG; it was time we put some of that firepower down range and onto the enemy. You don't join the British Army just for the pay. Make that especially not for the pay.

A Bruce Willis lookalike only smaller and without all the muscles, JC had originally joined the Pioneer Corps. But when the powers-that-be decided to amalgamate the Pioneers into the Royal Logistics Corps, JC and another Pioneer, Matthew Hull, had transferred across to the Household Cavalry. JC was a very easygoing bloke: he liked taking the piss and cracking jokes; if he ever left the Army, then he could try for a career as a stand-up comedian. In his dreams.

Now that we were out in theatre, D Squadron had divided into five troops of four vehicles. I was 3 Troop's CoH, or Sergeant equivalent. Lt Tom Long was the troop O.C. [officer commanding]. The Household Cavalry's designated combat role is mobile forward reconnaissance: scouting ahead of the main battle group, spotting the enemy, assessing his strength, disposition and readiness to fight, and picking off targets of opportunity when those presented themselves. But in Helmand province our role was set to change. Lt Tom Long and I reported to the TAC [battle group tactical headquarters] for an operational briefing. The TAC was the usual hive of activity – planning tables jammed in so tight together that it was hard to squeeze between them; throngs of people, most of them officers suffering from a greater or lesser degree of sleep deprivation; maps and lists and notices hanging everywhere; radios and computers; and several screens displaying UAV, satellite and other surveillance down-feeds (otherwise known as 'Kill TV') that were searching for and tracking the enemy. We still had no trade. But it was clear there was plenty of action in the offing.

Before deployment, the squadron had spent six long months training for combat: practising fire fight and anti-improvised explosive device [IED, or booby-trap bomb] routines; honing our gunnery and other weapons skills on the ranges; making our casualty evacuation [CASEVAC] procedures slick and quick; and going through endless scenarios designed to bring the squadron up to the peak of readiness. But now that we'd finally got out to Bastion, they were hitting us with a spell of relentless inactivity, otherwise known as acclimatization. We duly spent the first few weeks adapting to the blistering weather, avoiding sunstroke if possible, sharpening our battle skills and learning more about the enemy threat. But as each day went by and news of contacts between some of the other British units in theatre and the enemy came in, it grew clear that we were not engaged in some glorified nation-building exercise: we were at war.

With regular reports coming in that the IED threat was growing ever more serious and complex, we spent a lot of time in training to detect and clear concealed bombs and booby traps – sweeping for explosive devices with hand-held detectors, or what we called 'barmaring'. For the new conflict, we'd be using the latest Vallon detectors, which were a big improvement on previous types.

The squadron's Scimitar and Spartan armoured vehicles had to be prepped. We had to load the ammunition onto them and fire in the weapons: in the case of the Scimitar, which is a light-armoured vehicle slightly larger than a Range Rover only with a lot more killing power, that meant the cannon and the GPMG. With no turret, the Spartan has generally had to make do with a single GPMG.

The vehicles had been shipped to a Pakistani port in freight containers, and then driven from the port through the Khyber Pass and down to Camp Bastion on the back of jingly trucks – the high-sided, brightly painted lorries that the Afghans use to move heavy goods. Given it was a miracle that the trucks – and our wagons – had survived the journey without getting ambushed, hijacked or blown up, we had to check that the long journey itself hadn't done the armoured vehicles any harm. So it was out on the range to see if the guns still worked, zero them in, make sure the Tactical Navigation and Target Location System [TNTLS – the laser gun sight and ranging system for the 30mm cannon and the onboard Global Positioning System, or GPS] was working and accurate, give the engines a bit of a workout and so on. The TNTLS was the best and most brilliant upgrade to the Scimitar since its introduction to British Army service back in 1971 – once you laid the sight onto a target and lased it for range, then the Rarden would generally hit it. Not only that, but the TNTLS gave an instant GPS fix on a given target, which could then be transmitted by encrypted radio signal to other friendly forces like artillery and air. We played around with the system for a few days until its use became second nature. It was a good new toy, but it wasn't going to keep us amused for ever.

The Scimitar had been fitted with various other upgrades for service in Afghanistan besides the TNTLS: extra mine blast protection, the Bowman radio, an added layer of composite appliqué armour and, in some ways most importantly of all, the anti-RPG-7 'cage' or 'shopping trolley' armour. Welded all round the turrets and hulls to make RPGs [rocket-propelled grenades] explode before they could do any damage to the vehicle or crew, the cage armour was an absolute bugger to fit: getting it onto the wagons kept us busy for several days. For a start, the bolts never wanted to line up with the appropriate holes so we had a hell of a job wrestling it into place. Then the sun made the armour so hot you had to wear gloves to handle it; and once it was fitted, I thought the cage armour made the wagons look ungainly and ugly. But it was very shortly going to save not just my life, but the lives of many others.

What the wagons didn't have was any form of air-conditioning. In a country where high summer temperatures can top 50°C, and with the additional heat of an engine to deal with, things could get a little bit warm inside. But psyched up and raring to go as we were, prepping the wagons was just routine soldiering; as each day went by, the lack of any contact with the enemy was growing more and more frustrating. That sounds a bit gung-ho; but what made us especially keen-edged was the fact that while we kicked our heels in camp, some members of 16 Air Assault Brigade had already been out and taken on the brand-new enemy. One of the lucky people who'd been in a fire fight with the locals was Corporal of Horse [CoH] Shaun Fry, otherwise known as Sizzler.

'Sizzler' Fry and 'JC' Moses – who says the British Army doesn't have a sense of humour?

CHAPTER TWO

Judging by the briefings and reports we were getting, fighting was a way of life for most of Helmand's male population. They fought because they were from a different tribe or members of a different family clan; they fought to protect their interests in the drugs trade; they fought because they believed their religion commanded it; and they fought because the Taliban paid them. After six weeks in Afghanistan, my own impression was a lot of them shared a single aim: the burning desire to kill any foreign soldiers on their home turf.

Another thing that seemed to make the local males go looking for trouble was the majority Pashto-speakers' code of Pashtunwali. Some things about the Pashtunwali code were good. For example, all Pashtuns will go out of their way when it comes to hospitality: they'll feed, house and even clothe a complete stranger, and in some cases they'll even help an enemy in need. But there's another side to the code and that is the whole business of honour. In most parts of Afghanistan, one man only has to look at another man in the wrong way to start a blood-feud. Nine times out of ten, the vendetta spreads through the respective families and from there out into the wider tribal groups. If there's a woman involved in the dispute, the killing gets especially vicious, and the feuding can go on for generations.

*

Life on the Trowbridge housing estate in Cardiff where I'd grown up hadn't been quite as extreme as that but in some ways it had been almost as tribal. And there had been more than enough violence. My mother, Myrna, is Welsh, but my father, Vince, comes from an old Southern Irish Catholic family. Like kids from the other local Catholic families, I attended St Illtyd's Catholic High School in Rumney. Regardless of whether or not I actually believed the Pope always got things right, as far as a lot of the other local youths were concerned I was from a different tribe. That made me a target. There were times when I either had to let myself get bullied, or fight. After the first couple of scraps when I came home the worse for wear, my dad taught me a few moves. Teaching me to fight was his way of showing me love. The next time one of the local bullies tried it on, he got the benefit of my new education.

Sometimes, as in Afghanistan, the fighting on the Cardiff estates was over a woman, usually a woman from a neighbouring area. I mitched off school a few times when I was in my early teens – make that a few dozen times. It was usually because I was trying to avoid maths, or because I hadn't done the homework due in for that day. One time when I was 15, one of my mates had a dental appointment in school hours. I didn't need any of my teeth fixing, but I went along with Billy Dacey to keep him company. While Billy was getting his teeth sorted out, I waited down by the local rubbish dump next to the Rumney River: the truancy officers didn't go down there, it was far too rough.

While I waited for Billy to come back from the dentist, I bumped into a couple of lads who lived on the neighbouring Llanrumney estate. One of them, Curly, was my age – I knew him by sight from St Illtyd's. The other, a lanky kid called Tommo, was a year or two older. He went to Ball Road comprehensive. When I met them, they were both smoking. Curly held out a cigarette. 'Smoke?'

'No thanks – I don't smoke.'

'Why not? You posh or something? What are you doing over by Llanrumney anyway? You still seeing Pat Thomas?'

'Yes,' I said, and immediately realized that there was going to be trouble. Pat was my girlfriend. I'd been seeing her for about three months and she lived on their turf.

Curly said: 'Why don't you fuck off back to Trowbridge?' I knew Tommo fancied Pat, and I also knew she didn't fancy him. Curly was trying to look big in front of his older mate. With that, Curly took a swing at me. He caught me off guard, and his fist hit me on the side of the head. But the blow glanced off. He hadn't hit me hard enough to put me down. My father had taught me well: he'd shown me how to use my fists. I jabbed at Curly's nose with my left, landed a good one and followed up with a few more smacks in the face to keep him busy. Then, when he dropped his arms, I caught him in a headlock, bent him double and punched him in the face with my free hand. We wrestled to the ground, but I still had him in the headlock, and I was still thumping him. But then Curly reached down, grabbed half a brick from the dump, brought it swinging round and connected with my left temple. I saw stars and let Curly go. I stood up, thinking, 'Now would be a good time to fuck off', and started running up the bank. Curly was crouched down and bleeding from the punches I'd laid on him. I had him beaten, but I had an egg on my temple that felt bigger and more painful every time I touched it.

The next night, I'd spent a very pleasant evening at Pat's house. It was about nine o'clock on a February night, cold and dark, and a fine sleet was beginning to come down. I met up with Billy Dacey and a couple of my other mates. We were walking back home through the Llanrumney estate down Ball Road. There was a pub on the right called the Llanrumney Hall, and on the left there were some flats that had recently featured in a documentary about gangs and burglary. There was always a scrap going on outside the pub, caused by some of the local headcases. We were heading for Billy's house, hoping to get a cup of tea and something to eat. Looking up, I saw Curly, Tommo and a couple of their hangers-on walking towards us. Curly was sporting a split lip and a bruise or two. I knew it was going to kick off, but I didn't feel scared. Because I'd legged it from the first fight, Curly and Tommo thought they could have me.

'There they are,' I said. 'There's them two fuckers who attacked me.'

'I know them,' Billy said. 'That's Tommo and Curly, isn't it.'

I was watching the gang of four as they got closer. As we drew level, Curly sneered: 'There you are then, you yellow twat.' I kept my eyes on Curly – but it was Tommo who was fronting me up.

He said: 'I'm going to have you.'

I said, 'It's not you I want to fight – I want to finish off the fight with Curly.' I could see from the look in Curly's eyes that he didn't want to know. Tommo stepped forward. Without thinking, I kicked out. I caught him straight in the solar plexus. I'd never done any martial arts, but I'd winded him with a snap-kick to the gut from the standing position. As he bent towards me, winded, I grabbed hold of Tommo's back hair and kneed him hard in the face twice. Then the red mist came down. If he wanted to scrap then fuck it, I was going to destroy him. I sent upper cuts left, then right, then left again into his head. He went down and curled up in a ball. I thought about kicking him, but that wasn't my style. 'Stop, stop,' he gasped. He had no fight left in him.

I looked round for Curly. 'Now it's your turn.' He turned and ran.

As we watched him run, Billy Dacey turned to me: 'Where the fuck did you learn the kung-fu kick?' I hadn't learned it anywhere. It had come all by itself, fuelled by pure adrenaline. But even I had to admit it had been a great kick. We walked back into the Trowbridge estate and I went home. As far as I was concerned, I'd dealt with Curly and his mate and that was the end of it. Wrong again. Word got round the local area that I was some sort of kung-fu expert. Far from putting people off, it made some of them want to prove they could beat me. Sometimes, the Llanrumney estate was like the Wild West; it was lucky we weren't wearing guns or a lot of us would have been dead.

I was walking through the stretch of woodland between Llanrumney and Trowbridge a few days later when I saw a few of my mates at the top of the hill about 200 metres ahead of me. I was at the bottom of the hill, on my own. Suddenly two older lads stepped out of the bushes to either side of me: Curly's brother, who was 18, and his mate, who was a year younger. 'You beat up my brother. You think you're some kind of fucking kung-fu expert, do you?' His back-up moved round to my left side. I glanced up: my mates were too far away to help.

I said: 'I don't want no dramas.' But inside I was thinking, 'Oh, well – here we go.' I kept my eyes on Curly's brother. He was bigger and looked the more dangerous. But it was his mate who hit me first, stepping in and whacking a fist in my face that I hadn't even seen coming. I heard my nose crack as it broke. The pain of the blow blinded me, I couldn't see to fight back. Now I was helpless, they laid into me. My mates up on the hill – Steve Borgia, Jimmy Donovan and Billy Dacey – had seen what was happening, and started running down to help.

When they reached us, Steve said: 'If you two want to fight, you can fight the lot of us.' There was a bit of a scuffle, and then Curly's brother and his sidekick walked away.

As they went, they shouted, 'Tell Flynn to stay away from Ball Road.' I wasn't going to stay away. I wanted to see Pat. But I was going to be a lot more wary.

My mates picked me up, what was left of me. Blood had gushed out down my face and onto my shirt and I wiped it away from my mouth. 'My nose is broken,' I mumbled.

Jimmy said, 'Better get you home, then.'

When I got home, my dad looked at my nose. 'Clean break,' he said helpfully. 'There's no point going to the hospital – there's nothing they can do for that.'

He was right – when me and my mates finally got to the head of the queue in casualty, the doctor said: 'Nothing I can do for that, I'm afraid. Try and stay out of trouble for a while. It'll heal itself naturally.' I went home and sat in front of the telly feeling sorry for myself and plotting my revenge. As the years went by, fighting became a way of life. Maybe that's why I'd ended up joining the Army. At least when you're in the armed forces, you get paid for scrapping.

CHAPTER THREE

Back at Camp Bastion, the waiting game went on. We'd spent days out in the sunshine prepping the vehicles. We'd fired in the guns now, set the TNTLS laser-ranging and navigation units to the correct datum marks and as far as we could tell the systems were all working to the point where we – and they – were several shades of blue in the face. We were ready for war – but as far as the operational command were concerned, it seemed war wasn't ready for us. In the meantime, our frustration increased: target practice, emergency drills and routine vehicle maintenance weren't doing it for us. We had to get some trigger time soon. The daily Ops briefings made it very clear that enemy activity in Helmand province was intensifying all the time. The Taliban were carrying the attack to an ever-increasing number of our bases. Things were warming up.

One night while we were in the scoff tent, having our evening meal – 'we' being me, JC, LCoH Steve 'Squirty' McWhirter, and Coxy [LCoH Damian Cox]. While the rest of us sat down, 3 Troop's boss, Lieutenant Tom Long, came up with his paper plate of food and his plastic KFS [knife, fork and spoon] and then wandered off to fetch himself a glass of water. We exchanged glances: Tom had left his bag of plastic cutlery unattended for a moment. In the scoff tent, this was a well-known tactical error. One that deserved instant correction. Squirty leaned across, picked up the little bag containing Tom's diggers and snapped them neatly in half. Then he set the bag carefully back down in the same position as before. Tom came back. He ripped the bag open and shook it. Several small, useless bits of white plastic fell out. He went red. 'Who broke my diggers in half?' Nobody said anything. But the story shows how bored we all were.

As we were tidying away the scoff trays, someone said: 'Did you hear about Sizzler? He got injured in a contact up at Sangin.' Shaun Fry – Sizzler – was a JTAC, or Joint Terminal Air Controller, the person who calls in close air support [CAS] for front-line troops in contact with the enemy. I hadn't heard – and Sizzler was a mate.

'Is he OK? Where is he?'

'Over in the hospital. But I don't think it's life-threatening.'

I caught JC's eye: 'Are you thinking what I'm thinking?'

JC nodded: 'I'm thinking we need to go and see how Sizzler's doing. And I'm thinking if it was anything like the last time when he called in the A-10s up at Now Zad, then he's got a bit of a story to tell.'

Bearing in mind the old Army saying, 'The only stupid question is a question that you haven't asked', I was all for getting a combat download from Shaun – provided he was feeling up to it. The more we knew about how the Taliban thought and fought before we went out to meet them in battle, the better. From the background lectures we'd been getting for the past few weeks in RSOI [reception, staging, onward movement and integration – the Army loves acronyms] I knew that what was true about Sangin was true about pretty much the whole of Helmand province. Afghanistan produces more than 80 per cent of the world's opium supply, and Helmand grows and processes the lion's share of that. The place is pretty much a giant drugs factory. The amount of money the narco-terrorists make from the trade defies belief, until you see some of the palaces the war lords have built themselves: huge, wedding-cake complexes, bristling with guards and equipped with all the latest technology.

According to the UN, Afghan opium production in 2004 came in at more than 4,000 metric tonnes, earning the undesirables involved in it a gross income of more than $one billion. And as we were now discovering, the Taliban used some of the income from its share of the trade to help fund its military operations – against us. They collected protection money from the opium farmers; top-sliced a cut of the crop; and made yet more money from refining, transporting and selling the opium on to the next links in the chain themselves. The drugs then made their way out along well-trodden routes through towns that included Gereshk, Musa Qal'ah and Now Zad: which was probably the main reason the Taliban were fighting so hard to keep control of them.

I made a bee-line for the door. 'Right then – let's go and hunt him down.'

I'd first met Sizzler in 2002, when my wife, Shelley, and our three children were still living in Lincolnshire, running the post office we'd bought in the nine or so years I'd spent between spells of Army service. I'd left the Army in 1993 as a Corporal of Horse, rejoining as an Acting Lance Corporal of Horse in 2001. In the meantime, I started and ran successful business ventures – successful, that is, until they failed.

Having already served fifteen years in my first engagement, I only had seven years left before qualifying for what was then the maximum twenty-two-year term. But re-engaging meant I got to spend even more time in the Army – in fact, if I served out the whole engagement, I'd be well into my fifties. Encouraging older but much-needed NCOs to rejoin was a bit of an experiment at the time, and I was one of the first guinea-pigs to sign on under the terms of the new contract, which meant moving back to barracks.

The idea was that Shelley, my sons Liam and Sean and daughter Gabrielle would move down to join me; but at the time I'd gone back in, they were happy and settled in Lincolnshire and the children were in good schools. While I waited for my nearest and dearest to join me, I lived with the single men in Combermere barracks, the Household Cavalry's Windsor home. Shaun Fry was pally with JC Moses, who was already a friend of mine, and the three of us occasionally went out for a drink together. Which was how I'd got to know Sizzler.

The same height as I am, six feet two, when I'd first met Sizzler he'd been much like the rest of us: in good enough shape to pass the regular Army fitness tests, but not in tip-top physical condition – the beer saw to that. Then, in 2002, he started training as a Joint Terminal Air Controller [JTAC] in readiness for the Second Iraq War. It's a difficult, dangerous and very demanding job, and not all that many people can do it. When he came back to camp as a qualified JTAC, I hardly recognized him: he'd lost the extra stone or so of padding and turned into a lean, mean, air-power-controlling machine. This made him seriously valuable.

After the defeat of Saddam Hussein's regular forces in the First Gulf War of 2003, and when Iraq's Ba'athist-led insurgency kicked into high gear, Brigade sent Sizzler up to the insurgent-infested town of Al-Amarah to help out First Battalion, the Princess of Wales's Royal Regiment [PWRR] – the Tigers. And they needed help: hundreds of Iraqi guerrilla fighters had them under siege in the centre of town. Although he'd played second fiddle to a more senior colleague, Sizzler had put his hard-won JTAC skills to good use in action, calling in a fair few close air support missions, including five AC-130 Spectre gunship strikes. This had pleased him a bit. So when he got the offer to deploy to Helmand in spring 2006 as part of 7 RHA's [Royal Horse Artillery's] Fire Support team [FIST] with the first wave of 16 Air Assault Brigade, he'd jumped at the chance. Reluctant as the House-hold Cavalry was to let him go, they knew that Shaun Fry was the best available candidate.

At first, UK politicians, civil servants and even some senior British Army officers believed that British forces in Helmand would simply be protecting the PRTs, or Provincial Reconstruction Teams, which were there to deliver development projects. This rosy view of things turned out to be a little over-optimistic: no sooner had British patrols started probing the chaotic and largely lawless province than large groups of Taliban-led fighters started to attack them. The Paras, being

Paras, carried the fight. But with British Army boots in such short supply on the ground, they needed close air support. And that was where JTACs like Shaun Fry came in.

JTAC is one of the riskiest jobs in modern combat, if you chose to do it the way Sizzler liked to do it, on the front line, where the battle is unfolding, and not, as he puts it, 'sat back two or three klicks [kilometres] from the fighting on a hill, or in some Ops room somewhere staring at a computer screen'. He wasn't trying to be gung-ho in volunteering for service at the sharp end. Both his training and his time in Iraq had convinced him that by getting up close and personal to the enemy you can see exactly what type of close air support is needed and when. I knew how he felt – I don't like being stuck behind the lines at a desk, either.

With Taliban attacks increasing in ferocity and frequency across Helmand province, on 4 June 2006, Sizzler got his chance. Brigade tasked A Company, 3 Para, other specialist elements of the Parachute Regiment, a platoon of 2 Gurkha Rifles and Sizzler's fire support team with Operation Mutay.

Although most of D Squadron had only arrived in theatre several weeks after it had gone down, I'd heard a bit about Operation Mutay. It had started out as a simple plan: air assault in, cordon and search a compound on the eastern outskirts of Now Zad. Then they'd capture the Taliban commander Intelligence reckoned was in there; seize all his stocks of opium, weapons and ammo; and bring him back to Bastion to answer a few friendly questions. But the unexpected weight of enemy numbers; the unfamiliar and confusing maze of compounds, orchards, ditches, rat runs and other insurgent-friendly hang-outs that made up the town; and the Taliban's sheer tenacity had seen most of the assault units run into trouble. A large number of enemy fighters had outflanked 2 Platoon and Shaun Fry, pinning them down behind a shoulder-high wall. And then kept them under murderous fire from less than 50 metres away for most of the day.

In that contact, Sizzler had directed a pair of US A-10 close air support aircraft onto the enemy position at danger close range. The A-10s had strafed and rocketed the Taliban lines, allowing 2 Platoon to withdraw and regroup. But Sizzler and his boss Captain Armstrong, the Para FOO [Forward Observation Officer], had stayed behind until the last moment to make sure the A-10s hit the enemy, and not their own side. The Paras and Sizzler's FIST team had escaped Operation Mutay without death or serious injury, and killed plenty of Taliban. But now, at Sangin, they'd suffered at least three deaths.

CHAPTER FOUR

We made our way over to the base hospital. In those days, Bastion's hospital was housed in tents, and if you were being generous you'd have described it as makeshift. It reminded me a bit of the emergency field hospital in the old US TV series, *M*A*S*H*. With a more permanent building still not much more than a gleam in the Royal Engineers' eyes, the Bastion hospital mostly acted as a staging post: the medics stabilized casualties, and then shipped them back to the UK for further treatment. The treatment was good, even back then, given the conditions the medics had to work under. Nowadays, the whole medical picture at Camp Bastion has been transformed beyond all recognition. The hospital there is probably the world's best at treating every type of battlefield injury, from the most minor – like a half-severed thumb and frag, or fragmentation injuries – to multiple amputations, life-threatening burns, severe blast damage, gunshot, rocket grenade and shrapnel wounds.

I'd never been inside the hospital before. Some of the tented wards were set up for ITU [intensive treatment]. The guys lying in them had really bad injuries, such as limbs missing, or third-degree burns. Even before we'd heard Shaun's account of the battle for the Sangin DC, it was a shock to realize how ferocious things really were out there.

When we finally tracked Sizzler down, he was sitting up in bed, large as life. Larger, in fact: the fighting up at Sangin had made him look 'alley' – British Army slang for hard. It's impossible to fake.

Various people had been to visit him to say well done for the job he'd done on Operation Mutay, including Lieutenant-Colonel Tootal. Always nice to get some recognition, especially from a senior officer.

Sizzler had that thousand-yard stare behind his eyes – the kind you only get from being in combat. He also had no shirt on, just a tan-coloured Army combat vest, and as usual his sideburns and hair were that little bit longer than regulation.

At first glance he looked like the same Sizzler we'd always known; but if you knew him as well as JC and I did, you could see that something wasn't right. It wasn't just that he looked greyer and paler than usual, or that his body language was stiff: whatever had happened to Shaun up at Sangin had left its mark. He was still in his usual good spirits, but he had a massive white bandage on his right hand.

'All right, Shaun?' JC said. 'How's the hand? That fucking bandage is the size of your head.'

You don't want to go in too hard with the banter when people have been injured in combat – you never know how they're going to react. But I couldn't resist saying: 'Nice ticket home to the UK then, Sizz? Couple of weeks up at Headley Court, lounging around in the Jacuzzi getting pampered by the pretty nurses while the rest of us are stuck out here for another five months? All right for some.'

Shaun gave me a dose of the hard stare: 'The last thing I want to do is get on that bloody Hercules and go home, Mick.'

'Face it, mate,' I said, 'you're getting on the transport. You'll be back home in a couple of days. The rest of us will just have to stay here and do the job without you.'

Sizzler rose to the bait: 'Maybe so, mate – but I'll be back.'

'Have you been in theatre for thirty days yet?' I asked. 'Because if you haven't, you won't get that medal.' I knew that he'd been recommended for the Military Cross, one of Britain's highest decorations for bravery. But at the time, they'd had this stupid 'you have to be in theatre for thirty days before we'll give you a medal' rule. Thankfully, that's now been dropped.

'At least I've been out and done something. All you lot have done is bugger about here in camp.'

'Too true, mate – too true. It's driving us bloody mad. The wagons are about as ready as they're ever going to be – they'll have us polishing them next. Any idea when you're going home?'

'The air-med lift is going out tomorrow. When I get back UK-side, they're going to operate on my hand.' He waved the damaged paw like a grizzly bear trying to swat a wasp. 'I've lost all the feeling in it. But it's not major. Just that the tendons are severed. They're going to try and reconnect them. Have they given you wasters a mission yet?'

JC said: 'As it happens, we're detailed off to escort a re-supply convoy up to the garrison at Sangin and then help secure the DC. So we might finally get ourselves some trigger time with the enemy.'

'It bloody needs securing; the place is a pit and a hell-hole.' He gazed at us for a while without speaking. At last, he said: 'You say you want some trigger time. But like the old saying goes: "Be careful what you wish for."'

I said, 'Christ, Sizzler, that's the oldest one in the book.'

'Maybe it is. But I mean it. Some of the RPG-7 strikes smashed straight through these thick compound walls. That means they'll blow your little Scimitars to small pieces.'

'All right, we'll be careful what we wish for – now will you get on and tell us what happened?'

Talking about what's gone on in a contact can sometimes help you get over it. In Northern Ireland and the Falklands I'd seen close friends die horribly a few feet away from me. 'What happened then, Shaun?' I asked. 'Did you get fragged in the DC, or did it happen outside?'

Sizzler began slowly: 'We got called back to Bastion after Op Mutay. Then, a few days later, this other mission came up: Int said the Afghans up in Sangin had decided to kick off among themselves. From what we could gather, it was some kind of power struggle.'

Sangin didn't mean very much to me and JC. We'd had some briefings on the hot spots in Helmand province, but at that stage, to us it was unknown territory. A few small units of US recon troops had been up there to test the waters, but after getting on the end of a few horrendous fire fights, they'd pulled out again. The Americans, with their usual talent for the dramatic, had nicknamed the Sangin valley 'Death Valley'. Whatever you called it, I remembered that all the Int, the combat indicators and the reconnaissance missions told more or less the same story: a town of about 30,000 people that straggles along the cultivated and built-up area, or green zone, bordering the Helmand River, Sangin district was pretty much awash with raw, semi-processed, and refined opium. The district was a hotbed of enemy activity: hardcore and ten-dollar Taliban (they get paid ten bucks a day for fighting); insurgent and independent drug traffickers; and local tribesmen eager to take on anyone who basically wasn't them.

Since 16 Air Assault Brigade's arrival in theatre, the Taliban in Sangin district had carried out two separate massacres of local civilians, for offences like speaking to ISAF: 'International Security Assistance Force' (even when the victims hadn't actually done that); for being insufficiently Islamic; or for failing to show the Taliban sufficient support on demand. When twenty-seven villagers were killed in the second mass slaughter, Afghan President Hamid Karzai asked British commanders to put a presence in place at the Sangin Afghan National Police [ANP] compound, a run-down mud-walled building about half a mile from the town centre.

Karzai wanted the Taliban's rule of terror in the area stopped. No doubt a fair few of the local population wanted the same thing. But listening to all this, what I wondered most was, what were British forces in Afghanistan actually supposed to be doing? Acting as a kind of alternative police force and a prop for the national government? Defending the UK's national interest by fighting extremists offshore? Helping turn Afghanistan into a stable state? Or what?

As a JTAC and with fresh combat experience, Shaun had a better hook into the local intelligence picture at Sangin than I did. To help nudge him into talking, I said: 'Why the fuck are we getting mixed up in crap like that? Why don't we let the Afghans sort out their own shit?'

Sizzler said: 'It all comes down to the politics. I was attending an O [Orders] Group meeting on the eighteenth of June when a call came through the system: a man named Dos Mohammed Khan needed rescuing from the Sangin DC. Khan was governmental head of security for Helmand province. He was also a mate of President Karzai's. But according to the brief, a lot of the locals were extremely upset about some of Khan's activities. A rival clan chief and his followers had ambushed and killed about forty of Khan's men. It looked as if Khan himself was going to get it in the neck and the government wanted him out of there double-quick. The main problem was, the Brits didn't want to be seen rescuing an unpopular figurehead. Luckily for us, shortly before the rescue mission was due in, a group of the local elders grabbed Khan, took him to FOB [Forward Operating Base] Robinson a few kilometres to the south of Sangin town and asked the Afghan National Army commander there to lock him up.

'But that didn't solve the problem. Next thing, we heard rival warlords and insurgents were massing to take control of the Sangin DC. Karzai didn't want to lose his presence in the town, however flimsy. The Afghan Army's not up to speed yet. So the only chance he had of hanging on to the place was us – 16 Air Assault Brigade. Then, just to complicate the issue even further, Khan's son was shot and badly injured.

'A Company, 3 Para, got the live mission again and I went with the FIST team as before on Op Mutay. There was me, two Para MFCs [mortar fire controllers] and the boss, Captain Armstrong. We also had a specialist radio operator. The idea was to insert by helicopter at the DC before dawn; avoid contact with the enemy if possible; lift the injured kid and the police chief and extract back out of there a bit sharpish.'

Sizzler nodded at the cigarette packet sticking out of JC's pocket. 'I could use a cigarette. Have you got any smokes?' Reluctantly, JC held out the pack. We asked the pretty nurse who was dealing with Shaun if we could take him outside.

'Fine, but you have to bring him straight back to bed if he gets tired.' Medics quite often talk about patients as if they aren't there, or they're deaf or something.

'OK, no worries, we'll take care of him.' I tracked down three cups of tea and we stood outside for a bit. Then, spotting some green-painted, fold-up Army-issue chairs standing against a nearby wall, I grabbed three and we sat down. The sun was beginning to set, our shadows stretching out in the strong evening light. There was the usual background racket from aircraft, vehicles, and machinery as the camp went about its never-ending business.

We fell silent for some time. Then Shaun said: 'We got there at 0430. At first, it seemed like an easy job. The Chinooks came in and set down on an LZ [landing zone] to the east of town beside the Helmand River. We tabbed in to the DC. It was nice and cool at that time in the morning, which made a welcome change. The police chief was ready and waiting – he looked quite pleased to be getting out of Dodge. Which wasn't all that surprising: from what we'd heard, the local Taliban were coming in to saw his head off at any minute. The injured kid – Mohammed Khan's son – was lying on a stretcher in the compound. He was in shit state – they'd shot him in the gut. But he was still moaning and groaning so we all thought he'd probably live.

'At any rate, the Paras escorted Khan, the police guy, the injured boy and a few of their mates back to the helicopters, stuck them on board and off they went to Bastion, no dramas. We were all chuffed – we'd completed the mission in short time and not a shot fired. But then, because the job had gone so well and because President Karzai wanted it, Brigade tasked us to stay in place and hold the DC. If we pulled out, the thought was the Afghan Government would lose face with the locals. So we stayed.'

I could kind of see the sense in what Shaun was telling us: one of the main reasons we were in Afghanistan was to interdict the enemy;

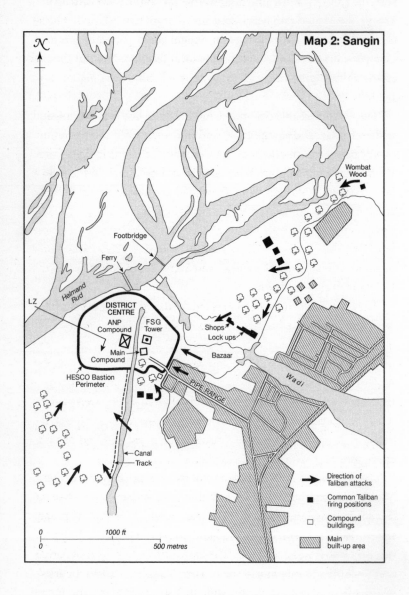

Map 2: Sangin

N

Wombat
Wood

Footbridge

Ferry

LZ

Helmand
Rud

DISTRICT
CENTRE

ANP
Compound

FSG
Tower

Main
Compound

Shops

Lock ups

Bazaar

Wadi

HESCO Bastion
Perimeter

PIPE RANGE

Canal

Track

Direction of
Taliban attacks

Common Taliban
firing positions

Compound
buildings

Main
built-up area

0   1000 ft

0   500 metres

seize the ground, hold it and then improve the country's infrastructure. This, since Afghanistan hardly had any to begin with, shouldn't be all that difficult. And sitting tight in Sangin for a few days meant A Company would be able to gauge the local reaction, find out the size of the Taliban presence, and estimate their ability and readiness to fight.

'There was just one tiny problem: kit. Since the original mission had been scheduled as a quick lift and shift – they told us a maximum of six hours – me and the rest of A Company had gone in light scales. We had hardly any of our personal gear and not much in the way of heavy weaponry. We had water, some food and ammo for the GPMGs and the SA-80s. But we hadn't even brought in our doss bags. The DC was a dump: it had a well for water and the only electrical power came from the field generators we took in and rigged up. There was a unit of about forty ANP in there who were supposed to be defending the DC and policing the town.

'They're rubbish: most of them spent the day lying around, smoking weed and planning who they're going to shag on Thursday night. As in, each other. Thursday night for the ANP is man-love night: we're talking eye-liner, flowers in the hair, jewellery, the lot. Mind you, the Afghan government doesn't exactly look after the police: when you talked to them, you found out that loads of them hadn't been paid for weeks. With the order to stay in place, we started sorting out the defences. It got dark at early o'clock; we had to eat and find our way around the base with our head torches.

'The compound is a weird shape, not rectangular like most of them. Most of the perimeter wall isn't all that high, either – and when we first got in there, one length of it was wide open. There were no proper sangars [fortified sentry positions] and no mortar pit. Luckily, for the first day or so it was dead quiet. The Paras put a couple of foot patrols into town and no one shot at them. There's a great big wadi (a dried-up river bed) about 250 metres wide that stretches to the south-east of the DC. The main bit of town was to our east. There's a bazaar there and a row of lock-up shops and garages.

'We started improving the sangars, dug foxholes around the perimeter and did what we could about the accommodation: the filthy bogs the ANP had been using were disgusting and the cooking facilities non-existent. There was this patch of grass in the middle of the compound: someone had been watering it, and whereas you couldn't call it a lawn, it was green and it was grass – and you don't get much of that in Helmand province. The Paras dug a mortar pit smack in the middle of it. It was the only spot in the compound from which they could get a 360-degree field of fire, plus the elevation needed to clear the walls.

'It was a good job they did get the mortars in: the place was basically waiting to get overrun. If the Taliban had attacked straight away, we'd have had a fucking job on our hands stopping them. We needed more heavy weapons and a lot more equipment – but Brigade was worried that if they sent in a Chinook with supplies, the Taliban would shoot it down. Which isn't all that surprising, when you realize we only had a few Chinooks for the whole battle group – and it was a good day if they were all working at the same time. Even then they struggle with the dust out here.'

Although the sun was beginning to sink, it was still hotter than a heat-wave in a whore house. Even in our camouflage shorts and fetching beige squadron T-shirts, the sweat dripped off us and down into our desert-issue boots.

'There's this building about fifteen metres high right next to the Sangin DC. We called it the FSG tower, because it's where we put the Fire Support Group. It's just outside and to the north of the main compound perimeter. The first time I saw it, it reminded me of those half-finished apartment blocks you see all the time in the Med: two storeys, brick-and-concrete fuck-ups with nothing in between the floors except for rickety pillars. The place was a shell – bits of wire sticking out everywhere. You reached the roof of the main building by two flights of bare concrete stairs. The floors were completely open to the world on either side; there was no front or back wall and no windows. The whole fucking place looked as if it was about ready to fall down around our ears.

'They'd plonked a small concrete blockhouse about two-by-three metres on the roof of the main building. Inside the blockhouse was a wooden ladder: you used that to get up through a trapdoor in the ceiling and out onto the roof. First thing, I got up there to see if it would make a good position for directing in air support. As things stood, it didn't seem like we were going to need that: the local pace of life was normal. People were going about their everyday business and there was no sign of Terry Taliban. From the blockhouse roof there was a superb all-round view of the surrounding area – it was a great position, except for one thing: there was hardly any cover: both the blockhouse and the main building below were wide open to attack.

'We'd hardly brought any defence stores with us: we had a few empty sandbags, but not nearly enough. We filled the ones we had and set up small, square sangars on the roof of the main building and the blockhouse. The walls weren't high enough to kneel behind – in fact they were barely high enough to cover your head if you lay down. But they were better than nothing.

'The FSG tower was a key local landmark. We could all see it made a perfect target, so it kind of worked for us and against us. Me and the fire support team set up on the main roof, and the Para snipers got settled into the sangar they'd built on the blockhouse roof. In the small room directly below them was a three-man LEWT [Light Electronic Warfare Team]: attached to A Company: two British soldiers and a local Afghan interpreter.

Intelligence reported that the Taliban were making threats like: "We're going to come in and kill all you kuffars [non-Muslims] – soon you will breathe your last." But by nightfall, when no actual attacks had come in, the guys were laughing and joking about it, saying Terry Taliban were full of shit. Quite a few of the lads were disappointed:

they hadn't joined the Parachute Regiment and gone through all that training to nursemaid injured kiddies and rescue policemen.

'None of us knew it then, but we were about to get into one of the biggest fire fights of our entire lives.'

CHAPTER FIVE

The nurse stuck her head out through the tent flap. Any minute now she'd be calling for her patient, like an anxious owner wanting her pet moggy in for the night. But Shaun wasn't going back to bed just yet: he was into it now, and we didn't want him to stop:

'Next morning, I gave the town a good going over through the binos. It still looked OK: the bazaar was open, there was a bit of trading going on; the locals appeared neutral if not exactly friendly, no one took a pot-shot at us and nobody out on patrol stepped on an IED. If there was going to be any trouble, we expected it to focus on the DC compound, as opposed to the FSG tower. The compound was where the Afghan National Police detachment hung out, so it was supposed to be the local seat of power.

'Then, come evening on the second day, a Taliban RPG gunner suddenly let fly from the lock-up garages on the far side of the wadi. The round missed anything serious, but the rest of the enemy at that location opened up with RPK and PKM machine guns and a couple more RPG-7 units. That set the pattern for the next two weeks: we'd send out foot patrols during the day to maintain our presence on the ground; then, as soon as it grew dark, the Taliban launched an attack. One that usually lasted until well on in the small hours. It was a brilliant system, absolutely guaranteed to stop any of us getting any sleep at all.

'But the weird thing was, instead of attacking the DC, they kept firing at the FSG tower. It was fucking annoying, and we couldn't understand it – why concentrate on the tower when they had a whole compound to play with? There were rounds whacking in all over the tower, RPGs flying in through one side of the gap between the two floors and out the other – it was mayhem. We called the contacts in; Brigade told us to sit tight and hold fast.

'Most of Terry's incoming was way off target,' Shaun continued. 'Our return fire was much more accurate. But then you'd get the odd fucker who knew how to use his weapon, and they were firing so many rounds you had to keep your head down. There was one good thing: at first, Terry didn't seem to realize we had night-vision kit. It was old school fighting, direct fire: we were blazing away, and the Para snipers up on the blockhouse were having a field day – they could hardly reload and fire fast enough.

'The Taliban had a basic grasp of infantry tactics, but at first they made some stupid mistakes, like not changing positions after firing, which made them easy to pick off. But they learned fast, and once they'd cottoned on they did pretty much what we'd have done: started probing at the DC from three sides in small groups. We suspected one of the ANP men had told them a few things: he kept coming up to the top of the FSG tower, viewing the sniper positions and anything else he could get his beady little eyes on. The second time he came up, we realized what he was up to and told him he was barred from the tower. But by then he'd already done us damage, reporting to his mates in the enemy camp. They kept nudging in, trying to find the weak points; work out how close they could get to us from each direction; find out the best attack routes and so on. They used the available cover really well, same as at Now Zad: even when you knew roughly where they were, it was difficult to spot them and lay on.

'At first, we were all quite pleased to be in contact. But as more and more attacks came in, we started to worry: there weren't that many of us, we were running out of stocks and Terry showed no sign of letting up. If he was going to keep coming at us, we had to have the heavier weapons: some .50 cals [Mk 2 Browning heavy machine guns]; a brace or three 81mm mortars; some Javelin missiles to knock out their hard points; and lots more ammo, water, sandbags and food. But we knew the Taliban had laid IEDs on all the approach roads, so bringing supplies in overland was extremely risky.'

We'd been talking for the best part of an hour already, and Sizzler had been doing most of it.

'You OK, Shaun?'

'I'm fine. But I wouldn't mind another brew.'

I went and fetched three more cups of tea while Sizzler had a bit of a smoke. Then he continued:

'A couple of days later, we found out why Terry was concentrating fire on the FSG tower and not on the compound: the same Afghan policeman had gone missing from one of the joint Para–ANP patrols. On the second night, he suddenly reappeared and asked to be let back in. There was something about him that didn't look right. So his mates asked him a few questions.

'He said the Taliban had threatened to kill him if he didn't talk. He'd given them an exact breakdown of our forces inside the DC: even drawn them a sketch-map. They were firing at the FSG tower because they knew some of our most important assets were up there – like the LEWT team, and the snipers. And the FIST team.

'The lesson we'd learned was that we couldn't trust the ANP. Loads of them in Sangin were from the same tribe as the local Taliban.'

The sun was low on the horizon, now, but Bastion still wasn't getting any quieter. As night air operations start to kick in, it often gets noisier.

'As the nights went by, the attacks got longer and stronger. We watched for muzzle flashes, or RPG-7 rockets launching, the usual. The Paras hosed Terry down with the GPMGs and the Minimis, whacked them with the mortars and sniper fire. Terry was firing back with light machine guns, RPG-7 and plenty of AK. We had nowhere to sleep; you slept where you could for the few minutes at a time it was possible. I slept on the roof of the FSG tower in the clothes I stood up in. Every time the Taliban attacked I sat up, grabbed my rifle, fired at the muzzle flashes and then tried to get my head back down when they gave it a rest. We were holding them at bay, but it was getting a bit ridiculous: as each night went by, the Taliban raised the ante that little bit more. We didn't just need the heavy weapons; we needed a truck-load of extra sandbags, a couple of tonnes of ammo and all the rest.

'Then, in week two we finally did get a re-supply: a couple of Chinooks brought in food, water, our Bergens with our kit and our sleeping bags. They also dropped off ammo, 100 empty sandbags and the icing on the cake, a couple of .50 cals and some heavy mortars. Terry went mad when the Chinooks came in; they were determined to bring one down. Intelligence reported the Taliban commanders getting very excited: "The birds [helicopters] are coming in, get ready to hit them, brothers." But as always, the transport helis came under cover of a twin Apache gunship escort.

'We set up the .50 cals; if and when the Taliban did launch their all-out attack, they would make a really big difference. Especially since our ANA spy, who was now banned entirely from the DC, hadn't seen and reported back on their arrival.'

Since the end of the Cold War, weapons like the Browning .50 machine gun that dated originally from World War Two had come back into their own. Small-calibre weapons like the SA-80 or the M16, which chamber a 5.56mm, or roughly .22 inch round, had been designed for use against Soviet forces: the idea being that it cost the enemy a great deal more effort, blood and treasure to deal with an injured soldier than it did to deal with a dead one. But in Afghanistan, against enemy fighters who had to be stopped dead in their tracks first time every time, larger calibre weapons like the .50 cal were a much better idea. From what Shaun was telling us, the Taliban didn't break off to treat their wounded when they were attacking. They just kept attacking – not least the ones who were off their faces on hashish and opium.

'The first day of July 2006 broke fine and clear. First thing, an enemy sniper took a pot-shot at one of our sentries. The Para was manning one of the heavy machine guns in the northern rooftop sangar. The Dragunov round smacked into the wall next to him and tore out a big fat chunk of masonry. The debris peppered his listening gear. When he came down to the RAP [regimental aid post] there was claret everywhere, all down his combats – it looked as if he'd lost half his head. Luckily, as soon as it had become clear the Taliban were interested in killing us, no one was allowed to go onto the roof of the FSG tower in daylight hours unless they were wearing full body armour and a helmet.

'In between ferrying sandbags up to the roof of the FSG tower, I kept up a to-and-fro with A Company's Int cell. I needed to know the up-to-date location of the main enemy positions, so I could fix them precisely for air attack. We were using MSTAR to help spot the Taliban. [MSTAR, or man-portable Surveillance and Target Acquisition Radar, is a small, high-definition radar developed for artillery use. We use it to track enemy.] The MSTAR system had detected enemy vehicles coming in from the north in ones and twos, driving to a pre-arranged spot and delivering the occupants. The system then showed these reinforcements forming up and rehearsing for a massed attack. But knowing the attack was on its way didn't mean we knew the exact moment when they'd launch it. It was all getting a bit antsy. They'd finished harvesting the opium, so they were hiring more and more spare hands as ten-dollar Taliban – we could see new recruits arriving in all the time.

'Just after nine p.m., the Para Int Sergeant called a snap briefing. The Int Sarge had been watching the MSTAR screen, and he wasn't overly happy about the view: the Taliban were massing in the gaps between the lock-ups, and at various points where they thought they might be hidden. It looked as if they were setting up for the promised massed attack on the DC.

'Intelligence reported that the Taliban commanders were checking that their units were ready: "Are you in position? Do you have the bread [ammo]? Do you have the watermelons [RPG-7s]?" At nine p.m. all the chatter suddenly stopped. It went eerily quiet. The silence ticked on for some minutes, then the Sarge said what we were all thnking: "It's imminent – they're coming."

'When he heard that, the OC gave the order: "Stand to!" Earlier that same day, we'd filled the extra 100 sandbags that had arrived in a spot of dead ground over by the Pipe Range; but the risk of sniper attack meant we could only take them up the FSG tower under cover of darkness. When they heard the "stand to" command, the Paras who'd been lifting and shifting the sandbags quit the FSG tower and moved directly to their ready positions. I asked the boss if I could get the guns [artillery at FOB Robinson] to lay down some illume [illumination] rounds. I wanted to make sure we'd be able to see the Taliban when the attack came in. The OC agreed. He also said he'd call Brigade, to try and get us some fast air. Neither was forthcoming: the air wouldn't become available unless and until we were actually under attack; and the guns wouldn't fire illume because a separate, nearby operation had priority for reasons that were beyond our need to know.

'I told the boss I was going back up on the roof. I started walking back across the compound. I could see all the lads standing to: manning the foxholes, the mortar pit, the sangars and the walls; getting behind their weapons and making ready.

'I was just coming up the last flight of steps to the roof. The LEWT guys were still inside the blockhouse. As I started walking towards the blockhouse door, additional intelligence was reported. The 'terp [interpreter] said, "The Taliban commander is telling his men: 'Get ready.'" When I heard that I stopped. Through the doorway, I saw the interpreter. He was staring at the wall directly ahead of him. It looked as if he'd just heard something really bad. His face changed and he pushed back his seat. Then he shouted: "They're going to fire!" Next thing I knew, I was knocked back on my arse and the world had caved in.

'I had no idea what had hit me – the blast just picked me up and flung me backwards. I hit something hard. I think I must have blacked out for a few seconds. When I came to, it felt like I'd been out for ever. I was lying on the top landing outside the LEWT room covered in dust and crap. Looking round, I saw I'd smacked into a wall. I sat up and looked down. There was claret on my combats, all over my legs. I felt them, but they seemed fine. I couldn't understand where all the blood was coming from.

'I felt dizzy, disoriented – but I knew I was up on the FSG tower. I also knew something really, really big had blown the massive smoking hole I could see in the wall ahead of me. Something like a recoilless rifle – or a 107mm rocket. I got up. I had a head torch on. It was risky, but I had to see what had happened to the LEWT guys. I switched the torch on and trained it round. The LEWT blokes were lying motionless. I crouched down but there was nothing I could do for them. The ladder to the roof was broken in two and there was a layer of dust over everything – big chunks of masonry and rubble everywhere. I thought: "Shit, they're all dead. Best not to hang around." I went back out onto the roof and shouted: "Medic!" a few times. Then I saw blokes lying around injured all over the place. A couple of guys were staggering around in a daze. There were still bullets and RPGs flying in, but no one was paying any attention. I could hear one of the snipers up on the blockhouse roof, he was shouting at the top of his voice. Then I saw why: blood was pissing out of his ears; the blast had shattered his ear drums. The medics raced up the stairs and started trying to revive the LEWT. Two of them were beyond help – they'd died instantly. The interpreter was barely breathing.

'When the rocket ripped the tower open, it had sent a huge shower of sparks flying up off the iron reinforcing rods. Using that and the hole they'd just blasted in the wall as aiming marks, the Taliban let rip with everything they had. They thought they could overrun us. So they went mad. We had incoming from all sides. We went mad back. We hit them with everything we had. The mortar team and the .50 cal gunners laid into the fuckers good style. The noise was absolutely deafening. It was absolute fucking mayhem.

'Finally I snapped to. My hearing roared back and I realized we were still under heavy fire. I dropped down behind the sandbags on the edge of the roof. Rounds were coming in through the hole the rocket had made and ricocheting everywhere. The incoming was chewing up the blockhouse walls, all these chunks of concrete kept hitting me in the face. The Paras were firing back burst after burst, the noise was absolutely fucking deafening.

'Then someone grabbed me by the shoulders and hauled me backwards off the roof – one of the medics. He said, "Where have you been hit? Where have you been hit?" He patted me down, trying to find the source of the blood. "Have you been hit in the leg?" I felt my legs again. It was true they were soaked in claret. But they were OK, I had feeling in them. "I don't think I have been hit," I said. "I'm positive I haven't been hit in the legs."

'He said: "Then where's all that blood coming from? Come with us. We want to check you out downstairs." The medics took me down to the RAP. As far as I could tell, every single one of the men who'd been on or near the roof when the rocket came in had been fragged. There was blood everywhere; the stairs were slippery with it. We got to the RAP and I sat down. Then they brought in three guys on stretchers – the LEWT team.

'It was really, really bright in the RAP. One of the medics said: "It's your hand, Sizz – your right hand." I looked down. It was true – my glove was absolutely soaked in blood. I just hadn't noticed it before. He cut it off. My thumb nearly came off with it – a piece of shrapnel from the rocket had ripped right across my palm and through the bit where the thumb joins on. The medic said it had sliced through the base of my thumb; he said it looked as if some of the tendons had been severed. He started trying to patch me up, but there were so many injured coming in, he kept having to go and look at more urgent cases.

'I stood up. The medic tried to stop me, but he was taking way too much time. I looked at the LEWT team interpreter. They were covering his face with a blanket. "Look," I said, "we have to get some air support, or we're all going to finish up like that." The medic went to deal with another casualty. On the way out of the dressing station, I bumped into the Intelligence sergeant. "Sarge," I said, "can you stick a bandage on my hand?"

'"OK, Sizz," he said, "no dramas. Come over here and sit down." He wrapped a massive amount of bandage round my hand and when he'd finished I stood up. He wanted to know where I was going. I told him I was going back up on the roof. I had to get back up on the roof and call in some close air support, as no one had yet replied to my earlier message on the TACSAT [Secure satellite radio]. He told me to take it steady, said it looked as if I'd lost a fair bit of blood. Next thing, the boss came up, Captain Armstrong: "Are you sure you're fit to go on?" I told him I was fine. I said: "Grab me some batteries, will you, Boss, and stuff them in my pockets?" The boss shoved a couple of spare TACSAT radio batteries into my combats; the last thing I needed was to lose comms at the critical moment.

'I went outside. It was still World War Three out there: if anything, the fire fight was worse than ever. There was a platoon of Paras bunched at the bottom of the FSG tower, ready to go up and reinforce it. The tower was still wearing a huge amount of enemy fire – the bullet and rocket strikes were showering debris down all over us. The platoon sergeant took one look at me, and then stuck a large gloved hand on my chest. "Where do you think you're going, Sizzler? You can't go up there – not in that state."

'I said, "I'm the JTAC – I have to go up. We have to get some air support. There's no one else to do it." He stepped aside and let me through. "Fair enough – if you're our only chance of air support, so be it."

'There hadn't been any more artillery rockets come in, but it was still raining RPG-7 and machine-gun fire like it was the end of the world. It was coming in from all points. When I got to the second-floor landing, I stopped. If you put the danger out of your mind for a moment, it was like watching the world's biggest and most spectacular firework display. There was tracer everywhere, orange from our side, green from theirs. It was crossing in the air and bouncing off anything that got in the way – rivers of it.

'Then I thought: "What the fuck am I doing up here? If I try and reach the roof I'll get killed." I stopped on the top landing. I didn't really want to go up. Then I thought about the three men who'd already died. If we didn't stop the Taliban, then more men would most likely end up in body bags. Perhaps we all would. I felt light-headed. But I thought, "Fuck it – I've got to get up there." So I climbed up the last flight of steps and ducked out onto the roof. The whole surface was slippery with spent cartridges and blood; there were empty ammo boxes lying around, used field dressings, shot-up sandbags, lumps of timber, concrete debris – and all these dark pools of blood.

'One of the Paras was still up there, a bloke called Taff. Taff said: "They're closing in on us. Look!" I took a quick squint over the top of the sandbags. I had to see where the enemy were and what they were doing. One group of Terry was still advancing down the wadi to the south-east; more groups were pincering in from the south and north. Some of them were closer now than 200 metres. I balanced the SA-80 on the sandbags with my left hand and got some rounds onto one of the groups. Then I remembered the SA-80 doesn't work for left-handed shooters – oversight of the makers and buyers. The way the spent cartridges eject, they could have gone straight back into my face.

'I stopped firing after the first couple of rounds. If we did get some air power, a lump of red-hot brass in my eye – or a broken mouth – wasn't going to help when it came to calling the strike in. I was wondering if I could find the TACSAT I'd dropped in the blast, and if I did, whether we'd ever get any support. Then I spotted the radio a few feet away. I crawled towards it, stuck the headset on and called Anvil One, [the main air tasking controller] at Brigade HQ: "This is call sign Hammer Four-Two. We're in a lot of shit – under heavy fire.

All positions are under heavy fire. It's coming in from all sides. We're in heavy contact; we have injured pax [personnel]. We need fast air." I wasn't overdoing it: the Taliban rehearsals had paid off. The assault was well organized: they were pepper-potting forwards, rushing us in small groups, firing and moving. Some of the enemy front-runners were charging across the wadi less than 300 metres away. I stuck a set of NVGs [night vision goggles] on my head and did a quick 360. The outlook wasn't all that good. There were large groups of enemy almost all the way around the DC, ghost figures flitting in the night, lit up only by the flash of explosions and tracer.

'I got back on the TACSAT and gave it another try. "It's horrendous here; we've got three suspected KIA [killed in action] and six casualties. We're being engaged from all positions, north, south, east and west; we're in severe danger of being overrun." I couldn't find my GPS – I'd lost it in the blast from the rocket. But I got Captain Armstrong on the radio: "Boss, give me the grid of the wadi to the east from your GPS. I'll confirm it on the map, and then I'll confirm it with Taff here. When one and one and one makes three we can give the air exact co-ordinates. If it ever arrives."

'It was still fucking bedlam. The Paras were still firing to all sides. Then we got some good news: an American B-1 bomber was returning off task to the north; even better, the pilot had been listening in to reports of the fire fight and he'd decided he'd quite like to join in. He came up in my headset and asked if there was anything he could do for us. He had a Southern drawl – was I glad to hear it. I said: "Can you ever, mate – what's the smallest ordnance you're carrying?" He told me he had one 500-pound bomb remaining. But he said he was on a radar suite, he couldn't see the ground or get us visual, and no one had given him a SITREP [situation report].

'I gave him a full run-down of what had happened: casualties taken, possible KIA; sketched out how and where we were still under enemy attack. Then gave him the grid, followed by the GPS co-ordinates after I'd double-checked them with the boss and with Taff. But then the

B-1 pilot said: "Isn't that kind of close to your position?" He was right: there was a real risk the explosion would cause own troops' death and injury. "Target is danger close, repeat, danger close," I said. "But we don't have any option. If we don't get something on the enemy now, they'll roll us up like a carpet. The grid's a good grid, the boss is happy, you're happy. We're going to have to drop it or we're going to get fucked." I marked our own position with fireflies [winking infra-red indicators that are invisible to the naked eye].

'The pilot came up on the TACSAT "Fireflies visual". There was a pause and then he said: "Affirm your grid. Affirm position of friendlies. Request clearance to release ordnance."

'Cougar Three-Five, this is Hammer Four-Two: you are cleared in hot, repeat cleared in hot, over?"

'He lined up for his bombing run, tracking north-west to south-east. He said: "Affirm cleared in hot. Switches to live. Sixty-second call."

'"Affirm sixty-second call."

'"Happy days, Hammer Four-Two. Running in hot. Looking for correction."

'I didn't need to correct his line of attack – he was bang on. By now, some of the Paras had joined me on the roof. I shouted: "Fast air in fifty seconds: get your heads down!" Then I smacked the PRR [personal role radio] and sent out the same message. We heard the engine roar as the B-1 came steaming in. Next thing, there was a massive, almighty explosion directly in front of us. The whole fucking tower shook. For a moment I thought it was going to collapse. A huge fountain of earth and rock flew up from the middle of the wadi a couple of hundred metres away. I tried to do a BDA [battle damage assessment] but there was so much fucking dust in the air. For about five minutes you couldn't see a thing.

'When the dust had cleared a bit, we saw Terry had dead and injured lying around all over the shop. Even the Taliban couldn't keep taking losses like that. But I wanted to make sure the fuckers went away and stopped playing. Next thing, a couple of Apache gunships came on task: I grabbed hold of them on the radio, talked them onto the wadi and they gave Terry some more good news. The enemy fire was much more sporadic now, but they had this one weapon that was still going. It had been bugging us all night. We couldn't be sure what it was, but most people thought it was a recoilless rifle: when it fired, it made this deep barking sound – like the old British Army Wombat. I'd never trained on the Wombat 120mm recoilless rifle, but I'd seen one in the Imperial War Museum at Duxford. It was basically an anti-tank weapon: in Taliban hands, a recoilless rifle was ideal for knocking lumps off mouldering old buildings like the Sangin DC and the FSG tower. And off us.

'I called up the Apache pilots: "Dragon Four Three, this is Hammer Four-Two: the enemy have a weapon system hidden nearby. It might be a recoilless rifle, on a flat-bed or under cover of some trees. We've been unable to locate it: can you see it and take it out?" The Apaches searched around, spotting and suppressing the remaining enemy attack groups. The Taliban were definitely starting to fall back, now, the extra firepower was beginning to tell on them. Then, sure enough, one of the gunship drivers spotted a Taliban team crewing a recoilless rifle. It was in a stand of trees about a klick to the north-east. The Apaches took the fuckers out of the game.

'After that, the Paras started calling the orchard where the gun had been hidden "Wombat Wood". The Apaches stayed on task as long as they could. But when they started to run low on fuel, dawn still hadn't broken. The flight leader said they had to go back to base and get some more fuel. He asked me if there was anything else they could do for us before they went. I thought for a moment, then I told him: "Yes: you can bring us the daylight – it's much nicer when they attack in the day, we can see them better." He said that was a bit above his pay-grade. They were heading back to Bastion, but they'd stay on comms with us. If we still needed their help when they'd refuelled, he said they'd turn round as quick as they could and come straight back. It was good to know we had the support. But the Taliban had melted away. For that night, the fighting was over.

'Shortly after dawn, a MERT [Medical Emergency Response Team] Chinook came in to pick up the dead and injured. Watching them load the bodies – that was grim. I didn't want to come back out with the dead and injured – not trying to sound like a fucking hero or anything. But the CO decided A Company might just have had enough, so B Company was going to come in as the RIP [relief in place]. But as far as I knew there was no replacement JTAC coming in with them. The Para doctor came and took a look at my hand. When he'd finished, he told me I had to go straight back to Bastion on the Chinook. I told him I was OK; I needed to stay on for a bit: if the Taliban attacked again, they were still going to need a JTAC. But the doc wasn't having any. He pulled rank on me – said my hand needed to be properly cleaned and if I stayed in Sangin, there was a very strong risk of infection. He also said I needed an immediate operation on the damaged tendons, or there was a risk I'd lose the use of the thumb. Then he told me I was exhausted. After the best part of a fortnight without any sleep, that was definitely true. The only thing that had kept me awake was coffee. In the end, the doc gave me a direct order: "Get on the first helicopter out of here and report immediately to hospital in Bastion." I went back out with the rest of the T2s [walking wounded] and climbed into a nice, clean bed in Bastion hospital. Next thing I know, I've got you two on my case.'

I knew Sizzler had played down his own role in the drama at Sangin. But his refusal to let his injuries stop him going back up to the roof of the FSG tower under enemy fire, and then directing in the air support, had most likely helped to save the garrison from annihilation. For his courage in the face of the enemy while injured and under fire, CoH Shaun Fry was awarded the Military Cross.

It was late now in the Bastion scheme of things, where everybody gets up at early o'clock. Time for bed. Sizzler had a long flight back to the UK on a Hercules the next day. We all got up and headed for some shut-eye. As I watched Sizzler going in through the flap of the hospital tent, I thought: 'We're going out on our first mission tomorrow. And if it's anything like what happened to Shaun up at Now Zad and Sangin, then we're in for a rough ride.' But I still didn't understand just how rough.

CHAPTER SIX

The next day, as scheduled, 2 and 3 Troops, D Squadron HCR left Camp Bastion as escort for the supply convoy taking food, ammunition, water and other essentials up to the Sangin DC, and covering the RIP, or troop relief in place. A section of 7 Troop RHA came with us, towing three much-needed 105mm light guns behind their Pinzgauer all-terrain vehicles. We set off in the middle of the night to second-guess the Taliban dickers (the spotters who note and report our movements) in and around Camp Bastion. Driving with NVGs over rough terrain, the going was extremely difficult – we were barely making more than walking pace. But then a bright moon came out, which meant we could take off the NVGs and see much better depth-of-field. That helped the convoy move a bit faster, until one of the guns got stuck in a patch of soft sand. So they weren't that light. Then, one of the Land Rovers got bogged in, and then another of the towed guns.

Being tracked vehicles with very low ground pressure – less per square foot, in fact, than a fully laden combat infantryman, the Scimitars and Spartans skimmed over the soft patches of sand with ease. But we were having to spend more and more time pulling the less well-adapted vehicles back up onto firm ground. The terrain kept getting rougher and rougher, and the maps we had were so lacking in detail and accuracy as to be virtually useless. On our own, the trip up to Sangin would have taken 2 and 3 Troops about five hours. Now, eight hours later, we were only just approaching the outskirts of Sangin.

We'd just learned the hard way that Land Rovers and other small, non-tracked vehicles were not suitable for the especially difficult stretches of deep, fine and very soft sand you keep meeting in Helmand province. The Scimitars, Spartans and other variants in the same CVR-T tracked combat reconnaissance vehicle family had proven their worth over icy, boggy ground in the 1982 Falklands War; now, more than twenty years later, they were excelling in the same way over reaches of talcum-powder fine sand.

Then, just when I was thinking what a good vehicle it was, my own Scimitar broke down. Its ability to cross soggy or sandy ground of one kind or another might be exceptional – its aged mechanical condition was not. We were on the up slope of a wide, steep hill, with the town of Sangin in sight through the NVGs a couple of kilometres to the north and east of us. It was just before dawn, about 0430 hours. The air was unusually cold: we were shivering. Even in summer the chilly night-time and early morning desert air can catch you out. At least being freezing made a welcome change from frying our nuts off. Then another Scimitar broke down. Then the Samson with the LAD [light aid detachment] which was supposed to fix the vehicles when they broke down, that fucker broke down too – there's irony for you. We tried to form a defensive triangle. But the three vehicles were too widely spread, stuck where they'd given up in less than ideal positions. Which made us extremely vulnerable to enemy attack. Even so, we couldn't let the breakdowns hold up the rest of the package. I told the rest of the formation: 'We'll stay behind and try to get these three wagons moving again. The rest of you need to crack on and get those supplies and the guns to the DC.' This got all-round agreement. The other five CVR-Ts rolled on towards town as an escort for the light guns and the supply trucks. We got down to the serious business of trying to repair ancient wagons that had ruptured their mechanical guts pulling every other bugger out of the mire.

The Scimitar behind me had no brakes and no engine. My driver Leechy, properly known as Trooper James Leech, could engage first and second gears, but we had no brakes; as for the Samson, it seemed to have suffered the mechanical equivalent of a hernia: it had no brakes but its engine worked when it felt like it. I still wanted to shunt the three vehicles closer together. But we only had one set of olly bones. Olly bones are what we call the metal A-frames we use for towing one CVR-T with another. The olly bone is hinged at one end, so that when the lead vehicle stops, the one that it's towing doesn't ram into it.

There we were, stranded on the side of a bloody great mountain. It was only after I'd had time to take a good long look through the NVGs that I realized how big it was. I could also see a hotchpotch of villages clinging to the low ground at the bottom of the slope, almost directly in our line of advance. I thought, 'We can't sit up here waiting to get whacked for the rest of the day. Let's at least try and get down off this mountain.' The Samson hitched up the olly bones and set off, towing the dead Scimitar behind it. I ground along behind them in first gear.

Very, very slowly, we bucketed and bounced our way up to the summit. Now we had a different problem: how to get back down a fucking great big slope without a single set of working brakes between us. Hmmm. Looking at it again, the descent struck me as even steeper than the climb – and we'd only just managed to complete that. The gradient was at least one in three, and there were huge outcrops of rock sticking up everywhere. It was tempting to go for it, though: extremely tempting. 'No,' I thought. 'We'd be mad to try going down that slope without any brakes between us. We'll lose control and crash. Either that, or one of the wagons will roll over and kill somebody.'

That settled it – we were going to try. I had one ace up my sleeve: my own working first and second gears. I told the other two vehicle commanders: 'You two stay hooked together, but with the Samson in front. We'll hitch my wagon to the rear end of the broken Scimitar with tow ropes. I'll go behind in first gear at the rear, and my wagon will act as a braking vehicle for both of yours. And everybody buckle up – harnesses on and fastened – it looks like it's going to be a very rough ride. All clear?' The other crews looked at me as if I'd gone completely mad. I was mad – mad to get on with the job and get into Sangin. But I was in charge of this three-wagon circus. And they knew that once I got a bit of a bee in my bonnet, it was generally useless to argue.

'Er – OK, Mick.'

'Marvellous – let's do it.'

We hitched up the tow ropes and made ready. Looking at the arrangement once we were all shackled together, I started to have serious second thoughts. Makeshift wasn't in it. I thought: 'This is ridiculous. This isn't allowed. It's not in the rule book – in fact, I'm sure there's a rule against it. Nobody's trained us to do this – this isn't a good idea.' It was just beginning to grow light, in that odd state of in-between that can play tricks on the eye. Just what we needed to make the trip that little bit more interesting. The slope ahead of us looked steeper than ever. But sitting where we were in a state of advanced mechanical breakdown, we were asking to get whacked.

We started off. The wagons ahead of me could still steer. But the plunge to the bottom of the mountain made the big roller-coaster rides at Alton Towers seem relatively safe. Plunge is an understatement: the combined 24-tonne weight of the two wagons I was trying to brake with my gears made us all skid and skitter over the lumpy ground. Over whole sections of the slope, we just slid down. I had the wagon in first gear, but I could smell the gearbox overheating. I kept thinking, 'Any second now, the cogs are going to strip clean off the gear wheels and we'll all roll down to the bottom and die.' It was like doing the giant slalom run at St Moritz, but in tracked armour. But against the odds and even with all of that weight tearing at it, my Scimitar's gearbox held good. We reached the bottom of the slope. I unclamped my fist from the grab handle, stood up and shouted: 'Is everyone OK?'

There was a long silence. The dust our tracks had thrown into the air settled slowly back to earth around us. My knuckles were still white from where I'd been gripping bits of the wagon. 'Is everybody all right?' The silence went on so long I was beginning to fear the worst.

Then there was the odd mumble of assent: apart from a few lumps and bruises where they'd been knocked against something hard and metallic, everyone was more or less all right. They were just collectively shrugging off the effects of being inside a giant cocktail shaker for several minutes.

I looked around. The compounds I'd spotted were now no more than 200 metres away, well within RPG and small-arms range: the edge of a village on the route into Sangin. The sound of gunfire carried clearly on the still morning air: most probably that meant that the rest of the column had reached their objective, and were enjoying a traditional Afghan welcome. Then I heard the rolling bass rumble of a fast jet. I thought: 'We got down the mountain in one piece. But if the Taliban decide to come out of that village and have a crack at us, we're an easy target. Nice to have some fast air on hand.'

The REME guys on the Samson set to and succeeded in fixing my Scimitar. Now we had brakes and a working engine at the same time: luxury. With the Samson towing the second Scimitar, which obstinately refused to let itself be fixed, we made our way through the outskirts of Sangin. To reach the DC, we had to drive right through the middle of town. But whether it was because they'd suffered so many casualties in the contacts that Sizzler had described, or because we had the Scimitars, a pair of Apache gunships providing top cover and a fresh unit of Para infantry to hand, the Taliban let us pass without firing a shot.

The people of Sangin, on the other hand, were anything but happy to see us. Their stares, as we drove through, were filled with hatred. That wasn't good – the idea was to win them over to the government side – hearts, minds, and all the other bits. Not so easy when they saw us as trouble. It wasn't difficult to understand their point of view: simply by being there, in many places we drew the Taliban in to fight. We responded to attack, and then they, the ordinary citizens, got caught in the crossfire. But despite the local anger and the loss of three men on the FSG tower, there was a positive side to the recent battle for control of the DC: despite being heavily outnumbered, A Company, Sizzler and ISAF: air power had given the enemy a bloody nose, and driven them back from the centre of town. It was just as well: by the time our convoy reached it, the garrison was almost out of ammo; down to its last few bottles of water; and scraping at its last stocks of food. I could see what Sizzler had meant about the ANP compound and the FSG tower – they looked as if they might fall down at any minute – something the recent rocketing and shelling had done nothing to lessen.

The good news was that the rest of 2 and 3 Troop had managed to get in with the supply wagons and the guns, and the fire fight I'd heard on the mountain hadn't been overly dramatic: the Taliban had only fired a few pot-shots at the column. The only real damage done had occurred when an attached Canadian unit driving LAVs [light armoured vehicles] had decided to split away from the rest of the column and strike out on a route of its own. The Canucks had run straight into an instant Taliban ambush: just add RPGs. Amazingly, the Canadians hadn't suffered any serious injuries. But the Taliban had managed to hit one of the LAVs with no fewer than fourteen RPGs, reducing it to a big fat heap of smoking scrap metal.

CHAPTER SEVEN

Back in Bastion, after successfully helping the garrison in Sangin to get fresh supplies, we did our best to repair all the broken-down wagons and get them rolling again. When the engineers were happy the vehicles weren't going to grind to a halt the second we got outside the gate, my boss, Lieutenant Tom Long, came to see me: 'We have a new mission. We're to drive up to Now Zad with all speed, link up with 1 Troop, and then help the Paras clean the Taliban out of the town.' A Household Cavalry unit was already in place on the summit of ANP Hill, the steep-sided mound that overlooked both the town of Now Zad and the DC; 1 Troop was acting as overwatch and fire support group for the mixed British and Afghan garrison.

The need for further action at Now Zad was pressing. At the beginning of June, a mixed force of D Company, 2 Gurkha Rifles, Afghan National Army [ANA] and Afghan National Police [ANP] officers had relieved the Paras then in position and occupied the police compound in the centre of Now Zad. Since then, despite Operation Mutay and to a certain extent perhaps because of it, the garrison had been under sustained and ferocious attack. In the course of the ensuing eight-week stand-off, the Taliban had been close to overrunning the stronghold many times. More often than they'd wanted, things had got so bad that the Gurkhas were picking up enemy grenades before they exploded and throwing them back over the walls. In the month of July alone, the Gurkhas had fired more than 30,000 rounds from their SA-80s, and getting on for 20,000 machine-gun rounds. The miracle was that, while they'd killed an estimated 100 Taliban foot-soldiers, the Gurkhas had not lost a single man. Jammy buggers.

The Taliban had not put their toys back in the pram and sloped off to practise basket-weaving after Operation Mutay. Instead, here they were again creeping forward through the rat runs that squirrelled between the densely packed compounds that surrounded the DC, and doing their level best to kill its defenders. Again. Once we'd joined forces with 1 Troop, we were to take part in a second joint operation with units of 3 Para to push the Taliban back from the District Centre. The idea, if possible, was to clear the enemy out of the whole area once and for all. I was looking forward to having a bit of me-and-them time with the Taliban. But given their persistence in the Mutay fighting and then up at Sangin, I thought the 'clearing them out once and for all' objective might turn out to be overly optimistic.

We set off from Camp Bastion in the early hours of the following morning with fourteen vehicles in the column. As the sun rose and began to bite down with its usual ferocity, our tracks chucked huge plumes of dust up into the stifling air. In an effort to mask our intentions from the ever-watching Taliban dickers, we took a deliberately roundabout route to the town. The plan was to move into the western outskirts of Now Zad mob-handed. Then 3 Troop – my troop – was going to move to the top of ANP Hill and stay in place there with four Scimitars and one LAD recovery Spartan.

We drove as fast as the stony, undulating ground would allow, reaching speeds of 60 kph on the flatter, harder stretches. In theory, the Scimitar can do up to 80 kph, but to reach that speed the vehicles need to be in tip-top mechanical order. But as we'd already begun to see, under the intense strain of the heat and dust in Helmand province, and constantly battered by the lumpy and horrible terrain, an increasing number of D Squadron's Scimitars and Spartans were ready for the knacker's yard.

As we neared the town, which lay some 40 kilometres north of

Camp Bastion, our interpreter started to relay the enemy chatter he could hear over the i/com scanner [listening device] we had with us for precisely that purpose. 'The special forces are coming to invade Now Zad with more tanks! They have more tanks, brothers, they have more tanks. Beware!' If you count the Scimitar as a light tank and the Household Cavalry as special forces, then they were right.

Now Zad sits in the middle of a broad valley flanked to the east by a green zone and the River Helmand. A short way beyond that, a ridge of sharp, jagged peaks spears up out of the landscape running roughly north–south. More hills and mountains surround the settlement on the three remaining sides. Once, not so long ago, Helmand province had been famous for the sweetness of its melons, grapes and peaches. Now, it was notorious for opium poppies and violence. Like Sangin and Musa Qal'ah, the town was a major staging post in the Taliban-controlled narcotics trade.

ANP Hill dominated both the town and the surrounding green zone. During its decade-long occupation of Afghanistan, the Russian Army had built a ramshackle base on the top, naming it the Shrine. The Shrine and the surrounding town had been the scene of murderous and ferocious fighting between the two sides. The main built structure on the summit was a long, low, thick-walled concrete bunker sitting on its eastern brow. The British units that had occupied the position since our return to Afghanistan had moved into the old Russian bunkers and trench systems. We'd begun the slow, difficult and backbreaking work of improving them, but there was still a long way to go. In the meantime, the accommodation, if you could call it that, was minging, horrible and really not all that good.

Leaving three of the RHA's 105mm guns as a separate fire support group on a bluff several kilometres from Now Zad, we hooked east at the last minute and drove in through a straggle of compounds, fields and orchards, skirted a few compounds and roared up to the top of the hill. Now we were in place there, our own mission – not to be confused with 7 RHA's longer-range artillery cover – was to act as a close fire support group for the upcoming clearance operation. Shortly after we set up shop, three companies of 3 Para, or about 400 men, inserted by Chinook to the west of the DC. Grouping into fighting platoons, they began sweeping through the settlement driving west to east. Compound by compound and street by street, the idea was to push back, arrest and if necessary kill the enemy; locate and confiscate any weapons and explosives that were found en route; and try not to get themselves killed in the process.

Our job in 3 Troop was to keep an eagle eye on the infantry and cover them as they completed this task. At the same time, 1 Troop was going to give the Paras 'intimate support': roll with the infantry, using its armour, cannon and machine guns as a protective, close-quarters shield. I watched through the Scimitar's commander's sight as the combined force reached the western outskirts of Now Zad. As soon as the first Para section entered the maze of compounds, it came under sniper fire. Someone yelled 'Contact!' on the radio. I scanned around hastily. We had to locate those snipers and kill them. But both for us and the assault teams below, the narrow, high-walled streets and alleyways between the compounds made it very difficult to see the enemy and fire back.

Jules Hoggarth, 1 Troop's senior CoH, who was leading the armoured column negotiating the rodent run below, called me up on the radio: 'Mick, we've got snipers firing at us – can you see them and engage?' We could certainly engage. But as always with snipers, even from our vantage point up on the hill, spotting them would be the real challenge. Our own counter-sniping teams were good: so good, that Taliban snipers very rarely took up position on buildings. Instead, they'd resorted to firing from the inner rooms of compounds, or through very small apertures cut through an outer wall. The shots kept on coming, but none of us could spot the enemy sniper. Frustrating – and annoying as hell.

'He's high – he's up on a roof,' Hoggarth transmitted. 'Look across the roof line to our east.' I scanned along the nest of compounds that

1 Troop and accompanying infantry were pushing through. The four Scimitars were in a narrow lane cutting through the area from west to east, with the Paras stacked up close to the eastern wall for cover. Then Jules radioed: 'We're taking more rounds, he's hitting the vehicle. Can anybody see where the fucker is?' The enemy sniper was good. Hoping to kill a vehicle commander or a gunner, he was repeatedly landing rounds on the turrets of the Scimitars. All four crews had their heads well down, but there was always the chance of a lethal ricochet. As I watched, Jules Hoggarth's vehicle came into view, but not the Para infantry I knew were advancing behind it – the walls of the lane they were stacked along masked them from view. I had a bad feeling there might be more than one enemy sniper at work.

Then I had a stroke of luck: making another slow scan of the most likely sniper positions, I spotted a big pile of tyres on the roof of a compound about 200 metres to 1 Troop's south and east. Peering through the sight on 10x magnification, I noticed a very slight movement from the middle of the heap. I laid the aiming circle onto the spot. If the sniper was on that roof and we could positively ID he was armed, then he was in for a nasty shock: for the Rarden cannon, he was at almost point-blank range.

A muzzle flash blossomed bright orange from the jumble of black rubber. A couple of seconds later I heard the sharp crack of a high-velocity rifle. Dragunov. 'I see the enemy sniper,' I told Jules. 'He's on a roof to the south-east of your position, range about 250 metres, in a pile of tyres.'

We might have spotted the bastard, but there was still a problem: some of 1 Troop's vehicles and a Para section of eight men were directly between us and the enemy marksman. I had the shooter directly in my sights, but he was also smack in my 'no-fire' line. A no-fire line is what it says: a line beyond which you cannot open fire without the risk of a blue-on-blue, or killing your own forces. The point Para section and Jules Hoggarth's lead Scimitar had crossed the line, which meant I needed special permission to open fire. The Para forward HQ was no more than 20 metres away to my left. I shouted across: 'I can see the sniper but I need clearance to engage over the heads of your troops.'

The Para RSM called back: 'Engage him! Engage!'

'I can't engage – they're into my no-fire zone. If I shoot any of your blokes, I'm done for.' The Para head shed [command] had a very quick chat among themselves. Then their FOO, a captain – it might have been Captain Armstrong – ran across to me.

'Is that where the sniper is,' he said, pointing. 'In that pile of tyres on the roof over there?'

'Correct.'

'Can you engage him with direct fire?'

'Yes: with direct fire, line of sight. We're going to use the 30mm and the co-ax.' I wanted to be crystal clear about what was going to happen.

'How close are you going to get to the lads on the ground?'

'My fire will pass about 10 metres above their heads. They'll hear my shots going over.'

The FOO called up the lead Para section in the lane. I listened in as he spoke. 'Be advised: call sign Three One is going to engage over your heads with 30mm and GPMG.' He turned to me. 'Engage.' He had the authority, I needed no second bidding.

'Reference tyres,' I told Jules Hoggarth. 'Watch my fall of shot. We're firing over the top of you now – keep your heads down.'

'You'll need to get this one smack bang on target,' I told my gunner Paul Minter. The nephew of the champion lightweight boxer Alan Minter, Minty shared his uncle's love of a scrap. He was from East London and he was now officially the main man – it was all down to his marksmanship. Minty opened up. I took a breath and held it as the first ready-use clip of three 30mm HE shells thumped out of the gun. I needn't have worried: Minty's shooting was well up to its usual standard. All three rounds slammed into the sniper's position. Old tyres and bits of rubber flew up to all sides as the high-explosive ordnance exploded in a lethal shockwave of metal fragments and blast.

Shouts and screams rang out from the enemy position, suggesting we'd hit the sniper. It also suggested there were more Taliban in the compound immediately below. Some of the tyres began to burn, sending up a thin, twisting pillar of oily grey smoke. The sniping had stopped.

Then a figure stood up from the pile of tyres: tall and thin, dressed in a black dishdasha and clutching a long rifle. The man turned and started to move. 'Fuck, he's still alive!' I said. 'The fucker's up and running. Engage him.' The sniper started loping back across the compound roof. Minter sent a stream of HE after him. Spotting the fleeing enemy, Jules Hoggarth's gunner joined in with short, well-aimed bursts of GPMG, leading the target slightly to allow for his speed of travel. A round thumped into the sniper, knocked him sideways and sent him tumbling. He lay face down at the edge of the roof, unmoving. 'Got him!' I breathed. A few of the Paras climbed up onto the roof. Eventually, they found the body, chewed up in the mess of old tyres, lumps of mud-brick and dust. They also recovered a Dragunov rifle equipped with a telescopic sight and a bipod, a pair of binoculars, a stash of ammo and a tote bag for the whole caboodle. The Taliban at Now Zad still had to learn one eternal truth of war: when there's armour in the offing, sniping is a mug's game.

We'd just got rid of the fiddler on the roof when I spotted the flash of an RPG launch. I slewed the turret round at maximum speed. A two-man insurgent team had just taken a pot-shot at another Para section, 200 metres or so ahead of the guys we'd just helped get rid of the sniper. The RPG gunners were in cover behind a wall that ran out at right angles from a compound almost directly ahead of the advancing Paras. One of the enemy was tall, dressed in a brown dishdasha and contrasting black turban. The second man was shorter, broader, and in shades of grey. But they were both looking for trouble and they were going to get it. Luckily, Laurel and Hardy had missed the Paras with their first shot. But the section they'd just tried to kill had little or no chance of spotting the ambush team – the sneaky bastards had pre-cut a small hole in the wall they were hiding behind. As I watched on 10x magnification, I could see the RPG gunners lining up to take a second shot. They were going to pop back over to the gap, give the Paras a second dose and then leg it before they got spotted and taken out.

The Paras might not be able to see them, but it was plain as the nose on a gnome that by the same token, the two-man Taliban rocket team had no idea we were tracking them from our overwatch position on the hill. Cat and mouse and cat – with the Scimitar as the biggest, baddest moggy on the block. Cool as ever, Minty had the pair smack bang steady in the middle of his gun sight. They were at just under 400 metres range. 'OK,' I told Minty, 'hit them with the GPMG.' Selecting the 7.62mm machine gun, Minty pressed the fire button. I watched as a stream orange tracer floated down and onto the enemy. The instant the rounds began to ping off the walls around them, they turned on their flip-flops and began to run. Fast. Damn it, we hadn't hit them with the first burst – it's incredible the weight of firepower people can sometimes survive.

Minty chased the fleeing men with a long, spiralling snake of bullets. The insurgents lifted their nightgowns and kicked up their heels: nothing like ten rounds a second plucking the dust up from around your feet to make you shift a bit. With orange tracer bouncing and ballooning up all around them, the Taliban made it round the far corner of the wall, scooted down a short stretch of adjoining alleyway and scuttled into an open yard. From our vantage, we could see that, apart from them, it was empty. Just before he pulled the heavy wooden door shut behind him, the taller of the two men looked back along the alleyway and smiled. I thought: 'You can smirk, you fucker – but guess what? We've still got you bang to rights.'

'Switch to 30mm HE automatic,' I told Minty. 'Aim for that door.' Minty selected automatic and opened fire. The first round hit the door, exploded, and turned it to matchwood.

I shouted, 'Automatic go on.' Travelling at more than 1,000 metres per second, the next five 30mm rounds flew in through the hole where the door had been, ricocheted, exploded and obliterated everything in the room beyond. The Paras came up and cleared through the compound. They found not just the two men we'd been after, but several more armed enemy fighters sprawled dead in the same room. Then we saw that the whole area of adjoining compounds was seething with Taliban gun-teams. With our own fire lending the same kind of support that had helped take the sniper and the RPG team out of the game, 3 Para and 1 Troop pushed the enemy right back out of town and into the green zone.

We'd killed at least a dozen Taliban in the course of the op, but to my way of thinking, that didn't mean that there weren't still plenty of them skulking around – or that they wouldn't be back for another bite at us once they'd treated their injured and regrouped. In case they did come back, Jules Hoggarth and 1 Troop were ordered to take up position on top of Now Zad hill as fire support group for A Company, 2nd Battalion, The Royal Regiment of Fusiliers [RRF]. The RRF had just come in as the replacement in place [RIP] for the Gurkhas.

We'd been expecting to stay and lend 1 Troop and the fresh RRF unit our continued support: having cleared the town of Taliban, it was a good idea to make sure they stayed out, and as always in battle, that meant firepower and lots of it. But then we got a new set of orders: head for Musa Qal'ah, and help oversee a newly-scheduled relief and resupply mission.

CHAPTER EIGHT

The brief was short, sharp and to the point: while we'd been trying to help deal with the problems at Sangin and Now Zad, the rest of Helmand province was going pear-shaped. An ever-increasing number of British units had run into serious enemy opposition. Top of the list of units in need of support was the coalition force defending the DC at Musa Qal'ah.

Lt Long led me over to a map. 'Our new mission is to make all speed to Musa Qal'ah: here, about 70 kilometres to the north-east. The garrison in there is PF [Pathfinders] and Danes. They're running out of ammo, food and water. They've been under siege for several weeks and they're hanging off their chinstraps. Our job is to help them push the insurgents back as far as we can from the DC; secure an LZ for an essential re-supply op; and then overwatch that – and the RIP – if and when they go in.'

'Are we going in with infantry support?'

'No – just the armour.'

That gave me something to think about. We'd just helped relieve the pressure on a beleaguered garrison at Now Zad – but that had been a combined armour-infantry op, as per the tactical manual. You don't send armour into a built-up area without infantry support: if you do, then you're asking for the armour to get hit. But that was exactly what they now wanted us to go and do at Musa Qal'ah: motor into what looked and sounded very like a fire trap waiting to happen, but without the Paras. It immediately struck me as a very bad idea. But as the man once said, ours not to reason why.

'The problem with operating in Musa Qal'ah,' Tom continued, 'is much the same as the problem we faced up at Now Zad: the DC is smack in the middle of town and it's surrounded by compounds, so the enemy can use those and the rat runs linking them to creep up close; it's very difficult to re-supply, and it's extremely difficult to defend. Not only that, but to the west, which is the direction from which we'll be approaching, there's a socking great green zone that gives a potential enemy near-perfect cover.'

I said: 'You're just trying to cheer me up, Boss.'

Lieutenant Long said: 'We'll be going in with elements of 2 Troop as a reinforced column of six Scimitars, four Spartans and three of the RHA's 105mm guns. Major Dick will be in command with SHQ Troop as per usual. I will be leading 3 Troop, ditto no change. We need to turn the vehicles round, tell the lads to get some rest and then get going first thing in the morning. If it does go ahead, which, as you know, will depend on things like helicopter availability and the outcome of our own part in the op, the relief mission is due in at 0600 the day after that.'

I glanced at my Army-issue wristwatch: it was seven o'clock in the evening. 'Less than thirty-six hours from now. No pressure.'

'As you say, Corporal of Horse Flynn – no pressure.'

I did a quick spot of extra homework. Despite the relatively short time UK forces had been in Helmand province, the problem at Musa Qal'ah already had a serious and complex history. Brigade had made several attempts to re-supply the garrison by air, but each time the Taliban had put up such a monumental barrage of ground fire from RPG-7s, machine guns and AK47 assault rifles, that the helicopters had been unable to get close. On 21 July, a month after the siege had begun, the Griffins, a squadron of Danish light-armoured cavalry, had left Camp Bastion on a mission to relieve the troops in place at the Musa Qal'ah

DC. Reinforced by British signals specialists, the column had reached the outskirts of the town, only to find that the Taliban had blocked the route ahead with barrels. As the vehicles slowed down to deal with the road block, the Taliban attacked from three sides. Heavy machine-gun fire and rocket-propelled grenades punched into the mixed force. The Brits and the Danes fired back.

A landmine exploded under a Danish Eagle armoured vehicle, destroying it and injuring its three-man crew. Their FAC called in an American B-1B bomber to suppress the attacking forces, then the squadron moved back from the Musa Qal'ah green zone to regroup. Five days after leaving Bastion, the Danish-led column finally managed to fight its way into the besieged compound. Which was pretty damned impressive, given the strength, determination and courage of the opposition – we love those Danes, they fight like fuck. Opening fire with everything they had in a mass attack, the Taliban gave the DC's new arrivals a warm welcome. In the ferocious close-quarter fighting that ensued, a Danish sergeant died.

The battle for the DC raged on until the end of July. Fighting for their lives, the Griffins and two dozen or so men of the Parachute Regiment's élite Pathfinder reconnaissance unit were holding out – but only just. By then, they'd been under near-constant Taliban fire for the best part of seven weeks. Originally sent in on 20 June to support a beleaguered Afghan National Police [ANP] unit that had been close to annihilation, the Pathfinders were still in the compound and still fighting; but as Tom Long had said, they were chronically short of water, food, and ammunition; physically and mentally exhausted, they were pretty much running on empty. Unless supplies and reinforcements reached the Musa Qal'ah DC in quick time, the garrison ran the risk of being overrun.

Now it was our turn to see what we could do. I've told this story before, in the first book I had published, *Bullet Magnet*. But I'm telling a cut-down version again because I found out a scrap or two of new information. One classic symptom of post-traumatic stress is the need

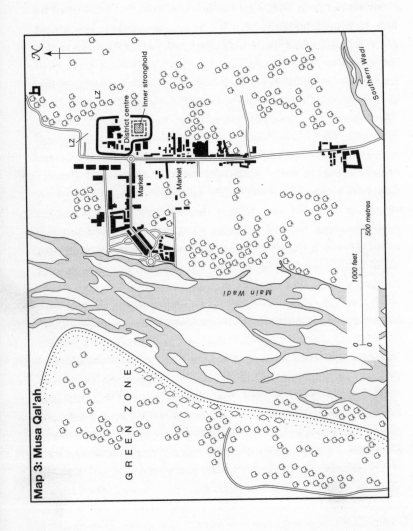

Map 3: Musa Qal'ah

to keep retelling the incident that upset you. Obviously, there's no way I'm suffering from anything like that.

We set out from Camp Bastion on 30 July. Since Musa Qal'ah lay only 70 or so kilometres from the base, that should have given us plenty of time to get up there and be in position at the DC to overwatch the scheduled re-supply mission. But although we made good speed for the first day, come evening, some of our vehicles caught the Afghan asthma again – dust got in the works and they started to break down. The next morning, as we tried to move towards an overwatch position just to the west of the Musa Qal'ah green zone, the Spartan commanded by JC Moses hit a Russian legacy mine. JC and his two crewmen were unhurt. But the blast disabled the Spartan, which in turn meant that the vehicle had to be denied – stripped of secret equipment and destroyed, so that it didn't fall into enemy hands. For various reasons, this turned out to be difficult, time-consuming and extremely frustrating. With the column now delayed by more than twelve hours, the re-supply mission was postponed until dawn on 1 August.

We reconstituted, left some of the broken wagons in the rear with SHQ [Squadron Headquarters], and pushed on towards the objective. As day broke on the morning of 1 August 2006, I led a column of five Scimitars and one Spartan down off the overwatch position where we'd set up a fire support group. We nudged forward into the western edge of the Musa Qal'ah green zone. The DC lay no more than four kilometres away, on the other side of the maze of beige-coloured compounds that sprawled along a line running roughly north–south a few hundred metres ahead of us. When an old tractor pulling a load of hay or straw chugged out of it without coming to any harm, we chose the middle of the three lanes that sliced through the built-up area.

We trundled up to the edge of a low hill facing the ragged sprawl of compounds blocking our path and came to a halt. I spent a few minutes taking careful stock of the lane and surrounding area. The lane was narrow and slightly sunken – not that much wider than the Scimitar. If the Taliban were going to hit us, then the lane was a good place to do it.

The eerie, brooding silence that had settled all around us was its own warning. Now would be a good time to send in the infantry clearance patrols that should, in the normal run of battle operations, have been working in tandem with us: flush out any enemy hiding in ambush and bring them under our guns. But SHQ kept on relaying the same message from Brigade back at Camp Bastion: 'Press on. Make all speed to Musa Qal'ah.' The relief and re-supply operation wasn't going to happen without the presence of our armour at the DC. The guys in there needed us. And there was no guarantee that any of the other routes through the green zone, which were in any case many kilometres to the north and south, would be any safer than the one I was looking at right now.

As my Scimitar nosed into the western end of the lane, I thought about getting Minty to hose down the whole area with fire from the Scimitar's co-axial GPMG: sweep the surface of the lane to see if that triggered any contact IEDs; put some fire into the olive groves that sloped up a gradual rise to form the lane's southern side and see if that forced any hidden enemy out of their lairs. But under the rules of engagement then in force, we were only supposed to fire if we'd been fired on, or saw an enemy in the act of aiming a weapon.

A ragged mud and straw wall formed the northern edge of the lane. Overgrown with trees and foliage, its top crumbled and serrated with age, it was a perfect place from which to launch an ambush. 'On,' I told Leechy. 'But take it steady.' We rolled forwards. I was hyper-alert, watching to all sides.

A brilliant flash of light filled the inside of the turret. On its heels came the thunderclap of a shattering explosion. A hurricane rush of blast rattled the Scimitar to its metal bones. The whole vehicle shook as if it had been grabbed by the scruff of the neck. I stuck my head up out of the turret hatch and snatched a quick look back. We'd rounded a slight dog-leg in the lane, and I couldn't see what had happened. But a great column of dark grey smoke was billowing up into the sky. Streaked with bright orange flares of flame, the towering, oily mass of slate-coloured fumes told me the worst: the Taliban had triggered an improvised explosive device: in all likelihood under the Spartan that had been directly behind us.

As I tried to decide what to do, a DShK 12.7mm heavy machine gun opened up from a hide at the eastern end of the lane directly ahead of us. The *dushka*'s big, 12.7mm (.50 inch) rounds smacked into the Scimitar's front end, jamming the turret. That meant we could no longer use it to train the 30mm Rarden cannon and our co-axial machine gun onto the enemy gun emplacement. But Leechy could pull the steering sticks to my command: make the whole vehicle turn on its axis. 'Right stick!' I told him. He hauled back on the steering-sticks. The Scimitar swung in a wild arc, way overshooting the target. 'Too much! Bring her back left a bit.' The tracks levered the vehicle round until our guns came to bear on the enemy position. 'Steady. On. Fire!' Nothing happened. Why hadn't Minter fired the main armament? I turned to see. 'Minty! Fire!' He was jabbing at the fire button, but nothing was happening: a *dushka* round had smashed the firing circuits. I smacked the palm of my hand down on the mechanical fire switch on the back of the Rarden's breech. Three HE 30mm rounds and a hosing of 7.62mm GPMG bullets thumped from our guns, smashing the *dushka* and shredding its crew. I saw one of them fall back to the ground, dead. Then, as if we didn't already have enough problems, the 30mm cannon jammed and refused to fire another round. Marvellous.

Now we discovered something else I'd managed to miss: the Taliban had pre-cut holes in the wall to our left to create killing (or murder) holes like the ones you sometimes see in medieval castles. Clever – and scary. Shoving weapons out through the newly revealed gaps, they opened up on us. An RPG-7 warhead smashed into the Scimitar's left side. The whole vehicle rang with the impact. The world turned a fuzzy shade of grey and then went to blackness and silence. When I came to, I had no idea what had happened. Was I still alive? I pinched hard on the top of my thigh. In return, I got a reassuring jab of pain. I was still feeling, still breathing: definitely still in the game. But I couldn't see anything. For a moment, I thought I'd gone blind. Then I realized: the shock of the RPG's impact had filled the turret with a dense cloud of fine dust.

It was game on. Unable to see what was happening through the turret's armoured glass vision blocks, I risked another lightning glance over the hatch rim. The cage armour we'd had fitted to the outside of the hull had buckled under the force of the rocket; but it had stopped the warhead punching through and killing us. More enemy fighters popped up from behind the jagged ramparts along the top of the wall, pouring AK47 fire at us in long, wicked bursts. The bullets smacked and thudded across the Scimitar's hull – but the showers of 7.62mm didn't worry me that much: unless we were very unlucky, the Scimitar could take that kind of incoming all day and survive. But the rocket-propelled grenade was a tank killer – and in comparison with a real tank, we were sitting in an eggshell.

'Smoke,' I thought. 'They've blinded us – let's return the favour.' I fired the pattern of six smoke grenades from the launchers on either side of the hull. Dense clouds of white phosphorus burst in the hot air, enveloping the Scimitar and screening the immediate area. The Taliban stopped firing for a few seconds while they tried to work out what was happening. Then a second rocket-propelled grenade smashed into our right-hand side, swatting the 12-tonne vehicle with pile-driver force. Again the world turned to dust and silence, and once again I wondered for an instant if we were all still alive. Then the grey-brown mist cleared, and I saw that, for the second time in less than a minute, the shopping trolley armour that they'd welded on for war had saved our lives.

We ground forward, weathering the metal storm of small-arms fire. Through the gun-smoke and dust, I saw a T-junction 20 metres ahead.

I wanted to reach the end of the lane – if we could do that, we might have some options. The junction came up. 'Stop!' I told Leechy. What was the best thing to do? We could turn left or right, but whichever route we chose there was every chance the Taliban would have set more IEDs; positioned more cut-off groups; or both. It was what I'd have done in their position. Best do what the enemy least expected: go back down the lane and have at them. All my focus was on getting the troop out alive. Most of the men under my command were in their late teens, the same age as my eldest son, Liam. And then there was the Spartan that had been directly behind us: I had to find out what had happened to that, and much more importantly still, what had happened to its passengers and crew.

'Turn around,' I told Leech. 'We're going back down the lane.' Leechy spun the Scimitar on the spot. There was a slight pause and then we lurched into forward gear. The moment they saw we were coming back at them, the Taliban along the top of the wall went berserk. Normally, they're ghost-figures: weaving and ducking, hard to hit, good at firing and moving and then popping back up in some other place you least expect. But now, a row of turban-clad fighters stood up in plain view and blazed away. The turret was still jammed. Perfect. And we still had no working main armament. But no fucker fired at me and I didn't fire back. 'Use the SA-80s,' I told my crew. 'Stick them up out of the hatches and fire blind. Let's try and keep their heads down.'

I poked my own rifle up out of the turret, pointed it in the general direction of the wall that was now on our right-hand side and squeezed the trigger. Minty did the same, Leechy was busy steering. But our joint spray-and-pray with the SA-80s didn't seem to be suppressing the enemy: if anything, they were raining fire on us harder than ever. The rounds slapped and stuttered across the hull, spattering like giant metal hailstones. I fired our last two remaining smoke grenades, but this time the enemy ignored the white clouds of phosphorus swirling to either side.

At that moment, a new enemy section opened up on us from the olive grove to our immediate left. I had a flashback to Sizzler, and one of the things he'd told us about the Taliban. They lured you into set-ups; they were always trying to funnel you into a killing ground like the one we were in now. I felt fury at being taken for a mug – but we'd had no option, we'd had to drive on. We were in a real fix: the enemy had really thought the ambush through. I got the sudden intuition that they'd sprung the same trap before: pulled the same trick on the Russians at this same spot. They were looking to lure us into a bottleneck, shepherd us like sheep to the slaughter, and then, when we were nicely sealed in on all sides, shoot the merry fuck out of the whole column.

As if to confirm the fact, another rocket-propelled grenade hammered into the Scimitar's right quarter, knocking it bodily round. The ancient wagon shuddered and groaned. For a moment, I was afraid the warhead had penetrated through and come into the hull. But once again the cage armour came good: we were still rolling, still heading back down the way we'd come.

We rounded the dog-leg. The Spartan was slewed sideways across the track directly ahead of us. Its commander had seen my Scimitar come under fire from RPGs and a heavy machine gun. Rather than drive straight into the ambush he'd told his driver, Martyn Compton, to stop and then reverse. The commander had made the right call: no point the whole column stumbling into a murderous trap. Better to reverse back out of the lane, regroup and call in extra support.

But as the Spartan rolled backwards, the Taliban exploded an IED directly beneath it. The blast had destroyed the vehicle.

'Foot down,' I told Leechy. 'Go for it!' I wanted him to drive past the burning vehicle, get us well clear of it and join up with the remainder of the troop at the mouth of the lane; then we could regroup and take the fight back to the enemy. But instead of stamping on the gas, Leechy trundled slowly up to the Spartan, tried to pass it on the left side, misjudged the gap and dumped our Scimitar into the ditch. The wagon lurched drunkenly to the left and stuck fast against the bank.

I looked out to my right: still caught in enemy crossfire, we were stranded directly alongside the blazing Spartan. I swore under my breath: the gutted vehicle was a ticking bomb – and it was almost within touching distance. 'Get out!' I told my crew. 'Get down in the ditch or we'll all get killed. Cover me: I'm going to take a look inside.' Leech and Minter tumbled out, took cover in the ditch and started laying fire on the Taliban. Marvellous.

Bullets plucked a neat line from the dust at my feet. I got down in the ditch next to Minter and Leech, raised the SA-80, took aim and fired at one of the shapes flitting along the top of the wall. He disappeared. 'Fall back with me to the end of the lane,' I shouted. At the same time I launched a red smoke grenade: it was all I had left, and the only way I could think to try and gain us some cover. The grenade hit the branch of an olive tree directly overhead, bounced and landed right back at my feet. At once we were shrouded in red smoke. Nice one. It marked our position nicely for the enemy, but now I couldn't even see Leech and Minter there in the ditch with me. AK47 rounds slammed into the baked earth all around us; more bullets whipped and cracked in from the olive trees. Firing and moving in turn, the three of us extracted to the end of the lane.

Lt Long had stuck his Scimitar's nose in the far end, its guns pointing back across our heads. I caught sight of the vehicle's gunner, LCoH Andrew Radford. Radders was dismounted, standing next to the Scimitar. He was staring back up the lane past me. 'Radders!' I shouted. 'What the fuck are you doing out of your vehicle? Get back inside, or you'll get killed.'

'No,' he said pointing, 'I can see someone moving up there. I think he might be one of ours.' I turned and looked. In the shadow of the first row of olive trees, 20 or 30 metres away, a still figure lay by the side of the lane. I studied it for a moment: there was no sign of a dishdasha, no RPG or AK47 on or near the man. Radders was right: there was a good chance he might be one of ours. In which case, we had to go up there and bring him back.

'Let's get him,' I said. We pepper-potted forwards, shooting and moving in turn. The Taliban still had us in enfilade fire from the wall to our left and the olive plantation to the right. They were bobbing up, firing a shot or two then bobbing back down. We fired snap-shots in reply, looking to make them keep their heads down, make them think before they showed themselves again.

A burst of gunfire poured from the mouth of a murder hole in the wall to my immediate left. I switched the SA-80 onto the gap and fired back. I couldn't see if I'd hit the hidden gunman but the firing stopped. A bullet whizzed past my head – a supersonic bee of lead. I glanced up the lane. The round seemed to have come from the far end. Fuck – a new enemy group was advancing towards us from up there, nine or ten men spread out in loose formation, firing AK47s from the shoulder and the hip as they came. I took a bead on the leader, steadied and squeezed off a couple of rounds. The impact knocked him backwards clean off his feet. I switched aim and double-tapped his right-hand neighbour. He didn't go down, but he flinched and dropped his weapon.

I sensed Radders next to me, leaning into his rifle firing aimed shots. The hardest thing to do when you're pepper-potting is to get your weapon steady on the aim when you stop and fire. Unless you can get nice and still and squeeze off the round, which is quite hard when your heart's pumping at about three times its normal rate and you can't seem to get a breath in your throat, then the chances are you're going to miss your target. The long days of training might seem tedious when you're out on the range, wet through and hungry and freezing cold – but if and when you do get into action they pay off.

With two of their number face down in the dust next to them, the remainder of the enemy section ahead of us faltered, crouched and then sprinted to either side. They wanted to get into cover. When they did that, they'd be back in the game. But at the very least, we'd given them something to think about.

We reached the man on the ground. A glance told me it was the

Spartan's driver, Martyn Compton. When the RPG had hit the Spartan's front end, the explosion had ignited the fuel in the engine next to him, drenching Compo in burning fuel. His whole body was burned scarlet. One of his legs lay twisted and broken. His eyes were fixed and unseeing, locked in a milky, unfocused stare. When I saw that, I thought: 'Martyn's dead.'

I knelt and tried to straighten his leg. At that, Compton's eyes came back into focus and he let out an agonized yell. Christ, he was still alive! I said, 'Let's get him out of here.' I bent, picked Compo up and laid him onto Radford's back. Compton was solidly built, but Radders took the weight with ease, bent his own body under it and set off back towards the mouth of the lane at a fast waddle.

I tried to stay with them, walking backwards and firing to all three sides. But the enemy could see we were there for the taking and kept up a steady rolling drumbeat of fire. I did my best to keep them all busy, but the effort slowed me right down. I was falling behind: there was a real risk I'd be cut off and surrounded at the heart of the trap. I hurried to catch up, stumbling as I tried to move backwards faster over the rutted ground. With a surge of relief, I glanced back and saw Tom Long's Scimitar right there behind me. Its Rarden and GPMG were spitting a firestorm at the enemy beyond. We needed the cover, but the rounds were passing so close to our heads that there was a real danger they'd kill us – and succeed where the Taliban had so far failed. I ducked under the hail of shells and shouted at Lt Long: 'Tom! Stop firing! Cease fire!'

I lifted Compton off Radford's back. Together, we laid him on the Scimitar's front decks. He screamed as the hot metal bit at his scorched skin. There was nothing else we could do – we had to get him out of there as soon as we could. I ripped my morphine syringe out of its coffin-shaped casing, tore off the safety cap, shoved the needle into Compo's arm and shot the contents into him. I remember thinking: 'Let the morphine work fast – please let it work fast.'

We jumped up on the Scimitar, holding Compton steady as it jolted into gear. The driver's headset had come disconnected, but I shouted steering commands in his ear. Narrowly missing a ditch, he steered us back out of the lane. The rest of the column had set up a helicopter landing site [HLS] in readiness for the medical emergency response team. As we reached the HLS, the Chinook carrying the airborne intensive care unit landed in front of us. The medics gave Compton immediate first aid, then got him on board and away to the hospital at Camp Bastion. I didn't know it then, but together with the third-degree burns to most of his body, Compton had taken two AK47 bullets through the leg. His heart had stopped twice en route to Bastion, but each time, by some miracle of skill and luck, the amazing MERT team had helped him cling to life.

With the injured man gone, we reached the top of the bluff where we'd left the fire support group. It felt as if I'd been in the ambush for ever, and at the same time it seemed to have gone by in a flash. The Quick Reaction Force [QRF] had just landed: 300 men of 3 Para to help us extract and then sort out the Taliban. I briefed the commanding officer, Lt-Col Stuart Tootal: 'We have to go back down there and make sure the Spartan crew are all dead or rescued. I could only be certain of two. Trooper Compton makes three. There may still be one man down there, missing.' When he'd heard me out, Tootal told me to lead the QRF into the compounds. We found and accounted for the missing vehicle commander. There was no point in wishing his death or the deaths of the other men away. All we could do now was mourn them.

CHAPTER NINE

With our ride reduced to scrap metal, Minter, Leech and I had had to hitch a lift back to Camp Bastion with the Paras. The Chinook was packed. It was oven-hot and I was severely dehydrated. Sitting there in the airborne mini-earthquake, I glanced across at Leech and Minter. They both looked like I felt – exhausted. Leechy had a glazed look that suggested he was suffering from delayed shock. Not surprising, given what we'd all just been through. Minter was perkier – all he wanted was the latest news on his beloved West Ham football team. I was desperate for water, but no one around me had a drop left. The Chinook thundered to a stop and we stepped out.

I tried to go and see Martyn Compton in the hospital, but they told me he was receiving treatment and to come back another time, so I made my way over to the accommodation pods, stepped in the shower and stayed there. The dust in Helmand province seemed to get everywhere: in the hair, up my nostrils, at the back of the throat. I spent a long time in the spray, struggling to wash away the dust and sweat. As I stood doing that, the contact we'd just been through kept playing over in my mind's eye. There were so many questions about it: why hadn't the Paras come into the green zone with us in the first place? Why hadn't we had a pair of Apaches providing top cover helped us get across that killing ground safely? Would moving north or south to try a different route through the zone have made any difference? Could I have done something different? Had I made a bad call going into that lane in the first place? I had plenty of questions, but no answers.

I chucked my grimy, blood-covered combats in the wash, had a cup of tea and sat down on the end of my bed. I thought: 'The worst thing is, I don't even know whose blood that is.' Someone said, 'You look exhausted, Mick – why don't you get your head down?' I put the half-finished mug of tea down; lay back on the pillow and closed my eyes. As soon as I did so, all the fatigue and the stress of the contact at Musa Qal'ah hit me a knock-out blow. The air-conditioning was out of action again – they'd switched off the generators to save diesel. It's so hot in the middle of summer in Afghanistan that even when you're lying down, uncovered in your skivvies, you immediately turn into a puddle of sweat. For once, I didn't notice. I just fell off a cliff into a deep, dreamless sleep.

When I woke up about eight hours later, it was early the next day. This time when I got to the hospital, the nurse let me in. Compo was swathed in bandages and inside a polythene tent. He was still unconscious, but he was still alive and that was more than a bit of a miracle. The nurse said that on top of his terrible burns and the AK47 round through the leg, he was going to need reconstructive surgery to his face. But to me, the fact that he was still breathing was the most important and amazing thing. Martyn had a girlfriend and a life waiting for him once they got him back home. It was really, really good that we hadn't lost him.

That same morning, Lt-Col Tootal summoned everyone who'd been involved to attend a debrief on the Musa Qal'ah ambush. We needed to come up with a new plan to relieve and re-supply the garrison. The problem was the same as it had been before our column had tried – and failed – to resolve it: the Taliban still had the DC in the grip of a ferocious siege; the Danes and Brits inside it were still heavily out-numbered; and they were still short of ammunition, food, water and just about everything else except fighting spirit. After we'd discussed what to do for the best, everyone present came to the same, resoundingly obvious conclusion: a much larger, combined air and ground force would have to be assembled in order to relieve the Pathfinders and the Danes, and with all possible speed.

The small Royal Engineers detachment at Musa Qal'ah had managed to repair a well inside the compound, which had been providing a limited supply of water. But the latest news was that the pump – held together by superglue and offerings to the gods – had again broken down. Slight in itself, the Int update nonetheless reinforced the point that all and any units taking part in the new relief operation had to be assembled in double-quick time. With every minute that passed, the garrison's predicament was worsening.

Early in the morning of Sunday, 6 August 2006, Brigade sent in the airborne element of the new attempt to RIP and re-supply the Musa Qal'ah DC, Operation Snakebite. Patrols Platoon went in first, securing a landing zone a short distance to the west of the town. With close air support from RAF Harriers and Army Air Corps AH-64 Apache gunships, three Chinooks then landed a mixed force of several hundred men: the lucky Royal Irish Regiment unit that was going in to replace the Pathfinders; B and C Companies, 3 Para; and a company of the Afghan National Army.

Setting out a day earlier than the main assault force so that we could reach the objective in time, the job of 2 and 3 Troops, D Squadron HCR was to secure the wadi leading in to the DC. The idea was for the Danes to break out down the lane connecting the DC to the wadi with their armoured vehicles and then link up with our armour. We'd then jointly establish a secure corridor for the Royal Irish to go into the fort and the Pathfinders to extract out. But we'd only just set out from Bastion on the new mission when once again our knackered old wagons let us down. Flogged to death even during the short time we'd been in Helmand province, choking on dust and creaking with age, four out of the five Scimitars in the column broke down completely. There was nothing for it but to turn around and tow them back to camp. D Squadron would be playing no further part in the relief mission. Like just about everyone else, I found that incredibly frustrating: we wanted to get back up to Musa Q and pay back the enemy with some lead. Why didn't we have any decent wheels?

With D Squadron out of the picture, a Canadian squadron in LAV III armoured vehicles took on the job of securing the wadi. I slipped into the TAC and listened in to the progress of the battle. Once they'd broken through the green zone and started linking up with the Danish troops, the combined infantry assault force began advancing on the Taliban with fixed bayonets.

Fighting through the residential compounds, gardens and orchards at very close quarters, and in some cases hand to hand, the battle group gradually pushed the enemy back. With temperatures soaring close to 50°C, food and water for the troops was essential. After some ten hours of intense combat, Operation Snakebite had succeeded. The Taliban had either been killed or cleared back from the centre of Musa Qal'ah. At last, the Pathfinders were able to extract from the DC.

Clearing the Taliban out of the town temporarily was one thing: holding the ground was another. One British officer likened ISAF combat successes in Helmand to 'mowing the grass'. To me, the Taliban were more like a particularly hardy and ferocious weed – as fast as you cut them down, they sprang back up again. They did now, regrouping, reinforcing and renewing their attacks on the Musa Qal'ah DC a day or two after the Operation Snakebite assault units had returned to base. There was nothing to admire about the Taliban – but they were some enemy.

Thirty-eight Royal Irish Rangers and the Griffins now defended the DC. Throwing back the new Taliban attacks with skill and determination, the Danes built ramps for their Eagle armoured vehicles so that they could make the best use of their remotely operated gun systems over the compound walls. The Royal Irish used their 81mm mortars with great accuracy, repeatedly smashing the Taliban out of the surrounding compounds when they encroached.

But the weeds kept on growing: on 25 August, with the district centre once again under siege, a new force of Paras and other units had to go back in, landing at the town in a second massed air assault codenamed Operation Atomi. Having either killed or driven back the latest batch of Taliban fighters, the troops left a garrison of several dozen fresh Afghan policemen to reassure the locals they were safe and secure. Given the reputation of the ANP at Musa Qal'ah and Sangin, some of us thought this was a bit like asking a shark to take care of your pet goldfish.

The next day, a 150-strong Taliban assault group welcomed the new ANP detachment with a massed all-round attack on the DC. The defenders called in an air strike. The A-10s responding to the call drove the Taliban back with heavy losses, but, true to form, the enemy renewed the attack at dawn on the day after that. In the fire fight that followed, one British soldier died. But the insurgents suffered far greater losses: Taliban dead lay where they'd fallen in the alleyways surrounding the DC. The garrison allowed the enemy in to pick up their dead, and everyone braced for a fresh round of fighting. But no one was winning: the battle for Musa Qal'ah had reached a stalemate: the Taliban weren't ever going to take the DC, but with their ability to call in seemingly endless reinforcements, we were unlikely to stop them trying. Only one thing remained certain: for as long as the stand-off lasted, people on both sides would keep dying.

CHAPTER TEN

While 2 and 3 Troops had been trying to help resolve the little local difficulty at Musa Qal'ah, 1 Troop had remained at Now Zad on the top of ANP Hill. It was time for a replacement to be made, and the lot fell to 3 Troop. But before we left we were hit with some awful news from Sangin that left the whole troop reeling.

Whilst we'd been knocking them back on their heels up at Musa Qal'ah, the Taliban had been busy re-attacking coalition and Afghan government assets in and around Sangin, especially the Royal Engineer contingent working to build a new FOB to the north of the town. They were building the new outpost a good distance from the existing DC so that the locals wouldn't think that British or other occupying foreign forces were running things in Sangin. As if they were that stupid.

Within a week of the work on it starting, all units in and around the new FOB came under Taliban attack: RPG, AK47, RPK: run-of-the-mill stuff, but to be resisted. Working with a platoon of Paras, 2 Troop, D Squadron HCR sent an armoured force protection patrol out to suppress the attacks. While 2 Troop and the Paras fought back, the engineers carried on building the FOB: you don't want to let the enemy see he's having an effect.

One day, the Taliban attacked in the cool hours immediately following the early morning call to prayers: post-prayer attacks get the day off to a good start for the insurgents – maybe it makes them feel as if they've achieved something. While the TIC [troops in contact, or fire fight] was open, the whole area around the new FOB was one big hive of activity, not least in the skies overhead: Apache gunships came on station; there were air strikes from fast jet and A-10s; battle group HQ was demanding an update every five minutes, and there were rounds and bombs flying about everywhere. In other words, it was busy. The numbers of enemy dead and injured began to mount. Later in the morning, the Taliban lost heart and withdrew. The TIC got closed and all units came back into Sangin FOB. In the course of the operation, which had otherwise been pretty successful, one of 2 Troop's Spartans broke a torsion bar.

Part of the vehicle's antiquated suspension system, torsion bars are steel rods that run between the chassis and the wheels. Unless they replaced it, 2 Troop would be one Spartan short – not good when there were so few available to start with, and given the high frequency of mechanical breakdowns throughout the ageing fleet. But replacing a torsion bar is difficult and dangerous. It means jacking 12 tonnes of armoured vehicle up and removing the crucial grub screws with an Allen key. Always assuming that you have a spare bar. With no spare available, 2 Troop had to take one of the torsion bars from a Spartan that was even more broken down. If they could get that to fit, then they'd have at least one working vehicle. Nothing like cannibalization.

The troop managed to get the Spartan back into the compound at Sangin. The ground in there was packed sand, but with a fine, talcum powder layer on top: not the same as tarmac or concrete when it comes to jacking up and repairing armoured vehicles. And more especially, not as safe. Lance-sergeant Lee Oakes, who was one of the fittest guys in the regiment, got under the vehicle and began trying to remove the broken bar. After a long time spent sweating and grunting under the Spartan, Oakes gave up trying to extract the grub screw and wriggled out. The heat in Helmand province in summer is so great that even when you're very fit, any sustained period of hard physical work saps the strength clean out of you. Thirty minutes working under an armoured vehicle in 40° heat feels like an eternity. Oakes had been under there for more than an hour.

One of the men who'd been watching Oakesy struggle said: 'It's time you had a break, Lee: let me have a go at it.'

For as long as it has been in service, soldiers have disliked using the jacking strut – especially on sandy soil of the type that is common in Helmand province. But being a good bloke, the volunteer slid in under the Spartan and took over from Lee. It was 1445 in the afternoon. The new man had only been under the Spartan for a few minutes when the jacking strut collapsed. The full weight of the vehicle fell directly on him, killing him.

Extremely saddened, we set off for Now Zad early in the second week of August 2006. Amazingly, this time out the troop suffered only minor mechanical failures on the way, nobody attacked us, none of the convoy hit an IED or a legacy mine and we got there in a matter of hours.

We'd made a few changes to the troop's personnel. Given his youth and what he'd just been through in the ambush at Musa Qal'ah, we decided to give my driver, James Leech, a break from front-line duties: he stayed behind in Bastion to work admin duties for a couple of months. Apart from one minor driving mishap, when he'd managed to get my favourite Scimitar stuck in a ditch, Leechy had done really well in the Musa Qal'ah fire fight. His replacement was Trooper Stan Stanforth, from Melton Mowbray. Tall and dark but missing out on the other bit, Stan's ambition was to become a farrier in the Household Cavalry. But while he worked on making that particular dream come true, I was lucky to have him.

When they did actually work as they were meant to, our light armoured vehicles were brilliant. After a few hours rattling our bones across the monotonous, grey-brown sandpit, we caught sight of ANP Hill. It looked exactly the same: as if someone had plonked down a huge pile of rock and dust, then hit it hard on the top with a shovel. Lovely – our new home from home for the next several weeks.

The first thing I did when we reached the top of the hill was to go and have a fresh talk with Corporal of Horse Jules Hoggarth, who'd been maintaining the DC overwatch position with the rest of his troop since we'd tried to help the Paras flush out and expel the local Taliban. While we talked, our troop leader, Lt Tom Long, had a meeting with his own opposite number, Lt Charlie Church. The first thing Jules Hoggarth said was: 'I'm sorry to hear about what happened over at Musa Qal'ah.' There was nothing I could say in reply. Losing three of our number had affected every single member of D Squadron – each in his own way. Musa Qal'ah was only about 20 kilometres away as the crow flies, so 1 Troop had heard most of the fire fight we'd had with the Taliban live on the radio net – not least because I'd left my chest pressel unit in the 'send' position for much of the time.

Hoggarth waved a hand that sketched out the sprawling, close-knit ramble of compounds that made up the town. Nothing had changed: the DC compound, with its mixed garrison of Brits and ANA units, lay smack in the middle, on the western side of the dusty, scabby main drag and a short distance from the foot of the hill on which we were now perched. The Gurkhas were pulling out, being relieved in place by 1 Royal Regiment of Fusiliers company [1 RRF] drafted in from their holiday complex in Cyprus.

The incoming Fusilier presence amounted to about 100 men in total – not very many. One rifle platoon plus their mortar section would join us up on the hill in defence of the Shrine. The remainder of the RRF – another sixty or so riflemen – would take over as the DC garrison. The Fusiliers had been told they'd only be in place at Now Zad for fourteen days, so they'd come in light scales, with very little equipment and not really enough in the way of heavy weaponry. Three months later, they would still be in Now Zad.

A bazaar that had done good business until the Taliban arrived but was now almost entirely abandoned, stretched down the street from the DC. That was about it for the town's stab at commercial enterprise. The Helmand River ran at the foot of a mountainous ridge to the east. With the summer heat going full blast, and Afghanistan suffering regular recent droughts, the watercourse had been reduced to a trickle. But when spring came, providing it remembered to rain again, the river would rush down the valley in a glacial flood, fuelled by the snow melt from the high peaks. One thing you're never far from in much of Helmand province is a mountain. Make that a range of mountains. It's like Switzerland, only with 45° heat and scorpions. Mountains surrounded Now Zad on every side, and if it hadn't been for the fact that we were at war, I'd have taken more time to admire the spectacular scenery. Most days, the air's so clear it looks as if you can reach out a hand and touch the distant, jagged peaks with your fingers.

'We've noticed a couple of things since we last met,' Hoggarth said. 'The Taliban use that dried-up wadi to the east over there as a highway. They go up and down it from here to Musa Qal'ah, Sangin and beyond, moving weapons, men and drugs.' I raised my binos and trained them slowly across the landscape, trying to get a new feel for the surroundings. At a distance of about 200 metres to the south-east of the town, I could see a cemetery. Prayer flags on tall poles fluttered from the new graves. With that graveyard full, the locals had tacked on an overspill cemetery, but that, too, had become overcrowded. The business in death was booming: packed tight together, a lot of the graves were fresh. If the Taliban decided to attack 3 Troop when we were up on the hill, we'd do our best to make them open up a new extension.

To the west of ANP Hill, barren, sand-coloured folds of land marched away towards the high ground: grey-brown slopes riddled with tunnels and caves where the enemy could hide. Jules saw me looking and nodded. 'That's where the Taliban run to when we've whacked them and they need to regroup. Once they've gone to ground up in the mountains, only the SF [special forces] can get them.' A lot of mountain ranges in Helmand province had cave systems that might almost have been purpose-designed to hide a guerrilla force. Some of the underground complexes were big enough to conceal a small army.

'It's been pretty quiet up here: maybe it was the clearance ops we did with the Paras, but we seem to have hit a lull in the Taliban attacks. The odd mortar or sniper round's come in, but nothing serious. In fact, the lads have been running a suntan competition.' I looked at the members of 1 Troop, saddled up and ready to go: they looked fit and relaxed, and all the ones who'd started out with white skin were now tanned a deep, golden brown. Swine.

'Obviously, we've done our best to support the garrison down in the DC. But when they do come in to take a pot-shot, the sneaky bastards creep through their rat runs between the compounds, which makes it pretty hard to hit them. They've got dried-up ditches they crawl through, storm drains and culverts and such-like.' I took a closer look at the DC. It was your basic Afghan fort, but at least the mud and straw walls were nice and high. The defences were very basic, but that didn't mean they were no good: heavily protected with sandbags and Hesco blast barriers, each of the four sangars had a sentry armed with a machine gun on watch twenty-four hours a day.

Jules led me across to the outermost ring of trenches that encircled the flat area on top of the hill. 'We're using the old Russian fortifications as accommodation. The Russkies burrowed right through the summit: the whole position's like a bloody rabbit warren.' Looking round the fortifications as Jules talked me through them, what struck me most was how much they resembled their First World War equivalent. Behind the perimeter trenches, narrow burrows and dugouts wormed through the top of the mound. Your average British Tommy on the Western Front would have felt right at home on ANP Hill, and been a lot drier into the bargain.

I stuck my head inside the nearest hobbit hole. Not far from the entrance, someone had cut a niche into the left-hand wall. A scattering

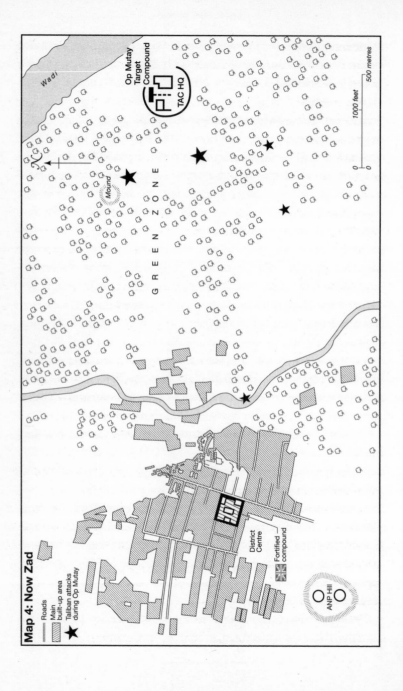

Map 4: Now Zad

Roads
Main
built-up area
Taliban attacks
during Op Mutay

Wadi

Op Mutay
Target
Compound

TAC HQ

Mound

G R E E N   Z O N E

District
Centre

Fortified
compound

ANP Hill

0   1000 feet
0   500 metres

of kit and a sleeping bag were laid out on the narrow ledge. As sleeping quarters went, it looked rough even for a tramp. 'Nothing like making yourself comfortable,' I said.

Jules nodded. 'You're right – it's a shit-hole – fit for spiders and snakes, not human beings. But we've tried to make the best of it. We've rigged up some showers, over on the other side: I'll show you.' He led me across to the lower western side of the summit. It was a far cry from my nice, comfy bathroom at home in Windsor: a makeshift contraption of wood and rope supported a couple of plastic shower bags, next to which was the shitters, or toilet. This consisted of a large wooden crate with a handy circle cut out of the middle placed over a pit in the ground. 'The worst job is having to burn the shit every two days – we pay the volunteers a few quid extra for doing that.' He pointed at the open section in the surrounding screen. 'As you can see, we deliberately didn't put any hessian up around the side that faces the mountains.'

'Why not?'

'The Taliban dickers watch everything we do from that side. We may as well give them something to look at. One of the biggest problems we have is getting water up here. There's no natural spring, so every single drop of the stuff has to be carried up. It's all bottled water, and it's too valuable for washing. We only get to shower once every three days, tops.'

'Any excuse for not washing, Hoggarth. Have you come under attack since you've been up here?'

'The Taliban spend most of their time hanging out in the green zone to the east. There are lots of them; their main forward lines are only about 400 metres from where we're standing and they're well dug in. All our efforts pushed them back a bit, but they keep trying to creep up again. They have a sentry screen out most of the time, and they use a team of motorbike dickers to report our activity.'

'Have you been in there? To take them on?'

'No. If you do decide to go down into the green zone, which I seriously don't recommend, then as you know, you'll need to be bloody careful.'

'OK. It doesn't look too complicated.'

'It's dead simple: the infantry down there in the fort are the good guys: there's a platoon of RRF in there with a forward air controller and some ANP. Half the time, the police are off hobnobbing with the enemy. It's the usual problem: we don't have enough boots on the ground.' I agreed with Jules: ninety or one hundred men including my own troop was a very small number when it came to controlling an enemy-infested town that was roughly the size of Maidenhead, only a lot more dangerous.

'The bad guys have us pretty much surrounded; they can come and go from their own lines as they please. All we can really do is sit tight and try to discourage them. It's basically like medieval siege warfare, right down to the crappy earthworks.'

'That's where you're wrong, Jules: there's no moat.'

'You're right – there's not enough water for a moat, more's the pity. But at least we hold the high ground.' That was the trump card: if we had to play the role of a besieged force, and we apparently did, then occupying the hill overlooking the town made all the difference. That, our armour, and the accuracy and range of the Scimitar's 30mm cannon. But Jules was right, we were effectively under siege. That's what happens when you don't deploy enough troops to do the job in hand: you end up stuck in one place, protecting yourself in small packets.

We weren't the only ones under siege. Intelligence suggested that a great many of the locals just wanted to get on with their lives; farm their crops and not get caught in the crossfire between us and the Taliban. But they were constantly getting harried – and killed – by one side or the other. In the case of ISAF, civilian casualties were always accidental. In the case of the Taliban, the killings were often deliberate and carried out in cold blood.

Jules said, 'One last thing, Mick, before we get going: thanks for taking out that sniper – he was a real pain in the arse.'

'Any time, Jules – you being a Life Guard, you'd still be looking for him now if we hadn't spotted him for you.'

'Fuck off, Flynn you old bastard – how are you going to get your wheelchair up here? There's no Stena stair lift up on the hill, you know.'

Waving us fond goodbyes, 1 Troop drove down the hill, formed up with the rest of the convoy that had escorted us up from the south, then began trundling south-east back towards Camp Bastion. A great swirling cloud of fine khaki dust flew up behind the vehicles, then joined up overhead to form a cloud that flattened and then slithered west in the prevailing breeze. Goodbye 1 Troop. I suddenly felt extremely alone.

Time to focus on the task in hand. The first thing to do was set up a ring of steel: place the Scimitars and the single Spartan in all-round defence at strategic points on the perimeter, making sure we had interlocking fields of fire that covered the full 360°. Nothing too complicated. But to begin with, we didn't add to the defences; as Jules had noted, the Russians and just about every other bugger who'd used the location had already tunnelled and entrenched the place until it looked like a big lump of Swiss cheese. What we did do was rig up awnings between the vehicles to give us a spot of shade, get the camping stoves going and make ourselves a brew. No point being British and not taking full advantage.

At first, all was quiet – exactly as Jules had reported. But then, at about six p.m., just before the call to evening prayers, I heard the familiar ugly whoosh of an RPG-7 launch: 'RPG!' I shouted. 'Take cover!' Fired from a nest of compounds about 600 metres to the south-east, the rocket grenade swarmed up the hill towards us. I watched as it streaked up into the sky directly overhead and then exploded in a spectacular burst of smoke and steel. The Taliban knew exactly what they were doing: when you fire an RPG-7, if the warhead hasn't hit anything in-between times, it automatically explodes at about 600 metres. The enemy were aiming the rockets at the airspace immediately above us, meaning to shower us with red-hot shrapnel. Everyone raced for the vehicles: it had to be safer under armour than out in the open, getting drenched in hot metal rain. The fusiliers ran for the trenches and tucked down under their hard hats. A second RPG followed the first, overshot to the west and exploded. No one was injured – but it was bloody annoying about the tea.

We stayed mounted in the vehicles spotting for targets. One of the good things – the only good thing – about an RPG attack is that the flash and back-blast as the rocket ignites, tends to make the firing point visible. Seconds after the attack started, our gunners were laying a wall of 30mm and 7.62mm shells and bullets onto the enemy.

Seated in the boiling Scimitar, I watched through the commander's sight as our gunfire slammed into the hazy shapes firing up at us from the compounds below. On 10x magnification, we could see them very clearly. Did the enemy somehow believe they were invisible? With rounds striking on and all around them, the enemy fighters broke off their attack, melting eastwards further back into the green zone. The fact they were cutting and running so quickly was probably a good sign: we might just have hit one or two of them. The Taliban like to dish it out, but they don't like to get it back.

'They're just saying hello,' I said, when the ruckus had died down. 'Leaving their calling card.' At the time, I truly believed that. If Jules Hoggarth had enjoyed peace and quiet for several weeks, then why should the local Taliban suddenly start a full-scale shooting war with us? The attack had probably just been a one-off: now they'd made their little point, with any luck they'd go back to minding their goats.

I was wrong. Early the next morning we were washing and shaving and brewing up. I'd just put some foam on my face when the enemy opened up with mortars. We were bantering and joking; the breeze hadn't got up yet and there was quite a lot of noise around the hill in the still morning air. We had our engines running to charge up the batteries and make a brew in the boiling vessels [BVs, or 'bivvies' – a small electrical cooking pot]. But the background rattle and throb of several Cummins diesels all running at the same time meant the first mortar rounds landed before we'd heard the pop of them leaving the tubes. As the first shell exploded in a shower of dirt and shrapnel, someone shouted: 'Mortar!' Thanks, pal.

Some of the lads still had their flip-flops and shorts on, aiming to get started on a suntan competition same as 1 Troop. But instinctively, I felt things were different: we weren't going to get a nice little holiday – we were in a fight, and it wasn't going to end any time soon. We ran for the wagons, jumped in, closed the hatches and switched the engines off. As I was running, I heard a soft pop. Peering out through the sight, I heard the deepening whistle of the incoming round. It landed on the south-western side of the hill, not all that far from our lines. Downright unfriendly.

Then an extremely loud bang shook the whole area. As the blast wave echoed and faded round the hills, I heard the same quiet coughing sound again. Another mortar bomb exploded about five seconds later, followed by another and another, and then so many in a stream there was almost no gap between the incoming rounds.

I hated the idea that all we could do was just sit there and take it. I thought: 'We could drive off the hill to escape the incoming, but then what? We'd lose the advantage of the high ground – and in the green zone, without any infantry support, we'd be sitting ducks.' So far, the Taliban fire had been inaccurate: it was obvious they were firing blind. With no forward observation officer to correct their fall of shot, it would only be luck if they hit us. But then, they only had to be lucky the one time.

We weren't used to mortar attack, so it took us a while before we were able to pick out the faint puffs of smoke or the ignition flashes that marked the enemy firing positions. Then one of the RRF guys suddenly did spot a flash. He opened up on the system with a .50 cal machine gun – exactly what we wanted, a nice big heavy weapon system whacking the enemy back. The Taliban mortar team was tucked in a small wadi about 800 metres to the east. I watched the tracer from the .50 calibre float out across the intervening distance and strike down into the enemy target. Then, spotting a second launch site, we laid a barrage of 30mm and co-ax on that. Under that withering return fire, one by one the enemy mortar teams fell silent. They stayed quiet for the rest of that day. But the peace wasn't to last.

From that morning onwards, we learned to run up our engines early, for the shortest time possible, and keep as quiet as we possibly could up on the hill to listen for the pop of the enemy mortars. The Taliban changed their own tactics after the first exchange of fire, falling back and regrouping at a range of about 3,000 metres. At that distance, they thought they were safe. They were wrong: the Scimitar's main armament, the 30mm Rarden cannon, can hit targets accurately out to some 4,000 metres. On the few occasions when they were stupid enough to come forward and try to infiltrate the DC, our 30mm cannon fire forced them back. More often than not, they carried their dead and injured out with them.

It became routine; every morning at around 0700, the Taliban hit us with a wake-up barrage of mortar fire. The only difference to the daily routine was the range from which they fired. Very quickly, we learned to judge the range of an enemy mortar by counting the seconds between the pop as it fired and the round landing. Practice making perfect, by the end of the first week, we could locate mortar teams and suppress them with return fire before they'd launched more than a couple of rounds.

But once again, the Taliban changed their tactics. The more experienced enemy teams began to dig out a pit before firing the mortar, and/or rigging a screen of sacking or branches over the tube to try and stop us spotting them. As ruses go, covering a mortar pit is risky: if a round hits a branch or any other obstacle on the way out of the pit, then it could explode and kill the crew. But the other change the enemy made was more sensible: they'd fire a couple of rounds and then shift the tube to a new location. It brought home the fact that the Taliban were adaptable and resourceful. They use everything and anything that comes to hand, including their wedding tackle: if their mortar tubes started to overheat, they pissed on them.

With attacks now occurring on a daily basis, we needed much better protection. Given how quiet it had been during 1 Troop's tour of duty at the Shrine, they hadn't felt the need to build any extra shelters. We, on the other hand, couldn't get them up fast enough. The boss called the lads together: 'Individual shell scrapes and firing trenches aren't going to save us from a direct hit. We've got to dig in – build ourselves a nice, big, well-covered super-sangar. That means timber; and steel supports if we can scrounge them up; and lots and lots of sandbags on the roof.' A groan went up: everyone knew they'd have to fill the sandbags by hand – a killer of a job in the punishing heat.

We set to digging out a rectangular pit about 4 metres wide by 10 metres long by 3 metres deep. Everyone went at it with a will, but in extreme heat and direct sun, the work was deadly. Given the strong risk of heat-stroke, I made sure the digging teams got good breaks at regular intervals. The boys didn't have to be told to drink water, even if it was boiling hot from the sun.

Then things got much worse: after digging down a few centimetres, we discovered to our horror that the fine sand gave way to solid bedrock. Digging sandy soil was one thing – but this was becoming a serious man-test. We'd been planning to use the spoil excavated from the pit to fill the 500 sandbags we needed to make the sangar secure – but the discovery that ANP Hill was made out of solid rock put paid to that idea.

Before hitting rock, we'd only managed to fill a couple of hundred sandbags. The other 1,800 were still piled up and waiting. How were we going to fill them? We realized the only solution was to drive a Spartan down the hill; find a large patch of soft sand; fill a load of sandbags and then drive them all back up again. That in turn meant manning a Scimitar in overwatch, to protect the sandbag shuttle vehicle and the teams filling them.

All that was far from ideal – but it had to be done. The troop set to, trundling up and down ANP Hill, digging, filling and lugging what felt like an endless pile of sandbags while a separate construction team got on with building the sangar. It was a bit like the old black-and-white film *The Hill*, set in a British Army prison in the Libyan desert and starring Sean Connery and Harry Andrews. Only it was probably hotter, and instead of being stripped to the waist we were all wearing body armour, helmets and combats. And the sand was more difficult to deal with: so fine in some places that we sank in it up to the ankles. When the breeze stirred itself to action, the dust seemed to go everywhere except into the bags.

It took us two days of hard labour to fill all the sandbags, transport them up to the top of the hill and get the sangar built. Under these extreme circumstances, I thought that was reasonably fast and efficient. But in the process, everyone involved lost the best part of a stone in weight. 'Shelley will be pleased if I come back leaner and meaner,' I thought. 'Well, leaner, anyway.' We went from drinking an average 20 litres of water per day each to swigging 25 litres. But drinking that much water flushes the foods out of your system, washing it clean of the vital stuff you need to survive, like salt and other minerals. The trick is to eat more, but extreme heat tends to kill the appetite.

All the time we were building the sangar, the Taliban watched us. But although it made us more vulnerable, for some reason they didn't attack. Then, just as we were unloading the last batch of sandbags and positioning them on the sangar roof, we heard the old familiar pop of a mortar round leaving the tube. The bastards were just trying to stop us from having a well-earned rest. They kept the attack going for more than an hour, but at least now we had a mortar-proof shelter. Or not: as soon as we got inside the sangar, we saw that the roof was sagging dangerously. The steel pickets we'd used might be good for fencing, but they weren't strong enough to hold up two tonnes of sandbags.

We had to get some RSJs, fast, or there was a risk that we'd be buried alive in our own shelter. We indented Camp Bastion's stores company for girders, but when none came we had to jerry-rig the whole roof with more pickets.

CHAPTER ELEVEN

Intelligence suggested that the Taliban forces newly pushed back from Musa Qal'ah had switched their attention to what they now saw as a softer target: Now Zad. It was quite hard not to take that personally: what had we done to deserve all the attention? But the more time we spent up on ANP Hill and the more intelligence we gathered, the clearer it became that Taliban forces switched from Musa Qal'ah weren't the only hostiles in the insurgent mix. After three months in Helmand, it was clear that all and any British Army units acted as a magnet for the Taliban. And not just the Taliban: local sources suggested enemy fighters were streaming in, not just from Helmand province and the rest of Afghanistan, but increasingly from Pakistan.

A few weeks later, the Taliban adapted their tactics yet again, attacking the Shrine from one side, and then, while we were busy dealing with that, launching a separate attack on the DC from another direction. Classic stuff, and from their point of view a good idea. Each and every time the Taliban attacked, the boys had to drop the Factor 20, whack on their helmets and body armour, jump in the vehicles and help the RRF to suppress the enemy. But with each day that passed, the task seemed to grow that little bit harder. The insurgents were pouring in resources, throwing more and more men and weapons into the mix: mortars, heavy machine guns, snipers and even the occasional 107mm rocket.

After a few days, most of us stopped jumping up and running for cover when the mortar rounds started landing. With no serious injuries on our side to date, and the Taliban routinely overshooting our lines, we were in danger of taking the threat a bit too lightly. You'd hear a pop, have a quick heads-up in the general direction to make sure the round wasn't coming your way, and then carry on with whatever you were doing. But in combat, complacency like that can be fatal.

The Afghan government had built a school about 300 metres to the north of the DC. Intelligence reported that the Taliban had occupied the main school building. Any doubts we might have had about that were dispelled when a 107mm artillery rocket fired from that location slammed into the DC's northern wall. More rockets followed when the enemy felt like it. Later that night, we saw lights flickering on and off inside the school. The enemy were still in there – and they couldn't be allowed to go on rocketing the DC at will. Brigade decided to call in an air strike. A pair of RAF Harrier GR7s came up from Kandahar airbase, lined up on the school, ran in and bombed it to dust. The Harrier crews shot battle damage assessment [BDA] footage that clearly showed bodies flying up as the bombs exploded. But I suspected they were ten-dollar Taliban, not the hard-core fighters we really wanted: part-timers who'd been lured to the school with the promise of extra pay and then sacrificed to make us look bad.

The only school for miles, and we'd destroyed it. What message did that send to the locals?

Shortly after first light the next day, I was having a wash and shave by the showers. Lance-Sergeant Metea, or 'Met,' a Fijian REME, was shaving over a makeshift basin just to the left of me. We'd just got the soap worked up into a nice lather when I heard the first pop of our regular morning wake-up call. The blade stopped dead on my face. I gazed up from the scrap of mirror nailed to the post in front of me. 'Incoming,' I said casually.

'Sounds like it.' The round started whistling towards us. Faint to begin with, the sound of its trajectory grew louder and louder. 'Could be a close one,' I said.

Met was a cool character. 'Could be very close. Maybe we should take cover.'

I said: 'Fuck it – I'm fed up jumping in the shell scrape because of these Taliban bastards. No fucking enemy's going to stop me from finishing my shave.'

'Me neither,' Met said. We carried on shaving. Three seconds later, I realized we'd both made a very big mistake. A small, dark object whizzed past my left ear and thwacked into the ground at my feet. I looked down. A set of tail fins was projecting from the ground between me and Met: if he'd wanted to, he could have reached down and touched them. I stared down at the star-shaped lump of metal. It looked extremely close, extremely large and extremely dangerous. But it had failed to detonate. I stated the obvious. 'That was fucking close.'

'Fucking was it.' We carried on shaving. Bravado was one thing. But there was a serious side to what had just happened: if the bomb had exploded, then it would almost certainly have killed Met, and either killed or seriously injured me. Even now, there was still a strong chance that it might explode. I caught Met's eye. 'Lucky, eh?'

'Fucking lucky.' We'd been fortunate in more ways than one: its failure to explode meant the enemy couldn't use the one accurate round they'd fired so far to register and adjust their firing co-ordinates. If they had succeeded in correcting fall of shot, we'd have been eating mortar rounds for breakfast.

In war, you need every ounce of luck you have to stay alive. This time around, fortune had smiled on us. Close shave wasn't in it: we'd bloody near ended up in small pieces, raining down on our own men. The lesson for us and everyone up on the hill that day was: don't ever think you can ignore incoming mortar fire: take it seriously. The macho stuff was way out of order: from now on, not only would I take cover the instant I heard the pop of a mortar leaving the tube, I'd make sure that everyone else in the troop did the same.

We piled a stack of sandbags around the unexploded ordnance [UXO] and cordoned it off. It sat there, festering, while we did our best to ignore it. But we needed to render it safe, immediately if not sooner – it was right in the middle of our lines. For that, we needed an Explosive Ordnance Disposal [EOD] officer, otherwise known as a bomb disposal guy. The only problem being, we didn't have one to hand.

Fed up with the early morning mortaring, I decided to put myself and my crew on regular dawn stag [sentry duty] for a few days: I wanted to try and eliminate the threat the instant it started – be in the Scimitar and ready to return fire. About three days after Met and I had our near miss, I was keeping watch one morning just after dawn when the Taliban fired their usual wake-up salvo. At first, in the uncertain light of the new day, I couldn't see any sign of the launch smoke. But that didn't bother me. What did bother me was the fact that, over the past few days, the incoming fire had been growing more and more accurate – witness the round that had nearly blown me and Met to shreds. I strongly suspected a Taliban FOO had eyes on us, and he was calling back by push-to-talk radio to correct shot. I heard a new pop, and started counting out the seconds between that and the moment the round landed: 'one, two, three, four, five . . .' A mortar bomb travels at about 400 metres per second. So the enemy team was about 2 kilometres away.

I scanned round with the commander's sight at that range. Nothing. I dropped the range a fraction and scanned again. A flash of movement in a dense stand of trees at the edge of the green zone caught my eye. I stopped the traverse and tracked the aiming circle very slowly back to the spot. A dark shadow flickered in the tangle of grey-green foliage. I upped the magnification to 10x. A man was perched high in the upper branches of an olive tree out there. Well concealed in the thick foliage, unless he'd moved at the precise instant I might never have seen him. But I had seen him. Which was bad luck for him, and good luck for us. The instant I could be certain I was looking at an enemy FOO, we were going to have the fucker.

The commander's day sight on the Scimitar works independently of the gunner's sight, but they both see the same thing through the thermal sights. I now switched the thermal image on; the fan whirred as it started up. In the cool dawn air, the man's heat signature made it easier to see him. Minty dropped the laser rangefinder onto the suspect and pressed the trigger. A string of numbers giving the location's range and GPS grid reference flashed up in the top right-hand corner of the sight: 1,800 metres. Extreme range for the General Purpose Machine Gun – but if we used the 30mm to good effect, then our friend was a dead man. I kept watching him. We needed a positive ID of hostile activity before he could be classed as a legitimate target. Another mortar popped in the distance. A few seconds later, the round landed 100 metres north of our lines. Immediately, the man in the olive tree lifted what looked like a large mobile phone to his mouth and spoke into it. He was passing fall of shot corrections back to the enemy mortar team. I thought, 'Right, you're a legitimate target. Fucking brilliant.' I said to Minty: 'Do you still see that guy in the top of the tree we just lased?'

'Yes. Is he a dicker?'

'Yes, he is. Lay onto him with HE.' The target moved a fraction: Minty brought the aiming circle back to bear exactly on him. 'On,' I said. 'Fire!' Minter pressed the fire button. The Rarden cannon thumped out one round of 30mm high-explosive. The shell hit the base of the olive tree. There was a flash, and large lumps of wood flew out in all directions, and for a moment I thought we'd blown the whole tree out of the ground. Monkey-quick, the enemy spotter tucked his radio into a pocket and started climbing down through the branches. Minty made a tiny correction on the cannon's elevation wheel and fired again. The second round exploded in the topmost branches. He'd bracketed the target – but the dicker was still climbing down the tree.

If we didn't get him soon he'd be down on the ground and running.

'Firing now.' Minty fired a third round. It hit smack on the trunk again. The spotter flew out of the tree. He landed on his back, lay dazed for a second or two and then sat upright. He looked a little the worse for wear – but we obviously still hadn't hit him.

'Right and drop,' Minty said.

I whacked another three rounds of HE in the loading tray. 'Loaded! Go on!'

Minty fired again. The dicker was scrambling to his feet. The next round landed almost on top of him. It blew his right leg off and launched the rest of him in the opposite direction. He tried to stand up, but then, almost in slo-mo, fell sideways to the ground.

At that, a second insurgent burst out of cover and ran up to his fallen mate. He wasn't there to help. Staring at the mess that had just been his buddy, the newcomer leaned down, retrieved the dicker's radio, turned on his heels and started to run. I told Minty: 'Select co-ax machine gun.' At that range, we wouldn't be able to follow the tracer rounds: the tracer would burn out before the business end of the bullet reached the target. But there was another way Minter could correct point of aim: the ground in the surrounding area was so dusty, as we'd discovered to our cost when trying to dig it, that each round would pluck up a gout where it hit. Minter fired a ranging burst. As wanted, each bullet kicked up a nice puff of dust. Head down and arms pumping, the fugitive was still running at full tilt. He could run: the soles of his sandals flashed pale as they caught in the clear morning light. But however fast he ran, he wasn't going to outrun our gunfire. And then, out of nowhere, I suddenly remembered the greyhounds.

CHAPTER TWELVE

At the age of 15, like just about every local teenager I'd been short of cash. My next-door neighbour, Charlie Crouch, owned a number of greyhounds. Sometimes, when he was busy, Charlie would ask me to walk the dogs. One day, when I brought his pack of three back safe and sound he said: 'You're good with dogs, Michael: if you need a job, why don't you go and ask for work at the Arms Park official greyhound kennels? I'll put in a good word for you.'

It was too good a chance to miss. The next morning, I went down to the Arms Park greyhound kennels in Cefn Mably, just outside east Cardiff. I mentioned Charlie's name and told them I was looking for work. To my slight surprise and great delight, they gave me a part-time job as a kennel lad. At that time, to make a bit of extra income, the Arms Park held greyhound race meeting on weekends and Wednesday evenings when there were no other sporting fixtures at the ground. All I had to do was exercise the dogs, feed them, and muck out their kennels. It was easy enough work, except for the exercising bit: three big strong greyhounds on each arm was a lot for a skinny little 15-year-old. If they spotted a rabbit, a smaller dog, or even someone walking they figured might be tasty, the greyhounds became an instant pack. Their instinct is to chase down other animals and rip them apart. Their ears would go up, their tails start to wag and I'd think: 'Oh fuck – what have they seen?' and hold on as fast as I could. The other slightly less attractive side to the job was the pay, which was less than brilliant. How to make more?

For several reasons, all of them good, the kennel lads weren't allowed to bet on the dogs. In the first place, we were under-age. Secondly, if the punters saw one of us placing bets on a greyhound, they'd bet on the same dog. As luck would have it, one of the other kennel lads had an older brother. The brother liked going to the dogs – he was a regular on race days. Brother came up with a plan: we'd tell him which dogs were likely to win; he'd place the bets; and we'd share the winnings. How did we know which dog was going to win? The answer was simple: we fed the dogs, and that meant we always knew how much food the dog had been given before a race. Each officially registered trainer had his own kennels.

There was a bread factory near the kennels, your bog-standard sliced white. The day before a meet, one or other of the trainers would pop round the back of the factory, pick up a batch of unwanted bread, and bring it to the kennels. Sometimes, if the bread was still fresh enough, I'd take a loaf or two home for my mum – we needed it. The dogs probably didn't, but sometimes the favourite for a race found he got half a loaf in with his feed. We always knew which greyhound got the white sliced.

Of the six dogs in a given race, only one or two would get the extra food. Any more than that, and it would have looked too suspicious. But if you give any greyhound an extra feed of white bread an hour before it races, it's unlikely to run its best. In fact, all it really wants to do is lie down and sleep it off.

Like the kennel lads, the trainers weren't well off; so like us again, they were looking to make the odd bit of extra money on the side. The plan wasn't foolproof – occasionally, a dog wouldn't run as predicted, or the dog we'd all laid money on would bump into another hound and take a tumble. But about eight times out of ten, the bread treatment worked. To help increase the odds even further in their favour, as well as feeding the fastest and best greyhounds heart-stopping quantities of white sliced, the trainers would deny one of the slower dogs its last scheduled feed before a race. The hungrier a dog is, the faster it tends to run. Rainbow Magic might be the favourite, but he was suffering from a serious digestive problem, whereas little White Lightning hadn't had his dinner that evening. Many people suspected the dogs were nobbled with chemicals, but from my own short time in the business, I can truthfully say that I never saw or heard of that. All it took was a packet of Mother's Pride. If you're thinking, 'no wonder greyhound racing's gone out of fashion', then I can only agree.

Our Taliban target was shifting so fast he'd reminded me of happy days at the dog track. But unlike the hounds, he wasn't going to get a tasty reward when the race was run. In fact, he was very unlikely to finish it. He might be dodging about like a mad March hare, but however much he twisted and turned, his chances of survival were getting slimmer: Minty was on good form. I watched the hot spot of his image through the thermal sight as he tried to get away. The heat signature of the 7.62mm rounds made it look as if a swarm of bees was chasing him. I watched Minty track the running man with the aiming circle, leading him very slightly to allow for the bullets' time of flight.

Spurred by fear, the dicker's mate was galloping towards the nearest compound. Our job was to stop him before he got there. Once inside, barring an air strike, he'd be safe: even our 30mm shells couldn't punch through those walls.

The runner was less than 30 metres from the compound; a few seconds more and he'd be out of our reach. To nail him, Minty used a technique our gunnery schools don't teach: hose-piping. In hose-piping, you watch your fall of shot and make corrections while continuing to fire. The regulation method is to fire a short burst; watch fall of shot; correct aim and then fire another burst. The reason gunnery instructors frown on hose-piping is because if you try it with an enemy at extreme range, you can end up using up huge amounts of ammunition.

But we didn't have the time to fuck about: with our man only a few metres from safety, we had to drop him. Minty kept his thumb on the firing button. Rounds thumped into the fleeing man: he tumbled arse over tit and collapsed like a puppet with its strings cut. Scratch one enemy forward observation team. We waited to see if he was playing dead, but he didn't move.

'Target,' Paul said.

'Target stop,' I replied.

In training they'd always give us another target, but in real life that doesn't always happen.

'That's one pair of spotters who won't be giving corrections for a while.' I felt as if I had to say that to justify what we'd done.

We climbed out of the Scimitar and put the petrol cooker on for a brew. Then we tracked down a packet of all day breakfast from the ration store: beans, bacon, sausage, reconstituted omelette, just what the doctor ordered. You can eat it cold, or you could if it ever got cold in Afghanistan in high summer. With their spotters dead, for one day at least, the Taliban stopped mortaring.

We established an improved stag routine for the regular morning and evening attacks: one Scimitar crew mounted up and ready to engage; one on immediate standby; the other two crews off duty and resting. Crews rotated states of readiness at two-hour intervals. By now, we'd trained every soldier up on the hill with us to use all our weapons systems, including the 30mm cannons: we needed every man there, including the REME guys, and we needed them competent. One factor that helped was that with the vehicles stationary, there was no need for a driver, which reduced the manning on the Scimitars to two per vehicle.

The Taliban must have clocked the new routine, because a day after we'd established it, they altered their times of attack: starting and ending the morning mortar barrage thirty minutes earlier. That way, they hoped to catch us at our moments of least readiness: at dawn and when the stag was changing over. But whatever the enemy did, we always had at least one Scimitar ready to return fire at a moment's notice.

I was on stag with my gunner late one night and all was quiet. The sky was clear, and there was a full moon. We were scanning with the thermal sights along the edge of the green zone to the east when a tiny white blob popped up into view. We call it 'white and black hot', but the thermal imaging system turns heat into a pale ghostly light, a distinctive greenish-grey against the background black. I said: 'Stop scanning, Paul: I just saw a white football shape – it might have been a head.' The turret stopped. We stared at the spot. I could still see the white blob, but I couldn't see a body attached to it. That was strange. It look like a human heat source: but if it was an insurgent, then where was the rest of him? I lased the object with the rangefinder. The readout came back at 1,400 metres. The blob disappeared. I was just wondering what to do when it popped back up into view again. It was a human head – and, I now realized, the body attached to it had to be moving around in a pit or foxhole. A man in a foxhole at the edge of the green zone: now that was very, very interesting – especially at two in the morning. The Taliban don't often like to fight after dark, but there's always the odd night owl. A second blur of white appeared near the first. The second shape was much bigger than the first – a whole human person, complete with arms and legs. The big blob walked up to the little blob, and then most of the big blob disappeared, too. Now there were two ghostly footballs sticking up out of the ground. I waited. Several minutes ticked by without any further signs of life. Then three human figures climbed out of what I'd now lay any money was a freshly dug mortar pit. A short walk from the nearest batch of compounds, and within spitting distance of tree cover, the spot was just right for launching an attack on our lines.

The three men walked over to the tree line and then stopped. Two of them bent down, ferreted about in the undergrowth and then picked up either end of a long, cylindrical object; the third man stooped and picked up a flat disc. A mortar tube and base plate. The trio now had my full attention. Then another three figures walked out of the green zone and joined them. I nudged Minter: 'See those six fuckers with the mortar?'

I sensed him nod his head in the pitch dark: 'Seen. On.' He settled the aiming mark in the centre of the group. We watched the six men carry the base plate and tube to the pit. One man climbed inside, while the others lowered the tube, the base plate and some other objects down to him. 'Got them,' I thought. 'They've been seen handling weapons and they still have the weapons in hand.' I called it in. 'Zero, this is Mustang Three One. Enemy position identified at grid reference Sierra Lima 42986354. Request permission to engage.' There was a short silence.

Then the RRF's company commander down in the DC responded: 'Three One, are you sure you have a positive ID on an enemy position?'

'Certain. We're looking at an enemy mortar team. Positive ID.' In the time we'd been talking, I'd become even more certain: as my eyes had adapted to the thermal picture, I'd watched the six suspects walk back to the cache in the trees, pick up a batch of mortar ammunition and carry it over to the pit. Zero knew I wouldn't be calling it in if I'd had any doubt about the target's legitimacy. 'Roger, Mustang Three One. Engage when ready.'

Great, we had the permission. But there was something else I wanted to do first. I hopped out of the Scimitar and walked over to the RRF's front lines. I found the unit's mortar commander, Sgt Gibson, woke him up, dragged him over to the Scimitar and sat him down in the commander's seat. I tapped the vision block. 'That's the thermal sight, Gibbo – take a look.' Gibbo leaned and put his eyes up against the scope. I said, 'As you can see, we've got visitors. They've dug a mortar pit and they've been busy moving weapons.' Gibbo was short and stocky with cropped ginger hair. Like JC and Leechy, he came from Manchester – by rights, they should have formed their own regiment.

Gibbo whistled gently through his teeth. 'I see what you mean. They're still at it – looks as if they're bringing in more rounds.' He glanced up at me, echoing my own thoughts: 'Fucking brilliant. Got them bang to rights. Let's have them.'

I patted the Scimitar's cool metal flank. 'If you jump out and tell Minty to jump back in, I'll see to it.'

Then Gibbo said: 'Hang on – let my guys register our mortars on the target first. There's bound to be more of the fuckers out there in the trees – the Taliban always work in groups. If any of them escape your fire, we might be able to give them a roasting. Let's see if we can't nab them all at the same time.' I thought about it for a moment, but that was all: Gibbo was right, it was a no-brainer. The Taliban tended to work in units of about twenty-five men. The six we were watching would almost certainly have back-up hidden in the trees.

Gibbo jumped out and roused his mortar unit. They made ready, laid one of the 81mm mortars onto the tree line just behind the enemy position and fired one round of HE to register. As soon as Gibbo fired, I told Minty to open up with the 30mm. The Taliban mortar teams had taken two weeks and more to get anywhere close to our positions up on ANP Hill. Gibbo's guys were landing rounds on the target by the time the third one had left the tube. Minty was pumping fire into the mortar pit and surrounding area. The white thermal blobs had disappeared. Gibbo fired six more mortar rounds. Then the whole hill opened up on them, their tracer following ours as we marked the target for them, blasting through the night sky and into the insurgents. The illume rounds fizzled out. We stopped firing to take stock.

Nothing moved in the target area. But the Taliban are hard to kill. To bring his machine gunners into play, Gibbo told a mortar team to fire a pattern of illumination rounds. After all the ordnance they'd thrown our way over the past few weeks everybody wanted a bit of that Taliban mortar team. The illume rounds swung gently to earth on the end of their baby parachutes, casting a brilliant white light. The RRF's .50 calibres and 7.62mm machine guns opened up, saturating the target. Then it went dark as the illume rounds hit the ground and ran out of juice. A few minutes passed. Through the thermal sights,

I could see a collection of grey-white blobs lying next to the enemy mortar pit. They were fading slowly to black – it's one way of dying.

But as predicted, they still weren't all dead. I saw a ghostly shape the size of a melon pop back up out of the hole and take a careful look around. Maybe he thought that because it had all gone dark and quiet again, he'd have a few seconds in which to regroup and take cover. The head turned into a body and the man climbed out of the pit. Then he crouched and reached back into it. 'Probably trying to help an injured mate,' I thought. Two more ghostly figures climbed out and stood for a second with the first. I told Minty to switch to co-ax machine gun. 'Don't open fire yet, though: wait on.' I wanted to see if the gruesome threesome would try to extract the mortar. It was essential we either destroyed or captured the weapon. The waiting time paid off: more men slipped out of the neighbouring tree line, ran up to the pit and started helping the injured get out. Next thing, I saw two men handling the unmistakable shape of a mortar tube. No point in delaying any longer. 'Fire!' I said. Minty's thumb closed on the button. The machine gun spat into life, punching 7.62mm into the enemy before they'd even heard the crack of the first rounds. Greenish-white bodies flew out and tumbled to all sides.

We had the 'terp listening in to the enemy i/com chatter. 'They're shouting,' he reported. 'They're screaming for doctors to come and help. They say they have many wounded. They want more men to come and help rescue the mortar tube.' Looking back through the sight, I saw three Taliban in the act of carrying the mortar tube away from the pit.

'Engage those three with HE,' I told Minty. He shifted his point of aim a fraction. The Rarden cannon roared into life, dropping the trio. I couldn't see what had happened to the tube, but still. 'Good shooting, Paul,' I said. At that range, through the night sights, it was excellent.

More ghostly grey-white figures started to appear at the edge of the tree line: reinforcements coming in to lift the tube as requested. 'Let them come,' I thought – 'the more the merrier.' I'd been on stag now for more than four hours, but my blood was up: the more of them that came to the party, the more we'd kill. They didn't seem to have cottoned on to the fact that our night-vision sights meant we could see them. The deep thump of an 81mm L61 mortar firing split the air, followed by another and another until the coughs merged into a steady barrage. Gibbo and the RRF were joining the party again. They walked HE fragmentation rounds along the wood line and then back through the trees behind. The big rounds soared up from the top of ANP Hill in volleys: a good mortar team can push out a bomb every four seconds. I watched as the high-explosive shrapnel smashed through and into the enemy lines. Tiny figures ducked and dived to earth, trying desperately to find cover, leaping behind trees and clumps of shrubbery that weren't going to save them.

Minter kept going with the cannon and the GPMG. Then I heard the distant rip of gunfire as a second Scimitar on the north side of the hill joined in – LCoH Cox and his crew. I did a quick assessment: enemy bodies lay scattered at the edge of the trees. There were more of their dead strewn around the pit. But with their usual combination of dogged persistence and semi-insane courage, the Taliban kept trying to retrieve the all-important mortar.

One after another, groups of three or four fighters assembled at the tree line, crouched, gathered themselves for the off and then hared for the pit. None of them made it. Each time they tried, we mowed them down. They were taking heavy casualties, and it was getting worse for them: the RRF's mortar fire was hitting them with deadly accuracy. We were cutting the enemy apart. I thought: 'They have to try something different. They can't just go on losing men at that rate: they have to execute a flanking manoeuvre or create a distraction.'

Just as I was thinking that, the Scimitar we'd positioned on the west side of ANP Hill came under small-arms fire – a flanking attack meant to draw our fire away from the mortar while they recovered it. Out of nowhere, Coxy had a fight on his hands. A small Taliban section armed with RPGs and AK47s was steaming up the hill towards him. They pepper-potted forward in loose formation, almost exactly as we'd have done: two or three men down and firing while the others kept up the charge, the front runners stopping to fire as the back markers ran through in turn. They were determined, but with the enemy showing up clear in his sights, Coxy's gunner, Rob Parry, began picking off the attackers at will. Coxy had help: with the new Taliban section now well within range of their weapons, the Fusiliers in the trenches on that side of the hill were putting down their own murderous screed of fire.

The Taliban were doing their utmost to recover the mortar – even to the point of sending men on a mission they must have known was suicidal. That told you how important the weapon was to them.

Long streams of orange tracer speared down the hill and into the flanking enemy. Rob Parry and the Fusiliers were keeping up a steady hail of accurate fire. The fusillade of 30mm and 7.62mm dropped one body after another. The Taliban charge faltered, broke, and the few who were left alive turned and ran back down the hill. All except one: a Taliban foot soldier decided to ignore the certain fact of his own death and keep coming. I watched as he climbed a low wall at the base of the hill. The insurgent was now directly below Coxy's position, looking directly into the mouth of his guns. Extremely brave, and extremely foolish: charging a Scimitar single-handed comes quite near the top in a short-list of bad ideas. As he started to run up the hill, a burst from the wagon's co-axial machine gun ended his solo charge.

Squirty McWhirter was at my elbow, trying to make himself heard above the din of the mortars and guns: 'Do we need air? Mick, do we need air?'

'Yes, let's call it in. Finish the job.' I called over to the RRF mortar team again: 'Gibbo – check fire on the mortars – Squirty's bringing in some fast air.'

We'd had so many contacts with the enemy by the end of our first week on Now Zad hill that we'd shot to the top of the air tasking priority list: Brigade had assigned two fighter-bombers to cover us round the clock. Or possibly not: at the very moment when we needed them most, it turned out they'd just been reassigned and there were no other aircraft available on task. I suddenly felt tired: make that dead tired, not to mention hot, thirsty, sweaty, half-mad on cordite fumes and covered in dust. I glanced at my watch: we'd been nearing the end of our two-hour stag when I'd first spotted the enemy mortar team. The contact had been rolling for another two hours on top of that. The trigger time had sped by. But now I thought the battle was over, a crushing wave of fatigue overwhelmed me. Climbing up on the Scimitar's back bins, Squirty shouted: 'Let me take over, Mick – you've done your stint.' He should have taken over from me two hours earlier, but there was no way I'd have let him do that, I'd been having way too much fun. I thought about accepting Squirty's kind and thoughtful offer. I was dog-tired – but I still didn't want to step down. Normally, you couldn't get anyone to go on sentry duty. Now, everybody was pumped up and nobody wanted to go off stag.

Instead of answering Squirty, I started throwing empty boxes out of the turret: we'd fired so much ammo the empties were threatening to bury us. 'Come on, Mick,' Squirty insisted: 'you've done your bit. Let someone else have a crack at them.'

I looked across at Minter. His eyes were fixed and staring, and no wonder: he'd been peering through a thermal vision block for hours on end. I said: 'Come on, Paul – Squirty's right. Let's go and get some rest.'

Squirty and Trooper Chalky White took our places in the wagon. Whilst we were walking back to the troop shell scrape, I heard Chalky shout: 'They're going back to the trench! They're going back to the trench!' He meant the Taliban mortar pit. Squirty told him to open fire. The Rarden barked into life again – how come the Taliban didn't understand when it was time to give up?

I followed Minty into the shell scrape. It took another hour to stop the Taliban – they kept coming and coming like soldier ants. I picked up a set of NVGs and slung them on: individual fighters had started trying to leopard-crawl from the tree line to the mortar pit; ants to the honey-pot, they just couldn't stay away. One by one, as they tried to make it across the gap, Chalky shot them. More gunfire crackled and ripped through the air. Our own mortars started up again, thudding away in a deep, staccato chorus. I lay down and closed my eyes. Immune to the clatter around me, I went straight to sleep.

Despite their massive losses, more Taliban reinforcements came up as the night wore on and took up position in the trees near the mortar pit. I was asleep, but Squirty got on the blower again and asked for another air strike. This time, he suggested the fast air have a go at strafing the enemy instead of bombing them as usual. A short while later, two US F16s came in at a shallow dive, one doing the actual firing, the second riding shotgun. As they came in they popped out a trail of thermal flares to confuse any heat-seeking Taliban surface-to-air missiles. The lead aircraft opened fire with its six-barrel M61A1 Vulcan cannon, spitting sixty 20mm rounds per second onto the target.

CHAPTER THIRTEEN

A couple of hours later, another pink dawn broke in the east and I woke up. The brown sandy earth began to bake in the new sun, the insects started chirruping again and the odd swallow reappeared, swooping and stunting in the blindingly blue sky. The first thing I did was raise my binos and take a look at the latest state of play along the north-eastern tree line. The enemy had stopped doing the suicide crawl. Had the Taliban really given up and gone away? It seemed a little too good to be true. Maybe we'd shot them all? Lt Tom Long was on stag, and I sauntered across to have a word with him: 'Has there been any movement at the mortar pit?'

'Yes,' he said. 'A number of women and children went up to it.'

'Did you open fire?'

Long shook his head. 'No.'

'That'll be the mortar gone, then.' I was right: under the guise of recovering their dead, the Taliban had sent a party of women and children in to pick up the mortar and then leg it as fast as they could into the nearest compound. If women are seen carrying weapons, then under the rules of engagement then in force we were well within our rights to open fire on them. No one did, because no one could. It was a tough one: the enemy would use that same tube against us as soon as they could. But the Taliban are no slouches when it comes to anti-Western propaganda: killing women and kids isn't the best publicity.

The rest of the day passed peacefully. The next morning, a strange procession appeared from the north-east: dozens of vehicles and what must have been getting on for 200 people tipped up at the cemeteries over to the south-east of the hill. The Taliban were burying their newly dead. Some of the vehicles belonged to known Taliban leaders. We knew this because aerial reconnaissance and other assets had tracked them from known enemy compounds in Musa Qal'ah, Sangin and Gereshk. It looked as if they were coming to pay their respects to someone important: one of their own, perhaps a leader we'd killed in the overnight fighting. The funeral rites started at ten o'clock. We watched as they put the men we'd killed into the ground. I felt nothing, no compunction; it came down to them or us. It was hard to tell how many fighting men the insurgents had lost, but even with a bit of healthy rounding down, we estimated they had at least thirty killed. We also knew from the radio traffic that they'd suffered a large number of injured. Now they were really fucked off with us. I said: 'There's going to be more trouble tonight – just wait.'

I was right in principle, but wrong about the time. Usually, the Taliban took the early afternoon off for a siesta. But at about two p.m., shortly after the funeral party had finished their tea and sandwiches or whatever it was they did for a wake, a Taliban section hopped out into plain view and started firing RPGs down one of the lanes that led directly into the DC. Bold as you like, it was more a show of force and defiance than a measured attack; a hit-and-run-and-hope-for-the-best. Firing on the attackers from the hill in support of the garrison, which also returned fire, I was pretty sure we inflicted yet more enemy casualties.

From intelligence reports, we knew the enemy hated the Scimitar, or to be more precise, the range and lethal accuracy of its 30mm Rarden cannon. Given the pasting they were taking, it wasn't difficult to understand why.

We were just thinking that we might have finally neutralized the Taliban indirect fire threat when we got an intelligence report to say that the mortar the women and kids had recovered was now in the hands of a specialist Pakistani team. The new team had been brought in to finish the job, the job in question being to dislodge us from ANP Hill, and kill as many of us as they could in the process.

We were sitting around eating breakfast and drinking tea the following morning when we heard the familiar pop of incoming mortar fire. But this time, it took about seven seconds for the rounds to land: the new team was firing further back, at about 4,000 metres. The first volley of rounds landed about 200 metres plus of our positions, on the base of ANP Hill to the west. The next volley landed about the same distance to the east. Without even thinking about it, I knew that the Int report was correct: we were now on the end of an experienced and much more professional mortar team. Who had just bracketed our position.

As expected, the enemy mortar team halved the distance by which their first two rounds had over- and undershot. The next two rounds landed almost on top of the super-sangar: good job we'd built the bugger. As our new Pakistani enemy warmed up, their fire grew even more accurate and better concentrated: so good, in fact, that while it lasted we were pinned down and unable to move. We'd have to do something about these guys: with rounds landing directly in the trenches, the only safe place to be was inside an armoured vehicle or crouched in the darkness of the sangar, blinking like a crowd of owls. Even then, we had to start shunting the Scimitars and Spartans around the hill to stop the mortars getting a fix on them.

The Pakistani mortar team were also much better at concealing their location, moving every time they'd fired a couple of rounds and making excellent use of camouflage. No matter how hard we tried, and believe me we tried hard, we just couldn't locate their position. Then, after a couple of days of highly accurate and seriously annoying bombardment, we got lucky. As the barrage began on the morning of the third day, one of our guys just happened to be looking in the right direction. He saw a wisp of smoke drifting up from the north-eastern sector of the green zone. All eyes turned to the spot he now indicated. We couldn't see exactly where the tube was – but knowing its rough location was good enough to call in air to help find it. If we didn't kill the new mortar team in short order, they were going to kill us.

LCoH McWhirter was already on the satellite radio to air tasking. He managed to grab a pair of Apache gunships on their way back to base from a separate mission. Circling overhead, the Apaches reported seeing two flat-bed trucks parked up near a compound at the location where the eagle-eyed RRF gunner had spotted the telltale fumes. But the gunship crews reported no sign of any hostile activity. That wasn't so surprising: the Taliban aren't scared of much, but they run from the gunships every time: drop their weapons; try to look like innocent farmers; hide; and generally try to make themselves scarce.

Tired of trying to spot non-existent enemy activity, the Apaches sheared away and turned for home. Fifteen minutes later, another mortar fired from the exact same spot as before. How annoying was that? Then we heard some good news: the Apache crews had filmed the mission. Reviewing the cockpit video back at base, the crew saw that there had been armed men in and around the flat-bed trucks all along: they'd unloaded a DShK 12.7mm heavy machine gun from one of the vehicles and concealed it in a canvas bag, then headed for the cover of a nearby cave. As they moved, it became clear they had AK47s concealed under their clothing. Why hadn't the Apache crews seen the weapons at the time and opened fire? The answer, as always, is that spotting enemy activity from the air and then being certain about what you've seen is difficult. The pilots only have a split second in which to make life and death decisions.

The footage meant the flat-bed mob had to be our Pakistani tormentors, and they were now a legitimate target. Responding to the call for immediate action, a specially trained reactive patrol operating in the mountains four kilometres or so to the north came to hunt down our friends with the flat-beds that same night. To avoid friendly fire, a wide area around the compound where the enemy had subsequently been seen going to ground was declared a no-fire zone.

The hunter force attacked at midnight. The next day, on the update, Brigade informed us that a number of Taliban had been engaged at the location. Estimates of enemy losses were unknown. The report on the outcome of the strike was way beyond my own need to know. But there must have been some enemy killed: that morning, another funeral took place in one of the cemeteries below our position. Only this time, there were far fewer mourners.

The really good news was that Brigade had stationed a drone above the compound to record the night-time contact. Better still, the UAV had stayed in position after the fire fight had ended. Forty minutes after the hunter force had pulled out, the drone's camera recorded fresh enemy reinforcements arriving at the target compound. The best guesstimate was that they were once again looking to recover the mortar. When it came to tactics, we'd learned the hard way that the Taliban are normally canny. But when they do make mistakes, they tend to make them big. They did now. What they should have done was pick up their weapons and then bug out. Instead, the new band of fighters settled down with their mates in the same compound.

Later that night, an AC-130 Spectre gunship came on task. A modified C-130 Hercules transport aircraft, the Spectre is a truly awesome weapon. Used in Afghanistan for ground and special operations support, it employs high-definition television, infra-red and radar sensors, and various other bits of wizardry to locate ground targets in any weather or cloud conditions, day or night. Depending on the variant, the Spectre has a frightening array of guns housed in the left side of its fuselage: a 105mm howitzer – not much smaller than the gun on a main battle tank – comes as standard. With that, the aircraft can carry two 40mm Bofors cannon or a pair of 25mm Gatling guns. The Spectre can either saturate a given area, or use its computerized fire control systems to engage targets with pinpoint accuracy. You really don't ever want to be on the end of it.

In the early hours, we woke to see the brilliant flash of explosions in the night sky. The Spectre was circling the enemy compound, systematically reducing it to rubble with the 105mm gun. We could hear the rounds hit home several seconds after they'd been fired: the impact of the big, high-explosive shells made the ground beneath our feet shiver. As the mauling took effect, the Spectre crew spotted several flat-bed trucks bugging out of the compound. Holding fire, they tracked the fleet of trucks to a second compound; waited until the Taliban had jumped out and occupied the building; then took aim and opened up again. The enemy on the receiving end of the aerial drubbing never even knew what had hit them. Like the sound of an A-10 tank buster, the rasping hammer of a Spectre firing is unforgettable. I was glad I was safely tucked up in my doss bag.

CHAPTER FOURTEEN

The combination of the Spectre and hunter force attacks had conspired to discourage the enemy. We knew that because, for four blissful days, we had another spell of perfect peace and quiet up on ANP Hill. No mortaring. No RPGs. Not even the odd sniper round. Then, early on the morning of the fifth day, we were sitting eating breakfast when we heard the distant, familiar pop of a mortar firing out in the green zone. Everybody dropped their plates and ran for cover. We'd been hoping we'd killed and injured enough of the Taliban to stop them attacking us with mortar fire ever again. But here they were back in business.

Lt Tom Long was on stag in his Scimitar with his gunner LCoH Andrew Radford. Part of the ring of steel, their wagon was parked up facing north-east on the brow of the hill, right on the edge of one of the infantry trenches. Tom and Radders listened as the mortar round whistled in towards them. The whine of the mortar grew so loud they thought it was going hit directly on the vehicle's turret. Instead, the bomb landed in the two-metre gap between the Scimitar's right-hand tracks and the neighbouring trench. Had it exploded, the round should have killed Radders and Tom Long outright, and injured or killed some of the adjacent Fusiliers. But once again, by some miracle of luck or enemy incompetence, one of the most accurate rounds they'd so far managed to fire was a dud. Just like the round that had landed next to me and Met, it buried nose-down in the earth and stuck fast, with only the tail fins left projecting above ground.

We'd piled sandbags over the first unexploded round so that if it did explode, the sandbags would absorb the blast – or most of it. And we'd moved the showers and washing area away from the dud as a safety precaution. But this second unexploded round was on a whole different scale of nuisance: right next to a trench; right next to the soldiers manning it; and within touching distance of Tom Long's Scimitar. The Scimitar was in an excellent position; we needed it to cover the north-eastern arc of fire. It was essential the wagon remain there. But if everything else had to stay put, then the unexploded round had to move. A quick check with Brigade confirmed that all EOD officers were fully occupied defusing even more dangerous unexploded ordnance elsewhere in Helmand province. There was only one thing for it: we'd have to move the unexploded bomb ourselves. Leaving it in situ was the riskier option. But how?

I wandered over to the trench to take a look. There was one very straightforward way of dealing with the UXO: get a lump of P4 plastic explosive, stick a fuse in it, trail out a length of detonator [det] cord and blow it up. We didn't need a bomb disposal officer for that, but we did need a person who'd completed a dems [demolition] course – and a lump of P4. Which for reasons best known to themselves, Bastion, in spite of repeated requests, had refused to send us. There was, in any case, a good reason for not exploding the mortar round *in situ* – if we did that, then the enemy would know they'd landed a shell in exactly the right position, and would use it as an aiming mark for a more accurate barrage.

I buttonholed Tom Long. 'There is another way we could get rid of it, Boss.'

'What's that?'

'I've got some paracord in the back of the wagon: we could tie a noose round the dud round's tail and pull it out.'

Tom Long stared back at me. Judging by the expression on his face, he thought I'd suffered a mental breakdown. 'Let me get this straight, Corporal of Horse. You want to tie a length of paracord to that unexploded mortar round, attach the paracord to the back end of your Scimitar, and yank the round out by force?'

'In a nutshell, Boss. Then we can tow it down the hill and leave it for the Taliban to recycle.'

'You're bloody not going to do that, Corporal of Horse – it's way too risky. If that shell explodes . . .'

'If it explodes, I'll be inside my wagon under cover. And provided the rest of you stand well clear, there shouldn't really be any dramas.'

Lt Long shook his head. 'Madness. No. Forget it.' But I didn't want to forget it. One way or another, we had to get rid of that bloody bomb.

Tom and I had been having the discussion inside the troop sangar. 'Anyone got a better idea how to move the twat?' I asked the onlookers.

Shakes of the head and blank faces all round. 'No.'

'You see, Boss, that's the only way to do it. Tie her to my wagon, rev up and yank her out by the tail.'

'No, Corporal of Horse – I still think it's a bad idea.'

But once I get an idea in my head, I don't like to be thwarted. 'Tell you what, Lieutenant – let's play scissors, paper, stone to decide. If I win, I get to give my plan a go. If you win, we leave the UXO where it is. OK?'

Lt Long studied me for a moment. Were we fucking mad? Not really: that mortar bomb could have exploded at any moment. At the same time, we didn't want to break SOPs [standard operating procedures] or standing orders. The balance of risk – and the more immediate need to maintain our protective ring of steel in the optimal position – won the day. With a shake of his head, he said: 'All right: let's be having you.'

I'd always been good at scissors, paper, stone in school – our troop leader didn't know it yet, but he had no chance. Balling our right hands into fists, we brought them down in front of us three times in quick succession. On the third beat, Tom Long called out, 'Paper!'

'Stone!'

He smiled triumphantly. 'Paper wraps stone – you lose.'

'We're not done yet, Lieutenant – it's the best of three, we agreed that.'

'No we didn't – I won and that's an end to it.'

I clenched my fist again: 'Let's do it.' Tom made a scissors, I stuck with the stone as before. 'Stone blunts scissors – one to me.'

'One all,' Long said. 'Final decider. No more after this one.' The troop looked on, intent. I met the boss's eye. I had the feeling he thought I was going to make a stone for the third time. In which case he'd choose 'paper' to defeat me. As our fists came down as one, I called, 'Scissors!'

'Paper!' he said in the same breath. I stood for a moment and looked at him. Now that I'd won, I was starting to have second thoughts – maybe our leader was right: yanking an unexploded mortar round up out of the ground by force was a little unwise. But there was no way of backing out now – it was my idea, I'd pushed Lt Long into deciding the issue by luck and I had to go through with it. I fished the length of dark-green paracord out of my Scimitar's back bin, warned Stan Stanforth I'd be needing him to man the driver's seat and strolled up to the offending round. It sat there, snug in its self-made burrow, looking very much at home at the heart of our lines. I said: 'You have to come out, you little bugger.'

I still didn't think it was the world's wisest plan. But I did think it was the only plan. I set about making preparations. The first problem was that we only had about 8 metres of paracord: not a lot, when it comes to towing lumps of high-explosive ordnance around the landscape: 18 metres would have been better. Everybody took cover in the vehicles, or got right back to the other side of the hill and dropped down in a trench. The best seat in the house was the command Spartan; you could see what was happening through the vision blocks. I could see Lt Long peering through them, keeping an eye on my preparations.

I made a small lasso in one end of the paracord, took a last look round to make sure that everyone else had taken cover, and strolled up to the dud round as casually as possible. I might be bricking it inside, but it was important to keep up appearances. The fucker was still stuck there; no one had moved it for me when I wasn't looking. The projecting fin was surrounded by rocks and stones – I'd have to clear them away before trying to snare it with the loop. Lying flat on my belt buckle, I leopard-crawled up to the round. As I lifted my head, the top of my dorsal body armour plate caught on the rear of my helmet and pushed it forward, forcing it right down over my eyes. I now couldn't see a thing – and I looked like a fucking idiot. 'Fuck!' Lifting my left hand, I grabbed the rim of the helmet and pushed it back. But the instant I let go of it, the helmet fell forward again.

Holding the helmet clear of my face with my left hand, I swept the ground around the UXO clear of debris with my right. Then I tried to chuck the noose over the fins. Lying flat and trying to throw with my right arm, I missed. Second time lucky. This time the noose dropped neatly over the tail fins. About fucking time: I was covered in dust, the sweat was dripping down my forehead and into my eyes and even holding my helmet back it was all I could do to see. With my body arched backwards, the plates of my body armour dug into me on both sides; I could feel more sweat soaking through my clothing beneath them. The sun was beating down on the back of my neck. It was mega fucking hot, and the ground seemed to be cooking my insides.

I thought: 'The fucking body armour's useless, anyway, given I'm so close to the UXO. So is the helmet.' I could feel at least thirty pairs of eyes watching me. I knew they all thought I was insane, not surprisingly: even I was beginning to have serious doubts about my mental state. But I kept coming back to the overriding fact: we couldn't risk the round exploding in the middle of our lines. The fucker had to go – it was the mortar round or me.

I gave the noose a series of gentle tugs to tighten it. So far, so good – come on, you bastard. I pulled one final time to make sure the knot was tight, and watched in disbelief as the entire noose unravelled and slipped off the end of the fins. I should have joined the Boy Scouts and learned how to tie proper knots. I flicked the sweat from my eyes, pulled the loose end of paracord up to my nose, rolled away, tied a new slipknot, rolled back over onto my belly and flicked the noose at the fins. It dropped on the tail first time. You see, it was only a question of practice. Holding my breath, I pulled the slipknot tight and gave it a firm tug. The noose held. I pulled the cord again, harder this time. The mortar round twitched in the earth directly under my nose. I went dead still.

The seconds ticked by. Everyone on the hill including me was waiting for the shell to explode. Nudging unexploded mortar rounds isn't a very good idea. I thought: 'Don't try this at home.' I eased backwards, climbed to my feet and retreated to a safe distance. 'Stan,' I called, 'mount up!' If I could, I'd have towed the dud round out on my own; but I couldn't drive the Scimitar and keep an eye on the UXO at the same time. Stan climbed into the Scimitar and fastened his hatch.

I jumped into the commander's seat. I knew that standing with my head out of the hatch wouldn't be the smartest thing to do. I thought: 'I'll keep an eye on the round through the rear sight.' I crouched down and tried to shut the hatch lid. But the Scimitar had been designed in the days when people wore berets, not helmets. With the hatch shut, there wasn't nearly enough headroom for someone with a big swede like mine, especially with the additional problem of a Kevlar helmet. I hunched and cocked my head to the side, but no matter how much I contorted, I still couldn't see the length of paracord or the unexploded round.

Still, I knew roughly where it was. And until we gave it a tug, the UXO wasn't going anywhere. 'OK,' I told Stan, 'start up!' Stan punched the ignition and the Cummins diesel shuddered into life. Just what we needed, more heat in the cabin, when the Scimitar already felt like an oven set for Sunday lunch. 'Select first gear,' I said. A loud mechanical clunk told me Stan had got us into first gear. 'Release the handbrake.'

Another clunk. They don't make them like that any more. 'OK Stan – nice and easy, now, take it forward.' We leapt forward faster than BBC *Top Gear*'s Stig off the starting grid. 'Slow down, Stan!' I shouted. 'Steady!' Stan slowed down. I was still hunched up and squinting like a bastard, trying to get an eye on the UXO. As we moved slowly forwards, the paracord came into view. Stan was doing a great job now, we were easing forward at the pace of a racing snail. Marvellous.

The paracord straightened and went taut. Then it went tauter still, until it was so taut you could have played Duelling Banjos on it. 'Why the bloody hell hasn't the bomb come out of the ground?' I wondered out loud. With all the extra armour and ammunition on board, not to mention me and Stan, the Scimitar weighed about 12 tonnes. The mortar round weighed a couple of kilos. With that much power and weight on the end of it, how could a lump of metal that size still be stuck in the ground? It defied common sense. There had to be some reason why the round was refusing to budge, but for the life of me I couldn't think what it might be. I really should have paid more attention in Physics lessons.

I was just beginning to think I'd have to get out and dig the round free of the surrounding earth, when the noose slipped off the end of the fins again. Fuck! The knot had come undone for the second time! This was getting ridiculous. 'Stop!' I told Stan. 'Reverse – slowly!' We reversed back about 5 metres. I jumped out, grabbed the paracord, made a new loop, got down flat on my belly and leopard-crawled back up to the UXO. The noose caught, brilliant – if only it held this time. When I was back on board, Stan put the Scimitar into first gear and edged us forward. The line went taut. Then it went very taut. Then it went even tauter. I was sure that the paracord was going to snap, I could actually see it twanging and vibrating under the strain. A split second later, the mortar round shot up out of the ground. I watched transfixed as it sailed through the air towards us.

'It's going to hit!' I called. 'It's going to hit! Stan! Put your foot down!' Stan understood there was a small problem – the tone of my

Wall of sand coming – sometimes even the weather was against us

Accommodation pod, Camp Bastion – all the comforts of home

Sangin DC

Below: Sangin overwatch

Sangin River crossing point: note massive dope fields in background

Sangin: ANA/British patrol returning to camp

ANP Hill, Now Zad: the Shrine – old Russian fortifications with new
British occupants

Me (left) and CoH Jules Hoggarth – handover on ANP Hill, Now Zad

Afghanistan, 2006 – Now Zad: ANP Hill seen from the District Centre

View from the top of ANP Hill

D Sqn 3 Trp catching the rays on ANP Hill: LCoH 'Squirty' McWhirter (2nd left, rear); my gunner, Trooper Paul Minter (middle rear); Lance-Sgt 'Met' Metea, REME (right, rear); Lt Tom Long (front centre); LCoH Andrew Radford (centre, behind Tom Long)

Unexploded 61mm mortar bomb smack in the middle of our lines, ANP Hill, Now Zad

Left: Close-up of the unexploded round – would you lasso this bomb?

Below: Afghanistan 2006 – targeting a recently bombed Taliban position through the Scimitar's sights, ANP Hill

The rush is on: Now Zad High Street during the January sales

Inside the super-sangar, ANP Hill: Trooper Chalky White (left) and Trooper Rob Parry

Above: Now Zad: Taliban rat run

Left: How to tell friend from foe? ANP unit in Now Zad High Street

Sgt 'Gibbo' Gibson, Royal Regiment of Fusiliers, and ANP police commandant, Now Zad

My driver, Trooper James Leech: 'Leechy'

LCoH Paul Harris, 'Harry 73' frying spam on ANP Hill

Major Bartle-Jones – 'BJ' – delivering ceasefire cash to Musa Qal'ah elders

Vehicle check point: world record for largest number of suspects in one pick-up truck – 24 men, plus the 2 women still inside

Shot up and bang to rights: searching a drug runner's pick-up, south of Garmsir, 2008

IED components found in drug runner's car: pressure plate attached to green battery pack

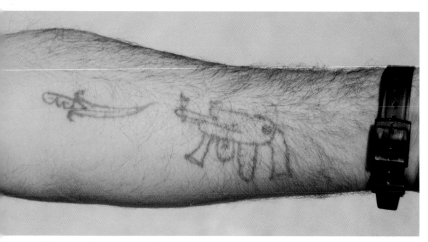

Tattoos showing the drugs runner has killed with an AK47 and a dagger

Not bad for a day's work: members of 1 Troop with 600kg of intercepted opium tar

FOB Dwyer: Jackals bring in the huge haul of opium tar

Wagon train: Jackals in close all-round defensive formation

LCoH Ashford's lucky day. The bullet passed through the bottom left-hand side of his armoured vest without injuring him

Gone fishing – for Taliban – near Marjah, 2008

Looking down the barrel, Route Cowboys

James Munday –
top skier, excellent
horseman and a
first-rate soldier
(Munday family)

Trooper James Munday, laid to rest with full military honours
(Press Association)

voice might have been a clue. He stamped on the accelerator. The Scimitar lurched forward. I glanced back: the mortar round was still hurtling towards us and just about to hit. I braced for the explosion. The round smacked into the ground about 2 metres behind the vehicle, bounced high up into the air, wobbled a bit and then thumped back to earth again. But there was no explosion. I thought: 'Thank fuck for dodgy Chinese ammunition.'

By now, Stan had us shooting down the slope at a rate of knots. When we'd made it to just over the halfway point, I told him to stop. The UXO was far enough away from our lines: even if it did eventually explode, it wasn't going to do us any damage. We could keep an eye on the round where it was, and if the Taliban tried to sneak up and recover it for possible reuse, we'd discourage them in the usual way.

I jumped out, cut the paracord and studied the round. I'd used up a lot of my Cardiff luck with that one. But at least now we were saved from the threat of an imminent explosion. I pushed a welding rod into the ground as close to the unexploded round as I dared, then attached a length of bright orange mine tape to the top of it, to mark the UXO as a hazard. The tape snapped and fluttered in the gathering breeze. I climbed back into the wagon and we drove back up the hill.

CHAPTER FIFTEEN

All the time we were up on Now Zad hill, the Taliban had two very simple objectives: the first was to overrun the RRF garrison in the DC compound and kill everyone inside. The second was to overrun ANP Hill and kill all of us up there. Our equally basic job was to thwart them on both counts. We kept knocking them back. They kept right on coming.

They tried attacking us from every different angle and from all sides at once, with various types of weaponry and in fewer or greater numbers. Each and every time, we used our extra firepower to beat off the attacks. In the meantime, we had to eat.

Compo rations are OK, but they wear a bit thin when the joker in charge has supplied only one of the available menus. Which was exactly what had happened to us: the twat who'd made up the load had given us six pallets of exactly the same menu, so for the whole six weeks we were up on the hill we had corned beef hash for breakfast and Lancashire hotpot as the main meal. A man can only take so much hash and pot, except of course if you're Dutch. After three weeks, we were all sick of eating the same thing. We fancied something fresh. One of the ANP officers nominally stationed at the Shrine with us said: 'No problem. There is a friendly village over that way; we can go there and buy bread.' He pointed to the settlement that lay a kilometre or so to the north-west. It was a hamlet, really: a tiny huddle of dusty brown compounds, home to a score or so families. Bartering for bread with the locals sounded like a good plan. We'd never had a serious and sustained attack from that quarter; we called it 'the friendly side'. Maybe we'd pick up some useful intelligence into the bargain while we were down there.

'Good scheme,' I told the policeman, 'let's do it.'

'No,' he said, 'I must go and buy the bread alone – otherwise, there will be a problem.' From our experience elsewhere in Afghanistan, we knew that nine times out of ten, the police pay the locals a pittance for any goods or services they buy on our behalf, and keep the rest of the money for themselves. We wanted the villagers to get most of the money.

We also wanted to buy a goat. We could slaughter it and make a nice, spicy goat curry. The local ANP made the world's most delicious goat curry. I'd tried it once and I was looking forward to repeating the experience. We'd get the goat first and ask the ANP to help us cook it later. But goats are a very big deal in Afghanistan: they milk them and trade them. They're one of the country's most valuable forms of currency, after dollars and opium. On due reflection, I decided it was probably best to stick to the bread.

The ANP man wandered off and told his mates what was happening. The police weren't happy with us going it alone. But then, there were little things about their behaviour that bothered us: like the fact that just before a Taliban attack came in, any Afghan policemen who were up on the hill with us would disappear down into the town on their Chinese-manufactured 125cc motorbikes and go to ground. Their sudden and timely disappearance was so obvious we used it as a combat indicator. The Taliban never seemed to harm the ANP; the officers came and went at will. You didn't need to be a genius to suspect there was a serious degree of collusion between the two sides.

We trundled down to the village in two Scimitars and a Spartan, leaving the rest of the armour up on the hill. The village lay in the lee of a cliff, at the mouth of a wide gorge that tapered away to the east. The ANP officer had called it correctly. The locals were very friendly:

the elders came up and greeted us, thanking us for keeping the Taliban away; and the kids were all over us trying to get bottles of water and boiled sweets. We shooed the children clear while the vehicles were still moving – experience in Bosnia and elsewhere had taught us that small children and moving tank tracks don't go safely together. But once we'd stopped we were happy to hand out the goodies. We didn't have a 'terp with us, so it was out with the phrase books and stumble through the Pashto for: 'Please may we buy some bread?'

The language business wasn't going too well. Then we spotted a woman actually in the process of making flat bread on a stone oven in a compound off to one side. We signed to her would she make some for us. She nodded happily. A couple more women and a girl came up to help. We gave them five US dollars. In return, they set to and cooked us a big pile of freshly baked flat bread. I tore a chunk off the first round and gave it a try. Delicious – proper food, I love it.

Five dollars was nothing to us, but to them it was a serious sum: Afghanistan is one of the world's poorest countries – the average annual per capita income is only about one US dollar a day.

Well pleased with our early morning expedition, we shook hands with the villagers, carried out a short local patrol, rolled back up the hill, brewed up some tea, sat down and set about scoffing the bread with the latest batch of Lancashire hotpot. The stew tasted exactly the same as the last lot, but the fresh bread made all the difference.

Three or four days later, we decided to go back down to the village for some more bread. But when we reached it this time, the atmosphere was entirely different: everything was silent, no kids came running out to meet us, and when the adults caught sight of us, they turned their backs and hurried away. Odd. And very worrying.

I thought: 'Something's going to kick off in this village. Best try and find out what.'

We had an ANP officer with us who spoke a little English. When we'd tracked down a couple of the village elders, he acted as interpreter. 'Can we buy some more bread?' he asked.

Both elders looked at us askance: 'No.'

'Ask him why not? What's the matter?'

There was a short conversation, then the ANP man turned back to us. His mouth was set in a grim line. 'After you'd gone last time, two of the village elders went into town with the dollars you paid them. A gang of Taliban grabbed them and beat them to find out how they'd got the money. When the elders confessed, the Taliban decided to set an example – teach the people not to deal with us. Two days later, they came back here in the night and dragged the same elders out of their homes. They made them kneel down in front of their families and then they shot them.'

'Fuck!' It was all I could think at this horrible news. 'Fuck!'

'Now the Taliban are playing games with the villagers – they tell them they will come back and hurt them again soon.'

One of the other villagers came up. Pointing to a tiny graveyard off in the desert to one side, he said: 'There is what you did – look.' Two fresh mounds covered in stones to keep the animals from digging marked the spot where they'd buried the dead men; prayer flags fluttered from long poles stuck in the graves.

We drove back to the Shrine. What a fucking nightmare. Talk about winning hearts and minds. Two days later, I was still thinking about what had happened when a bloody great 107mm artillery rocket came hurtling in at our lines. Then another exploded on the north-facing slope. Next thing, a heavy machine gun opened up on us.

Artillery rockets are a relatively scarce resource for the Taliban – when they fire one at you, you can be certain they're very upset. Mostly of Chinese manufacture, as Sizzler and the LEWT team had discovered to their cost in Sangin, the 107mm rocket is a serious threat. When it explodes, the 8.3kg high-explosive fragmentation warhead fires more than 1,200 pieces of shrapnel over a lethal radius of 12.5 metres. The Taliban either fire them from the rocket's dedicated tripod mount, or improvise by building a mound of earth. The rockets aren't very accurate, but then with a 12-metre kill radius, they don't really need to be.

The enemy fire was coming from a compound on the edge of the same friendly village where we'd bought the bread. Strange. We put down a serious amount of 30mm and GPMG in return. Then the Fusiliers opened up on the enemy with .50 cal and mortars. I watched our HE rounds smacking down into the compound and ricocheting around the walls: the insurgents holed up in there were taking some serious stick. A few seconds later, the fire from the compound suddenly stopped.

Watching through the commander's sight, I saw a gaggle of villagers pour out of the compound's main gate. They were yelling and waving their arms. Then I saw that some of them were carrying more of their number who were injured. With a terrible feeling, I realized what must have happened: to punish the villagers further for trading with us, the Taliban had driven into the hamlet, herded all the villagers they could find into the compound and lured us into firing at it. Whatever it might or might not have done to the Taliban gunmen, our return fire had terrorized and injured innocent civilians.

Letting rip with a last volley of heavy machine-gun fire, the Taliban started moving out of the back end of the village. They were headed for the safety of the mountains. I thought: 'We should mount up and move to cut off that group of fuckers: teach them a lesson.' But the boss vetoed the idea, and he was probably right. In all likelihood it was a come-on; there'd be IEDs and more insurgents waiting if we gave chase.

The ANP went down to find out the details of what had happened. By sheer good fortune, we hadn't actually killed any of the villagers; but a couple of people had nasty injuries. We offered them medical treatment, but they refused. The incident made us feel like anything but heroes. We were in Afghanistan to try and help the government keep the rule of law, not to harm civilians. But there was no way we could have known the Taliban would stoop so low. The ANP officer who'd told us we might be able to buy bread in the village came up to me. Speaking through the interpreter, he said: 'I told you I should have handled it.' I had to restrain myself from giving him a good slap.

We'd just found out the hard way that the Taliban would stop at nothing to prevent friendly contact between local people and ISAF forces. The villagers were so traumatized and afraid by what had happened that they packed up their portable belongings and quit the hamlet early the next morning. We watched them set off in a convoy of ramshackle pick-up trucks, old tractors and trailers. From that day till now, the village lies abandoned.

The moral of the story is that you can try to win over the local population, but you have to be really careful how you go about it. Growing up on the Trowbridge estate in east Cardiff, I'd learned the hard way that violence breeds more of the same, and that what might seem at first like a small and unimportant incident can lead swiftly to major trouble.

CHAPTER SIXTEEN

Still under regular attack, by the beginning of our fourth week on ANP Hill we'd fired so much ammunition we were starting to run short – in the case of the 30mm, we were down to between twenty and thirty rounds per vehicle. The infantry wasn't that much better off: close to running out of .50 link for the Browning heavy machine guns; 7.62mm for the GPMGs; and 5.56mm for the SA-80s. The mortar guys weren't exactly weighted down with spare rounds to fire, either. Under favourable security conditions, ammunition is brought in by vehicle. But in a minor emergency of the kind we now had, and with the overland lines of supply wide open to attack, the RAF provide what's known as an Eagle's Lift. But the communication wires got crossed somewhere: the Chinook that came in later that night arrived with lots of ammo for the infantry – but no 30mm for the Rarden cannons.

After two more weeks of playing tit-for-tat with the Taliban, we were drawing near the end of our six-week stint at Now Zad. I'd noticed that when it was quiet, and when we were all in the troop shell scrape having a bit of a banter, one of our number was always conspicuous by his absence: Trooper Chalky White. 'Where's Chalky?' I asked Coxy, the second time I realized Trooper White was missing.

Coxy put on an extreme version of Chalky's West Country accent: 'I'm not coming out of this here hole, because I likes it in here.'

The next time it was quiet on the hill, I walked over to Chalky's foxhole. He looked like a hobbit in a burrow. 'Chalky,' I said, 'come and have a chat with the rest of the lads in the scrape.'

Chalky shook his head. 'I'm staying here.' Pretty soon, the rest of the troop noticed Chalky was missing and started trying to talk him out of his hole. The more Chalky resisted eviction, the harder we all tried. He was like a badger: he'd only come out at night. Then he'd get a wash, have his rations and do what he needed to do. But as soon as it was daylight, he'd get straight back down in his burrow again. Worried the banter might get a bit out of hand, I went back to try to talk some sense into him. 'If you don't start mixing in with the rest of the troop, Chalky, the piss-taking's going to get a lot worse.' Nothing would budge him.

When I couldn't get him to come out, a little bit of the devil in me decided to wind Chalky up. I started a rumour going that because of the death of one of the lads in 2 Troop at Sangin, someone would have to stay behind when our tour of duty ended. I let it be known that as the most junior member of the troop, Chalky was the man who'd have to remain in place.

'Do I really have to, Corporal of Horse? It's not fair. Can't we pick straws?'

'No, Chalky, sorry – it's you. Anyway, I thought you liked being up here. You spent a lot of time making your trench nice and comfortable.'

The other lads picked up the story and ran with it: 'We'll send you some ciggies when we get back to Bastion, Chalky, no worries. And I'll make sure you get your mail after we've read it, and your parcels from home.'

Every time Chalky was in earshot, Radders even started singing a pop song, but with a few of the words changed: 'What's that coming over the hill, is it a mortar, a mortar?'

Chalky wasn't impressed. He obviously wasn't trying to gain favour or anything like that, but all of a sudden Chalky started mixing with the rest of the troop. I kept the wind-up going until 4 Troop, with JC Moses large as life to the fore, arrived to relieve us. We mounted up on the wagons, all our gear packed and ready to roll. Chalky was still in his burrow, looking very sad and sorry for himself. At the very last moment, I told him to grab his kit and throw it on the wagon. He leapt out of his hobbit-hole, ran for the Spartan and jumped aboard. I never saw a Trooper look so happy. But it didn't stop him swearing about the twats in his troop as he mounted up.

CHAPTER SEVENTEEN

'MOG' [Manoeuvre Outreach Group] is a new-fangled name for an old idea: manoeuvre warfare. The main idea behind manoeuvre warfare is to find, dislocate, disrupt and destroy the enemy by means of speed, mobility, and surprise – all things the Scimitar light tank was designed for and is very good at. Success in manoeuvre warfare relies heavily on unit commanders making rapid and good local decisions both before and when in contact with the enemy. You have to keep the initiative; keep up the tempo of attack, and keep the enemy going backwards.

In the case of Helmand province, the more specific job of the MOGs was to deny the Taliban freedom of movement; push attacking forces away from the platoon houses, FOBs and patrol bases; interrupt enemy supply lines; act as a surveillance screen and maintain a visible ISAF presence out on the ground. To me, the MOGs were a development of the long-range desert patrols carried out by special forces units in World War Two.

In the early days of Task Force Helmand's deployment, MOG outreach patrols had visited remote villages and Bedouin encampments providing quick-fix solutions to local problems and delivering basic medical care. But Taliban aggression had quickly put paid to the hearts and minds stuff. Several months on, our new mission was to flush out, harass, disperse and diminish the enemy forces surrounding Musa Qal'ah; to help relieve the pressure on the DC and surrounding area;

and generally convince the local non-Taliban nationals that we were there to stay, that we could provide them with the security they needed, and that, when that happy day arrived, we could make their lives better in other ways. But the security bit came first. It was an independent, roaming brief, of the kind I like best.

We were halted one day in an empty patch of land to the west of Musa Qal'ah having a brew when we spotted four figures wavering towards us out of the midday heat. I put the commander's sight on them. Instantly, the shimmering outlines resolved as three young children and a middle-aged man. But there was something very odd about the children: looking closer, I saw it was their skin colour. Black nationals are rare in Afghanistan, but the kids limping along beside the man looked as if they were of African origin. That was very strange. As they drew near, I saw why the kids had black skin – the poor little things had terrible burns. They were brothers, aged about ten, eight and six. Our interpreter explained that the boys had found and started playing with some kind of unexploded ordnance out in the desert. The munition had ignited, covering them in burning chemicals. But with the extraordinary strength and resistance to pain that many Afghans seem to possess, the kids had walked five or six kilometres with their uncle to seek medical help.

These kids were hard as nails: even with 70 per cent burns and their skin charred black, they'd walked over rough terrain to get to us. It was only by pure chance that they'd bumped into us. Mind you, wherever we are, the locals within a ten-mile radius seem to know exactly where to find us. They track us with smoke signals as we pass through the villages, by flying white kites or by push-to-talk radio.

Worried that if the Taliban found out they'd been in contact with ISAF troops they'd kill the whole family, the parents had decided not to come. Why they thought the uncle might get away with it is anyone's guess. The MOG's medical team took one look at the severity of the burns and called in the MERT Chinook. While that was on its way, they gave the children emergency first aid. The MERT came in and airlifted the kids back to Bastion hospital. The two elder brothers survived. The youngest died.

Once we'd dealt with that emergency, we carried on with the patrol. The MOG was made up of two troops of D Squadron, HCR; three WMIK 'Wimmik' Land Rovers with RHA reconnaissance teams onboard; and several RHA Pinzgauers, three of them towing 105mm guns. The MOG's SHQ with a Spartan and a Samaritan tracked field ambulance were bringing up the rear. There was also a vehicle transporting a Desert Hawk UAV, or spotter drone.

We began to cross a wide stretch of flat, featureless land to the north of Musa Qal'ah. About 500 metres to the east, I spotted some old fortifications dating from the Russian occupation, including the remains of slit trenches and scrapes where the Russians had positioned their armoured vehicles to keep them hull down to reduce the risk of RPG strikes. From hard experience, we'd learned that more often than not, the Russians had protected their positions with minefields: we'd suffered a number of deaths and injuries from triggering these legacy devices. Strong in my mind was the memory of JC's Spartan hitting a Russian legacy mine on the bluff overlooking the Musa Qal'ah green zone at the beginning of August.

As a routine precaution, I radioed the rest of the column: 'We've got old Russian positions 500 metres to the south-east of us. Be careful to stay exactly in the tracks of the vehicle ahead of you.' At the same time, in a precaution born of long training, I told Stan the man to stop the Scimitar. The closer we got to the old Russian lines, the worse I felt about the risk of running over a mine. I was just thinking, 'It might be a good idea to retrace our tracks altogether and go round by another route,' when a three-man RHA reconnaissance team in one of the Land Rovers behind us suddenly swung out of the column, accelerated and overtook us in a cloud of dust. I stared in astonishment. I'd just advised everybody to stay in line and in the tracks of the vehicle ahead while I worked out whether it was safe to continue as we were or to go back.

Speeding on along a parallel track about 50 metres off to the east, the Land Rover hit a long-buried Russian mine. The explosion flung the vehicle high into the air, catapulting the RHA men out to the sides. Two of them hit the ground with a crunch and began screaming. The third man lay quiet and still.

The whole column came to an immediate halt. The nearest vehicle to the scene of the explosion was another of the RHA's WMIK Land Rovers. Its three-man crew jumped out and started working frantically to clear a safe route up to the injured.

The Samaritan at the rear of the column came forward on the proven track to assist. LCoH Andrew Scott, aka Trigger, was in command. The chief medic on board was Paul Hamnett. The armoured ambulance stopped and then started reversing. It meant coming very slightly off the safer track, but we had to get medical help to those three men as soon as possible: every second might make the difference.

Hamnett climbed out onto the vehicle's front decks. He was just about to jump down when he noticed a round object lying in the sand at his feet: another Russian anti-tank mine. If they'd kept driving for one second longer, they'd have hit it. Scott and Hamnett climbed down off the Samaritan with extreme care.

There was a stiff breeze blowing that day. As we scrambled to help the injured men, the scouring wind uncovered a third Russian mine. I looked around: more and more shallow indentations were appearing in the ground as the wind did its work. We'd driven into a huge Russian minefield. We could mark those devices and either deal with or avoid them. It was the mines that we couldn't see we had to worry about.

Hamnett ran forward and made a quick examination of the injured men. When he'd done that he sent: 'Call the MERT. One of the casualties has a suspected broken back. The second is bleeding profusely from both legs; the third man's unconscious, I think he may have suffered internal injuries.' He placed tourniquets around the thighs of the man whose legs had been shattered.

The MERT Chinook arrived. Paul and his team strapped the three casualties into the yellow trauma stretchers to reduce the risk of further injury, and then lifted them into the back of the Samaritan. By now, we'd cleared an HLS, but for safety reasons we'd positioned it 300 metres back from the known minefield. That meant driving the injured across to the site – another necessary, calculated risk. Once they were safely onboard, the MERT took off and headed back to Camp Bastion. Later, I heard that despite Hamnett's best efforts, one of the three men had lost both his legs. The blast had broken the second man's back, leaving him paralysed from the neck down.

We still had to deal with the damaged Land Rover – we couldn't just leave it for the enemy. SHQ tasked one of the RHA's three 105mm guns to come up and do the job. The crew set up. Laying the field gun's sights directly onto the mine-blasted WMIK, they opened fire. The gun was less than 200 metres away from a stationary target in broad daylight. Normally, the L118 gun is a highly accurate weapon. But the first shell missed its target by some distance, exploding harmlessly in the desert beyond. Maybe the WMIK was a bit too close?

The gun team laid on again. There was a loud bang. I looked front, fully expecting to see bits of Land Rover flying around the local area. But for the second time, the shell missed. This was getting silly. Still, third time lucky. When the third round missed the WMIK, my patience snapped. We already had the Scimitar's armament laid onto the damaged vehicle. I told my gunner: 'Fire at those jerry cans on the back of it.' True to form, Minty hit the target with his first round of 30mm. The vehicle started to smoke. I didn't like firing at one of our own vehicles – they're not human, but you get attached to them. In this case, however, it had to be done.

The WMIK was still smoking, but still hadn't gone up. I said, 'Give it a couple of bursts with the machine gun. The tracer should do the trick.' As the neat cone of 7.62mm fire worked across its mine-blasted carcass, the WMIK burst into flames and then exploded. Bits of it fell back to earth and bounced around the landscape. Job done.

I wasn't angry with the guys who'd been blown up. They were gunners from the Royal Artillery, not used to going forward in open territory, more used to supporting from a few miles back. For them it was a very hard learning curve. I'd learnt my skill threading through minefields in the Falklands War. One of the hardest lessons had been seeing my troop leader's Scorpion blown up directly in front of me.

CHAPTER EIGHTEEN

By now, Major Will Bartle-Jones [BJ] had taken over command of D Squadron from Major Dick. I'd first met BJ in 1999 when I'd gone down to Cardiff to watch Wales playing rugby. I was a civilian at the time, but I met up with my old mate Jimmy Evans and the boys in the Prince of Wales pub near the bus station. Jimmy introduced me to BJ, who was in a very smart three-quarter-length camel coat. I liked him straight away: he was friendly, but his manner made you want to respect him. After the match we moved to a club called Kiki's in town. By now it was 11.30. Then we suddenly noticed that BJ had an exceptionally nice-looking woman on his arm. 'This is Caroline,' he told us, 'my fiancée.' The boys started muttering and looking daggers. The number one rule is, what goes on tour stays on tour; followed closely by the second rule which is, never bring your missus or your girlfriend with you. We only started talking to BJ again after he got in two very large rounds of drinks.

It was close to kicking out time. 'Right,' I said, 'time to move to Caroline Street for chicken curry off the bone.' We all picked up our coats except BJ – his lovely new camel wool had disappeared. We searched the club but we couldn't find it. BJ was fuming. He asked the bouncers if they'd seen anybody leaving with it. 'Sorry, mate.' We went outside into the shopping arcade. BJ was still moaning about his coat when we spied the best-dressed tramp in Cardiff begging in a doorway.

'Oi, that's my coat!' BJ said. We all started laughing. 'Give me that coat back!'

'No chance, butty bach, my friend from the club gave it to me. It was a present. There's my friend there.' The tramp pointed at one of the lads, Spandley, who was pissing himself laughing.

BJ had to buy his coat back off the tramp for a tenner.

In the six weeks since the Musa Qal'ah DC had been relieved, the combined force defending it, Easy Company, had repulsed more than 100 Taliban attacks. But with air re-supply still the only viable option, and still as difficult and dangerous as ever, during their time in the DC the company had only been re-supplied six times. Of those drops, one had overshot the drop zone by several hundred metres, re-supplying the Taliban with food, water and ammunition. By 8 September, with the 81mm mortar team down to thirty rounds and out of fresh link ammunition for their Minimi light machine guns, the defenders had to fill old ammo belts with 5.56mm rounds left behind by the Danes.

If things were still sticky for the Brits in Musa Qal'ah, they were even worse for the Taliban: their repeated attempts to storm the coalition garrison had left them with an estimated 1,000 dead and many more injured. Everyone could see that the battle for Musa Qal'ah had reached a stalemate, from which neither side was likely to emerge victorious. With their town centre largely destroyed and abandoned, the bazaar closed, unable to conduct trade or any normal pattern of life, the locals had had enough.

Attacks on coalition forces elsewhere in Helmand province continued with the same relentless ferocity. Shortly after the ceasefire agreement, the main contingent of 3 Commando Brigade Royal Marines arrived at Camp Bastion to take over duties as the battle group. It meant that we'd shortly be returning home. But first, we had to go and pick up 4 Troop, Household Cavalry, from Sangin.

Quitting the MOG patrol box to the west of Musa Qal'ah, we made a brief stop at Now Zad to join forces with 1 Troop. Then, as a column of some dozen armoured vehicles, we feinted north of Sangin, before turning back south to take up position a short distance to the north of the town. It was meant to be confusing. But that's impossible with an 800-metre cloud of dust following you everywhere.

The Sangin FOB sits at the western edge of the town, near the eastern bank of the Helmand River, which dawdles past at this location in a series of curling meanders. A flat plain about one kilometre wide stretches west and north from the FOB, then rises to a long escarpment about 150 metres in height. This bluff is cut in turn with mainly north–south running wadis, but its key advantage, from our point of view, was the fact that it overlooked the FOB across the broad flood plain to the south and east. In other words, the escarpment was a very good location from which to cover 4 Troop's extraction. We halted at a point almost due north of the DC to regroup.

Two Chinooks came in as we made our initial assessment, barrelling in fast and low towards the FOB. As they skirted a village a couple of kilometres to our east, a salvo of RPG-7 rockets streamed up at them, followed by long bursts of automatic weapon fire. Two AH-64 Apache helicopter gunships riding shotgun on the Chinooks returned fire, their 30mm cannons scything through the compounds below wherever and whenever the pilots spotted enemy.

Right from the moment Sizzler and 3 Para had gone in there, Sangin had been a rats' nest. Six months down the track, if anything the enemy presence in the area was bigger, better organized and even more dangerous. But we, too, had poured in reinforcements during that time; and we, too, kept up a rolling programme of tactical improvement.

The biggest problem with the extraction plan as it stood was the fact that in order to reach us, 4 Troop would have to negotiate and then ford the river. That made the column vulnerable. Armoured vehicles have to slow right down when they're crossing any depth of water; the crew's attention is focused on doing that, and it's more difficult to watch for and engage the enemy. In the days before we arrived to help them extract, 4 Troop had recced what at first they took to be a suitable crossing point. Examining their choice from higher ground, I told BJ and Tom Long: 'The crossing point they've chosen there is too high risk. That village' – I pointed at the compounds from which the enemy had fired at the Chinooks – 'is much too close: lots of compounds, plenty of cover and protection, perfect for a Taliban ambush. We need to find 4 Troop an alternative route.'

Just then, one of the vehicles behind us threw a track: we had to stop and secure the area while the crew fixed it.

After inspecting the area again, Tom Long and BJ agreed with my assessment. With the Scimitar now back on its tracks, SHQ Troop stayed in overwatch near the village, while 1 and 3 Troops went back west along the river to search for a better option. As we moved, we saw various bits of long-dead Russian armour and equipment lying around the local area, rusting slowly back into earth that was almost of the same colour. A few hundred metres later, Lieutenant Charlie Church found 4 Troop a much more suitable crossing point, at a much safer distance from the enemy-held compounds.

As we relayed its exact location to 4 Troop and began to take up station, we spotted a Taliban dicker on the hillside above and to the north of us. How could we be sure he was an enemy spotter and not a harmless shepherd? In the customary dishdasha and turban, the man was hiding momentarily in the undulating ground to our front, then standing up, watching our movements and then passing information via a push-to-talk radio: the 'terp, who was listening in on the i/com, could hear every word he said: 'The Americans have tanks; they are on the hill overlooking the river' and so on. (To most Taliban, all ISAF forces were 'American'.)

I gave BJ the news: 'We've positively identified a dicker, we can hear him passing info about our movements and I'm about to engage him.'

BJ acknowledged this with his usual economy of words: 'Roger. Out.'

'OK, Minty,' I said, 'let's see what range he's at.' Minty lased the target, who was 650 metres away, well within machine gun range. But he kept ducking down behind the rocks. 'Take him out with the main armament,' I said. Paul squeezed the fire button. The round smacked out across the intervening 650 metres and exploded next to our friend. I didn't see the shell actually hit him, but he disappeared from view.

'Automatic, go on,' I said.

Minty laid back on with the aiming mark and squeezed off the remaining five rounds. 'Gun empty,' he shouted.

We still couldn't see the dicker so we moved up to see what had happened to him. But when we reached the spot we couldn't find any trace of the man. Maybe he'd picked up his skirts and run away? Or maybe a couple of his chums had come and helped him escape?

When 3 Para pulled out they'd left a fair bit of weaponry and kit behind, there being no point in lugging it all the way back to the UK, and among the weapons now available for use was a batch of MILAN anti-tank missiles. The MILAN had originally been designed to knock out Warsaw Pact main battle tanks in the Cold War. But as a young Scorpion gunner in the Falklands War, I'd seen first-hand how effective the missile was at destroying enemy bunkers and infantry.

Just over a metre long and with a 7.2kg shaped charge HE warhead, the MILAN was old tech: the operator guided the missile to the target by wire, which meant he needed to maintain a clear line-of-sight to the target, which in turn put him at risk after launch. But although it had been superseded by the Javelin, the MILAN still packed a mean punch. We strapped, bungeed and otherwise cobbled several of the 3 Para's cast-off MILAN launchers to the superstructure of the Spartans.

BJ now gave QBOs [quick battle orders] outlining a new plan: 1 Troop would cross the river and meet up with 4 Troop as they came out of the FOB. My troop (3 Troop) would remain in overwatch to provide covering fire in combination with SHQ Troop to the east; and the RHA's guns up at FOB Robinson would lend additional support as needed.

As 4 Troop left the FOB, they came under intense enemy fire from the maize fields and compounds to the south of the DC. The Taliban love maize: in daylight hours, the tall, densely packed stalks allow them to move around unseen; they pop out of the field edges, fire and run back in to hide from return fire. In Afghanistan, it's always a bit of a relief when the maize crop is in.

Gunfire barked out from the other nest of enemy compounds to our east. I heard the bang and whoosh of RPG-7s launching. Under heavy fire, 1 and 4 Troops drove west from the FOB and headed for the new crossing point. Calling in artillery, the FOO directed smoke rounds in from FOB Robinson to give cover. As we scanned the broken landscape, we saw that much of the enemy firing was coming from a compound half-hidden in one of the maize fields. BJ came up on air: 'Lay down fire onto that compound, and onto the enemy extracting from the maize fields.'

We'd broken down our arcs of fire so that each vehicle covered a specific area. I told Minter: 'Enemy building ahead and right: HE, go on.' Minter started pumping fire into the target compound. At the same time, the squadron SCM, Dean Goodall, fired a MILAN missile from the SHQ position. The MILAN travels at about 600 kilometres an hour, or one kilometre every six seconds – on a good day, you can watch its progress. This was a good day. The missile swooped down towards the target, did a little shimmy as Dean corrected his point of aim, and then slammed into the compound. Designed to penetrate up to a metre of rolled armour, the MILAN brushed the thick, mud-brick walls aside as if they weren't there. Several kilograms of shaped high-explosive anti-tank charge exploded on contact with one of the inner structures. Most of the building vaporized. At the same time, the maize field surrounding it caught fire.

Long tendrils of orange flame snaked skyward from the tinder-dry stalks. Whipped by the breeze, fire and smoke engulfed the enemy within, forcing them out of cover. As they came running out into view, we dosed them with HE and co-axial machine gun; racing down the field boundary for all they were worth, the insurgents looked like nothing so much as human rabbits.

The enemy mortar team had stopped firing. There was smoke everywhere now, the white phosphorus from the shells mingling with the dark-grey clouds swirling up from the burning cornfields. We kept up a barrage of 30mm and co-ax to keep the Taliban on the run. With the enemy on the back foot, 1 and 4 Troops began to cross the river. As the shreds of the enemy we'd driven from the maize fields met up with their southern group, the FOO we had with us called in close air support. A Harrier appeared low and fast from the south-east, dropped a 500lb bomb smack in the middle of the newly massing insurgents and then wheeled away.

Charlie Church led the armoured column into the river. Hitting an unseen trough, the Scimitar began to slew round: for a moment, its crew thought they'd lost control. Then, spotting ripples that indicated a shallower reach, Church told his driver to veer right and step on the gas: as the tracks bit on the shallower section, the vehicle dog-legged and drove out to safety on the opposite bank.

One after another, 1 and 4 Troops' Scimitars forded the Helmand. But then, missing the safe track by the same narrow margin as Charlie Church, the last but one vehicle in the column got stuck. Water surged up the Scimitar's sides, threatening to engulf it. As it struggled to break free, I started to worry: how the hell were we going to extract a stranded Scimitar out of the river? The second we started trying to do that, the Taliban would see their opportunity, regroup, and come down on the column.

But then, with the same aplomb and skill as Charlie Church and his crew, the driver managed to swing the vehicle's nose upriver, find a toe of shallower ground and manoeuvre the Scimitar out of danger: its nose broke the current and it surged out. Scanning round from our higher vantage, I could actually see enemy dead where they lay at the edge of the maize, in and around outbuildings and among the village compounds to the east. As 1 and 4 Troops climbed the relative safety of the escarpment and turned west, we started up and followed in their wake, firing as we moved at any remaining hostiles. There were few targets: far from regrouping, the Taliban were slinking away to their dens. We might still not have won the war; but they'd lost the latest round in the battle for Sangin.

When we reached the pre-arranged holding area we found a number of 'drops' or flat-bed transporter trucks waiting, in case any of our vehicles developed mechanical trouble. It was just as well: suffering from severe mechanical breakdown, two of the Scimitars had only just made it to the RV – they had to be loaded onto the drops and carried back to Bastion. The rest of the column limped along in escort.

We'd had a fairly busy time of it on Operation Herrick 4: in the seven months between April and October 2006, 16 Air Assault Brigade had lost nineteen men killed and had many more injured: fought 500 contacts; and fired almost half a million rounds of ammunition. It was easily the most intense fighting British forces had seen since the Korean War. My first tour of Afghanistan was at an end.

CHAPTER NINETEEN

We reported back to Combermere barracks before leave, expecting to return to normal duties. But, not for the first time in my Army career, the colonel of the regiment had other plans. A day or two after we arrived back, Major-General Barney White-Spunner arrived in camp to take a medals parade. As 'Gold Stick' or Colonel of the Blues and Royals, Princess Anne had been intending to take the medals parade, but the Gold Stick has to stand in for the Queen on official duties and Her Majesty had a cold; so General Barney had to take the place of Princess Anne. On the day, I lined up and stood at attention with the rest of the squadron.

Barney walked up and down the ranks, stopping now and again for a chat and to give out the medals. I wasn't expecting a medal, but the general and his aides halted in front of me. I'd known him from the time he'd been a young troop leader in Northern Ireland and I thought he was just going to say hello. He asked me a few questions about our tour of Afghanistan, which I did my best to answer. Then, all of a sudden, an aide handed Barney a Staff Corporal's rank slide. The General handed me the rank slide, stepped back and held out his hand. 'Congratulations, Corporal Major Flynn.' (As a Staff Corporal in the Household Cavalry, you get called Corporal Major. It's to do with horses – and Queen Victoria.) The promotion came as a complete surprise. I was delighted – until I remembered it was the tradition to buy everybody in the mess bar a drink when you received promotion.

Because of the medals parade, that meant I was going to have to buy a round for nigh-on 300 people. That was going to cost me a fucking fortune, and wipe out my pay increase for the next three months.

A few days later, BJ called me into his office: 'Sit down, Corporal Major. You've been away a lot – you've seen a lot of action, but you haven't seen much of your family. The Colonel thinks you could do with a bit of a break from regimental duties. How do you fancy a posting to the HCR and Royal Armoured Corps recruiting team down at Bovington?'

I said, 'I'd quite like to go back out to Afghanistan with the squadron when it goes out again in eighteen months.' I'd joined the Army to fight, and despite – or because – we'd lost colleagues and friends, the Taliban were an enemy worth fighting.

BJ had thought of that: 'Don't worry, I'll make sure that you're back with the squadron in a year from now, and you deploy with the rest of us. But a recruiting stint will give you time to recharge your batteries – and see something of your family.' I stared at the squadron leader in astonishment. It was true I hadn't seen anything like enough of Shelley and the children in recent months. And you only get the one chance to see your kids growing up. In my many years of service, the British Army had changed a lot when it came to family welfare.

It was strange being back at the Armour Centre in Dorset. In the time since I'd done my own initial training there in 1976, the whole atmosphere of the place had changed. There was a much greater emphasis on professionalism, and much less by way of unnecessary bullshit.

Now I was going down to Bovington as a member of the Household Cavalry recruiting team, Shelley and I decided to sell the shop and post office in Lincolnshire. When we'd done that, she joined me with the family in Lulworth camp, where we moved into a married quarter. The Cove Hotel just down the hill was handy for playtimes. We could walk there on a summer's evening and share a bottle of wine while our teenage children did their own thing safely in boarding school.

Seeing more of my wife and family sounded great on paper, but the reality was different: the recruiting team spent so much time on the road drumming up business, I actually saw less of Shelley and the kids than I had during the six-month tour of Afghan. But that tour was my biggest recruiting weapon. At some point, most would-be recruits wanted to know the answer to the question: 'What's it like being in battle?' The Paras, the Marines and the Household Cavalry had fought in every major British Army conflict since and including Northern Ireland. With combat experience in that scrap, the Falklands War, the Second Iraq War and now in Afghanistan, if I couldn't give the youngsters some idea of what it was like to be in battle, then it was time someone else took on the job.

One day in January 2007, I was talking to a group of school leavers who were thinking about making a career in the Household Cavalry when a trooper came up and beckoned me to one side: 'There's a phone call for you, Sir – it's Major Bartle-Jones.' As soon as he said that, I knew I was being called back to Windsor. I was right – the Squadron wanted me to take over command of 3 Troop.

The MoD prefers not to send young, inexperienced troop leaders into dangerous war zones if that can possibly be avoided. Taking over the troop and going back for a second bite at the Afghan cherry in place of a younger man suited me just fine. By the time I reached the end of my eighteen-month recruiting stint, I knew I'd be ready for a change.

A few weeks later, Shelley and I walked down the hill from the camp to the Lulworth Cove Hotel. We pulled up a bottle of their best Chardonnay and took it to the beer garden. It wasn't actually beer, but we didn't think the management would mind. A side order of mussels in cream with a big chunk of fresh home-made bread and butter helped things along nicely. It was nearing the end of September and we managed to catch a bit of the late summer sun. I'd been putting off telling Shelley that the squadron wanted me to go out to Helmand again in the spring for as long as I could, and at least until December: there was no point making her worried for longer than was absolutely necessary.

We were talking among ourselves when I heard a voice calling: 'Mick! Mick!' I looked up. It was Pete Townsend, a LCoH from D Squadron; his wife, Louise, and his brother, whose name I never found out. Pete and Louise actually lived in Lulworth, and had been out fishing on their boat.

I said: 'You all seem a bit merry: is it something you caught?'

Pete said: 'No, we didn't get a bite all day – we've been drinking the local nightrider [cider].' They came up to our table and sat down. Then Pete said: 'Mick! You must be chuffed to fuck!'

I said: 'What, Peter? What are you talking about?'

'I've seen your name on the ORBAT. You're coming out with us on Herrick Eight.' I glared daggers at Pete, trying to warn him to shut up. He kept beaming at me: 'That's fantastic news, though, isn't it – what do you think?'

I looked across at Shelley. She was giving me the wifely stare, headlights on full beam. I could almost feel the guilt written on my face. I said: 'I'm sorry, Shell – I was just trying to find the right time to tell you.'

Pete suddenly realized he'd made a gaffe. He looked stricken. 'Er – would you two like a drink?'

I said: 'I think we're going to need one. Best make that another bottle of white wine.'

When we did get a chance to talk it through alone, Shell saw that in some ways I could hardly refuse the call – BJ had asked me to deploy with the squadron, and I really, really wanted to go.

A few weeks later, I drove up to Windsor with a fresh batch of potential Household Cavalry recruits to show them round the barracks. While they were doing that, I had a meeting with my old friend and acquaintance Steve McWhirter. I said: 'They've made me 3 Troop's leader in place of younger man.'

He said: 'I know and in your case, being younger isn't difficult. I'm going to be your Corporal of Horse.' I couldn't think of anyone I'd rather have with me. We had a bit of a chat about what was required for the upcoming deployment, what sort of mechanical state the troop's vehicles were in and so forth. After that, I went and had a chat with BJ, who'd been busy that morning getting the latest update from Brigade HQ in Colchester. He asked me if I could join a big pre-deployment squadron exercise in November. 'No, sorry Sir – I'm committed to the recruiting team at Bovington until early January.'

When I arrived back at Combermere barracks in January 2008, I discovered that during the autumn exercise, the squadron had decided it made no sense for two experienced senior NCOs like Corporal of Horse McWhirter and myself to be in the same troop. So I moved across to take command of 1 Troop, while Squirty continued in his role as 3 Troop's Corporal of Horse. Although I was sorry to lose Squirty, with the new deployment looming ever closer we needed to spread the love – distribute the people with combat experience as widely as possible.

When a squadron's about to deploy on a tour of duty, it's usual to have a bit of a get-together for wives, families and other loved ones over a buffet lunch. I was standing in the mess in Combermere barracks, chatting to D Squadron's new SQMC Jules Hoggarth and his wife Julie. Someone else came up to talk to them and I turned away. I bumped into Harry 27. I'd known Paul Harris senior – Harry 27 – almost from the beginning of my Army career, even before going to Northern Ireland in 1978 at the age of 18.

Shortly before I'd rejoined the Army in 2001 after my eight years out in civilian life, Harry 27 had reached the end of his statutory twenty-two years' service. He'd married twice during that time: his second wife, Pauline, was with him at the get-together that day, and so was his first wife, Sue. (There's a strong family tradition in the Household Cavalry: divorcees are welcome. It's not like the Roman Catholic Church.) I'd watched Harry 27's sons grow up, and it hadn't been all that big a surprise when his younger son, Harry 73, had also joined the Household Cavalry.

Why were the Harris family members referred to by numbers, and not by their names? It's an odd fact, but a great many people with the surname Harris join the Household Cavalry; the number system is the best way of distinguishing between them.

Harry 27 fixed me with a bit of a look. 'Mick,' he said, 'my boy Paul's in your troop. You're taking him out to Afghanistan with you. Make sure you look after him, won't you?' As my senior corporal and my most experienced commander, his son Paul was a key member of the troop. He was also a trained FAC. His seniority and skills made it more likely that Harry 73 would stand in harm's way when we deployed to Helmand province, and not less. I met my old friend's gaze. He was smiling. We both knew he was asking the impossible when it came to guaranteeing his son's safety. But before I could stop the words coming out of my mouth, I said: 'Don't worry, Harry – I'll look after him.'

The next day, another member of my new command, Trooper James Munday, came to see me. Everyone in D Squadron knew Trooper Munday by his nickname, 'Magpie'. Magpie looked worried, and that worried me. I knew and liked James. He was one of D Squadron's brightest and most promising soldiers – and from a professional point of view, he had absolutely nothing to worry about.

I'd first met James when I moved back to Windsor to take command of 1 Troop in January 2008, by which time he was a qualified Scimitar driver and gunner. A talented horseman, he'd joined the Army in February 2005 and had been posted straight to the Household Cavalry Mounted Regiment in Knightsbridge on completion of basic training. Trooper Munday was also very good at downhill skiing, and when you came up against him on the rugby field, you knew about it.

He said: 'Can I have a word in private, Corporal Major?' We went into the troop leader's office and shut the door.

I looked across at James. 'What's up?'

'I'd like to talk to you about leaving the Army, Sir.'

That stopped me dead in my tracks: soldiers like the man in front of me were exactly what the Army needed. And I wanted James to serve in my troop. 'What's brought this about? Is something bothering you?'

'No, it's nothing like that. I love the Army, but I've done my first year of A-levels. I was thinking about going back to college and getting better qualified.'

'Let me tell you something, James: when I first joined the Army, I wasn't all that happy – but when you get your first stripe – your first promotion – it gets a lot easier. With you, that's going to happen pretty soon.'

That news obviously surprised him. 'Is it?'

'Yes, it is. Look, all the hierarchy in the Squadron think you have the makings of a very good NCO. What that means is, within five or six years, you'll be a troop Corporal of Horse earning £40,000 plus, and you'll have a cast-iron pension at the end of your career. Not only that, but under the present rules, you'll be able to retire at 40 – which is still young enough to do something else in civilian life.'

I let him think about that for a moment. Then I said: 'If you do leave the Army, you'll have to spend at least a year doing your A levels, and then another three years at university. And even after all that, you'll probably come out and get a job that will only pay you about £25,000. Unless you're really lucky, it will be two or three years before you start earning any real money.'

I could see my argument was making an impression on James Munday. But then, I didn't want to push him into doing something that he wouldn't want to do. 'The best thing is, you go away and have a serious think about it, then come back and see me in a week or two. OK?' He thanked me and left. Three days later he was back in my office. He said, 'I've thought it over, and I've decided I'm happy in the Household Cavalry, and I'm happy here in Windsor. So I've decided to stay in.'

'That's excellent, Trooper Munday – really good news. All you have to do now is knuckle down like you have been doing, and within five or six years you'll be a troop CoH.' I watched James Munday walk out of my office – a straight-backed, straight-talking soldier in the best tradition. And if I could only have foreseen what was going to happen, I'd have called him back in.

CHAPTER TWENTY

For obvious reasons, I'd been watching events in Helmand province closely in the run-up to our second tour. Early in 2007, the usual mix of extremist opposition to the ISAF presence, drug-trafficking interests and tribal rivalries had caused the ceasefire we'd helped conclude at Musa Qal'ah to break down. On 2 February, a group of between two and three hundred insurgents stormed the DC, disarmed the ANP garrison, razed many of the government buildings to the ground and executed Haji Shah Agha, the elder who'd led the ceasefire negotiations we'd helped protect. Seizing control of the town, the Taliban had immediately begun reusing Musa Qal'ah as a base for offensive operations; imposed strict sharia law and extorted money from the local population; and set about forcibly recruiting young men and boys into their ranks.

It sounded like a total disaster, but the truth was slightly different: British and other ISAF forces had stayed close to Musa Qal'ah, using MOGs to keep an eye on the Taliban, interrupt their supply lines and keep them off-balance as the opportunity arose. Despite these efforts, there was no doubt that by the end of 2007, the town had become a kind of trophy for the Taliban – and for us. We couldn't just let them sit back and use it as a major hub for drug-trafficking, terrorizing the local population, interrupting legitimate trade, and generally making their own special brand of trouble. Nor could we let them trumpet their defiance of the democratically elected Afghan government. We had to convince both the townspeople and the wider population of Afghanistan that they, and not the Taliban, were the real power in the land. In short, the Taliban needed knocking back.

On the afternoon of 6 December 2007, a combined force of British and Afghan Army troops led by the Household Cavalry battle group under the command of Lt-Col Smith-Osborne launched a three-pronged assault on Musa Qal'ah from the south. Later that same evening, several hundred US troops landed to the north of the town. Fighting the estimated 2,000 Taliban defenders right through the night, the jaws of the ISAF vice started closing. The problem was IEDs: with plenty of time to prepare before the offensive started, the Taliban had sewn hundreds of improvised explosive devices in and around the town.

Defusing the hidden devices slowed the assault to a crawl. Even so, by the end of the second day, the combined assault had pushed the enemy back from the surrounding villages and advanced to within two kilometres of Musa Qal'ah town centre. Determined to keep control, the Taliban poured reinforcements into the area. On 12 December, four days after the assault began, Taliban forces abandoned the town, retreating northwards into the mountains under harassing fire. As a political gesture and an acknowledgement of their fighting contribution, ISAF commanders asked the Afghan troops who'd taken part in the assault to take formal control of the town and raise the Afghan flag over the DC. So much for background developments. Now it was our turn to show what we could do again.

On arrival in Camp Bastion to begin our six-month tour of duty on Operation Herrick 8 in the first week of May 2008, we found that the original camp had been linked with a new one, Bastion 2, to form a giant super-camp about 4x6 square kilometres in size. And even that wasn't big enough: the civilian contractors who'd taken over from the Royal Engineers were in the process of making the base even larger.

Bastion now housed and protected more than 3,000 British personnel, together with 1,000 or so servicemen and women from other countries, and hundreds of civilian support staff. Most of the accommodation in the camp was the same as it had been on our first deployment: polytunnel-style 'pods', tents, and the odd shipping container. The view around the camp was also unchanged: a brown, beige and khaki sprawl, with a backdrop of dark-grey mountains glowering in the distance. One new addition was a trailer that made pizzas, which, we were told, had been very tasty – until the truck had been struck by lighting and set on fire, putting it out of action.

The tented accommodation had come on quite a bit in the two years since I'd been away: in place of the old hot and sweaty canvas affairs, we now had white, double-skinned super-tents made of a thick, weatherproof nylon-based material. The air-conditioning also worked much better, which was a relief, and the camp had far more real buildings made of things like bricks and wood. Gymnasiums, or at least tents with running machines and weights in them, were another big improvement: without somewhere to work off their excess energy, young soldiers tend to go a bit mad. It was hard to remember the old camp hospital with any great fondness, but it had in any case more than doubled in size and was now housed in a dedicated new building.

We spent a couple of weeks acclimatizing and taking ownership of the Scimitars we'd be using on Herrick 8. Then, allotted the Now Zad/Musa Qal'ah/Nawa AO, or area of operations, the squadron got its first mission: our task was to head up to FOB Edinburgh, 50 kilometres or so to the north-west of Bastion between Musa Qal'ah and Now Zad. Part of a ring of patrol bases and FOBs that were gradually being established to protect Musa Qal'ah District Centre and prevent the Taliban coming back in to retake control of the town, FOB Edinburgh sits on the western side of the local green zone at an altitude of more than 1,000 metres.

In a fully working Scimitar, the journey up to FOB Edinburgh normally takes six hours. But the vehicles we were using were so old, and had seen so much hard service in the two punishing years of daily and relentless duty in Afghanistan's heat and dust, that they were now very difficult to keep going. As we immediately found out, mechanical breakdowns were now so frequent that despite our best efforts to fix the given problem and forge on, it took us three days to reach the FOB. That works out at an average speed of less than 20 kilometres a day. As each vehicle broke down, a second working wagon had to hook up and tow it, then that one would break down and the whole process had to start over again. The REME light aid detachment team travelling with us worked wonders – and worked their tits off – trying to keep the convoy rolling; but there was only so much they could do with what was essentially shagged equipment. By the end of the third day, when we finally reached the FOB, we were all just about dead on our feet with fatigue, and the sheer frustration the journey had induced was sapping our collective morale.

Then, just to make a perfect end to the journey from hell, my own Scimitar seized up as we drove in through the front gates of FOB Edinburgh. It stuck there and refused to budge, blocking the entrance. We had to get a bulldozer to shove it into the base for running repairs.

After twenty-four hours to recover, repair the vehicles and reconstitute, we set out from FOB Edinburgh on our first Herrick 8 MOG patrol. The basic mission was resoundingly familiar: to deny the Taliban freedom of movement in and around the area to the north of Musa Qal'ah, and allow law-abiding Afghans to go about their normal business. Corporal of Horse McWhirter was senior NCO of 2 Troop; then came 4 Troop, followed by SHQ Troop. 1 Troop was bringing up the rear. With the ever-present danger from IEDs, a two-man barma team swept the ground ahead of the squadron on foot for mines, marking a safe lane for the column as it advanced. At walking pace, we reached a wadi about 20 kilometres north of the FOB. Squirty took his Scimitar east across the dried-up watercourse, reaching the other side without incident. Sticking closely to Squirty's tracks, 4 Troop's commander, Lt Rolly Spiller, followed in his Spartan. As the driver, Trooper Baker, pulled the vehicle's steering sticks to take it around a slight dog-leg, the Spartan's back end strayed less than half a metre out of the marked route. Straying a tiny bit off-line like that is inevitable sometimes when you're trying to steer an armoured vehicle. It was bad luck, not bad driving.

A metre below ground, the pressure plates of a long-buried IED closed together. The firing circuit made, triggering a huge explosion. Blast punched the rear end of the 12-tonne vehicle high into the air, catapulting Lt Spiller and the vehicle's operator, LCoH Anthony Todd, out of their hatches. They smacked into the ground about 10 metres out to the vehicle's front and lay where they'd landed, too shocked and dazed to move. But worse was to come. The passenger in the rear of the Spartan's cabin had taken the full force of the blast. He'd died instantly. The Afghan interpreter who'd been seated opposite suffered severe burn damage to his lungs, but he lived.

Our very first patrol back in theatre, and we were straight back into it. When the IED exploded, I'd been at the top of the wadi's western bank watching the squadron's rear arc. Keeping a wary eye out through the commander's sight in case the Taliban tried to take further advantage, I saw a plume of black exhaust smoke swirling towards us. Gradually, the image resolved into a battered white minibus laden with Afghan men. Fumes billowing from its overworked and ancient engine, the vehicle kept appearing and disappearing in the smoke.

I immediately alerted the rest of the MOG. The Taliban liked nothing better than to strike at a unit busy dealing with the aftermath of a mine or IED strike. Expecting imminent attack, we laid the 30mm and the GPMG on the approaching minibus. The vehicle slowed when its occupants saw us, then veered away to the east of our position. One of the men on board the vehicle waved. It looked as if he and his mates might just be innocent travellers. That was a relief – we had enough trouble to deal with already. With the minibus disappearing back into the heat haze from where it had come, I told Stan Stanforth to spin the Scimitar on its axis and then take us back out the way we'd come in, being careful to roll exactly in our own proven tracks. When we were clear of the wadi, we stopped and helped clear a secure helicopter landing site: the MERT Chinook was already on its way to treat and evacuate the injured.

Then call sign 33 Alpha, Squadron Corporal Danny Hitchings, arrived at the HLS with the squadron ambulance. We helped get the injured to a suitable area for boarding the MERT when it arrived. The Chinook thumped in to land, sending up the usual brown-out. Even before the dust had settled, Danny was organizing people to help the injured onto the helicopter.

Given the high risk of further IEDs at that location, Brigade sent out a specialist EOD team. Part of the Joint Force Explosive Ordnance Disposal Unit based at Bastion, they jumped off the Chinook and set to work. When it comes to danger and sheer balls, the work the EOD teams do is hardcore. And after two years in Afghanistan, they were getting really good at finding and disabling enemy explosive devices. So good, in fact, that they were slowly defeating the Taliban's latest tactic. As a result, coalition EOD teams had shot to the top of the Taliban's kill list. The EOD officers were helping us stay alive. Our job, as they worked to clear the ground, was to return the favour. In this, we had good help: alerted to our predicament, a unit of 2 Scots based at FOB Edinburgh moved to our assistance with a troop of Warrior AFVs.

The EOD team uncovered the pressure plate device that had triggered the blast. The Spartan's right-hand rear track had strayed barely 15 centimetres outside the bounds of the marked safe lane. A tiny distance in relation to the size of the vehicle. But enough to kill one good man and seriously injure another. The IED – it was definitely a Taliban device, and not a Russian legacy mine – had torn a long split in one of the vehicle's metal walls. If the bomb had exploded further forward under the engine block, the crew – and the vehicle's passengers – might all have survived.

We spent the night keeping an eye on the damaged Spartan, then fell back to FOB Edinburgh at daylight, once a recovery vehicle had arrived.

With another vehicle destroyed, we fixed up the remaining wagons as best we could and then went back out on patrol. We drove up to Musa Qal'ah, following the wadi north-east, cutting straight through the town centre and then emerging out into the badlands on the other side. We were probing for the FLET, or forward line of enemy troops. But for once, the Taliban didn't want to come out and play. Deprived of entertainment, we turned and headed back down to FOB Edinburgh. That was easier said than done: even over what was a relatively short distance, we once again suffered continual and near-catastrophic mechanical breakdowns. At last, much later that same night, we limped back into the forward base.

Next day, we began the not very long but extremely slow and painful journey back down to Camp Bastion. With one vehicle after another breaking down and grinding to a halt, we once again had to play a kind of mechanical leapfrog with the column: using vehicles that were still operational to drag or tow the ones that had given up the mechanical ghost. In 2006, on Herrick 4, the journey between FOB Edinburgh and Camp Bastion had taken us five hours. This time, it took five days.

Fixing the ancient rolling stock proved to be almost impossible: crucial spares were either completely unavailable or extremely hard to come by. After three days trying to fix them, we still only had about 50 per cent of D Squadron's armour fit for operational use. Major Bartle-Jones decided that something radical had to be done – as in, getting a core fleet of armoured vehicles that was serviceable for more, and not less, of the time. We were supposed to be in the cavalry. If we'd wanted to spend our time on foot or fixing broken wagons, then we'd have joined the infantry or the REME.

BJ went to see the Brigade commander. 'Sir, the vehicles we have – the Scimitars and Spartans – are no longer fit for purpose. It's got to the point where we can no longer carry out our designated operational role. Or for that matter, any role. We have to re-equip.'

The powers-that-be decided to keep the best ten vehicles of the Scimitar and Spartan fleet out in theatre, and then, having raided the remaining wagons for spares, trickle them back to the UK for a complete overhaul. Half D Squadron – 1 and 2 Troops – would now re-equip with a brand-new vehicle in service: the Jackal. Fantastic. For their part, 3 and 4 Troops would continue to operate the Scimitars – and good luck to them.

I had nothing against the Scimitar – when it worked, it was a great vehicle. But at the same time, like everyone else I'd grown sick to death of the incessant breakdowns. Off with the old and on with the new; I was looking forward to trying out the Jackal. There was only one small problem: looking a bit like a jeep that's overdosed on steroids, at 7 tonnes unladen, the Jackal was a heavy vehicle in its own right. Despite the fact that we were in a war zone, health and safety regulations dictated that any of D Squadron's drivers who didn't already have a heavy goods vehicle licence would need to get one. So we had to send fourteen of our men back to the UK.

All fourteen drivers passed the HGV test, including Trooper James Munday. But they'd trained on trucks and not on the Jackal. So when they came back clutching their shiny new HGV licences, they had to undergo yet another driving course in Camp Bastion.

The Jackal, when I tried it out, struck me as fast, rugged and reliable. It came with a GPMG fitted as standard in the front commander's seat, and either a .50 cal heavy machine gun or a grenade machine gun [GMG] mounted on the rear pintle. For its relatively light weight, the vehicle was well armed. Its small size, high speed and good manoeuvrability would also help keep it – and us – out of trouble. But sitting in it, I felt that the Jackal, which was open-topped with a roll bar and plate steel doors, didn't provide enough protection for the crew. The Jackal also had no cage armour – and at Musa Qal'ah, I'd learned only too well how important that was in protecting against RPG attack. Used to having an armoured shell and a turret, I felt more than a bit vulnerable: not just when it came to potential RPG strikes, but also in the case of shrapnel, bomb-blast or sniper fire.

At least I'd be occupying the commander's seat – the rear gunner was even more at risk. His position above and behind the central roll bar gave him an excellent field of fire, but if the vehicle overturned, then he either had to jump clear or hunker down inside and hope for the best.

Under normal circumstances, it takes two weeks to get qualified on the grenade machine gun. But because of the delay in getting people qualified to drive the Jackal, there was now an official hurry-up: we learned to strip, clean and operate the GMG in the morning of one day. Then, that same afternoon, we did the same for the Browning .50 cal heavy machine gun. The next day, we took both weapons out on the range at Camp Bastion and practised firing them. Now that's what I call a fast weapons course.

I already knew how to operate the .50 cal from my days as a Chieftain tank gunner, so I had no trouble getting back up to speed on the weapon. The Mark 2 version now in service had some improvements on the old model I'd first met as an 18-year-old, not least of which was the ACOG, or Advanced Combat Optical Gunsight. Also mounted on the GMG, the SA-80 and the GPMG, the ACOG's 4x optical magnification and all-round user-friendliness made it easy to acquire targets and then hit them.

But some things about the .50 cal were still the same: I hadn't forgotten the almighty, teeth-jarring recoil when you opened fire. The first round from a Browning .50 machine gun is always the most accurate; when that one's gone, the weapon bucks so hard in your grip you do well to stay on the aiming point. Like all machine guns, except in extreme circumstances the weapon was best fired in short bursts, laying back onto the target between times.

The GMG was new to me, but it was simple to operate, easy to clean – and, once you got the hang of it, meant you could hit targets out to two kilometres with an awesome amount of firepower: 340 high explosive, 40mm metal fragmentation grenades per minute, or more than five rounds a second. The GMG wasn't just a ferocious weapon in its own right – it was also very useful when it came to marking a target for other weapons. Marvellous. By the end of day two on our snap weapons course, I was looking forward to using the GMG in the field. As things turned out, I wouldn't have to wait long.

Given that different driving and weapons skills were needed to operate the Jackals, we had to make a few changes to the troop crewing lists. As a result, my new troop Corporal of Horse was none other than my old pal and drinking buddy, 'One Shot, One Kill' JC Moses.

CHAPTER TWENTY-ONE

While we were busy sorting out D Squadron and learning to operate the new vehicles, an almighty ISAF operation got underway to move a giant new turbine up to the Kajaki dam.

Part of the general coalition effort to convince Afghans they'd be better off living in a Western-inspired democracy with electricity, and not under unelected Taliban rule without it, the turbine, once installed, would provide many megawatts of extra power to the local grid. With a height of 100 metres or so, the Kajaki dam is located in the north-eastern corner of Helmand province, about 25 kilometres north of Sangin. As well as providing electricity to some 650,000 people, the dam helps irrigate almost 2,000 square kilometres of what would otherwise be arid land. With the new, third turbine in place, its output would increase significantly, pumping electricity to an additional 1 million people. But the Taliban, who apparently want the country to moulder in a kind of medieval chaos so that they can exploit it for their own ends, didn't want the third turbine to be installed. In fact, they didn't want any hydro-electricity flowing from the dam at all. What they really, really wanted was to blow up the turbine house and, if possible, destroy the entire installation. We knew this because they'd launched repeated attacks not just against the dam itself, but against the ISAF base and the patrols we'd established to protect the installation since arriving in Helmand province.

The threat to personnel at or near the dam was very real. Back in the days of the Russian occupation, a mujahidin unit had overwhelmed the Russian defenders in place, trapped the Soviet engineers in the upper floor of an accommodation block, tortured their guards to death on the floor below, then broken in and killed the engineers – slowly. Not what you'd call a desirable outcome. And one we were keen to avoid repeating.

More than a year before British forces had officially deployed to Helmand in 2006, a Royal Marines commando unit, breaking the operational ground as they often do, had established a forward operating base hard by the dam. Determined to oust the Marines, the Taliban mounted a major attack on them early in the New Year of 2007. In the subsequent fighting, units of 42 Commando repulsed the insurgents, held the dam, cleared a number of enemy cave complexes in the local area and then flushed the Taliban out of the nearby compounds. But a few days after the Marines had driven them out, the Taliban started trying to creep back in. Since that first engagement, with an estimated 700 enemy fighters in and around the FOB and more insurgents arriving from Pakistan and other provinces in a steady trickle, enemy attacks on the dam had kept on coming.

D Squadron's Jackal group deployed to the south of Kajaki on Route 1 about 20 kilometres east of Gereshk at the beginning of July. Located at the northern end of the Sangin valley, FOB Kajaki was then the most remote British base in Helmand province. The landscape was extremely rugged and wild. Some might say attractive, but I love Britain – give me Dartmoor, the Brecon Beacons or Hyde Park any day.

With the turbine operation scheduled for the end of August, our job in the Jackal group was to recce and mark out a safe route for part of the massive turbine convoy's journey to the dam. We were also to reinforce security in the southern Kajaki area, act as a reconnaissance screen, keep the Taliban at arm's length, and if we did come in contact with them, prevent the enemy from flanking the turbine convoy or getting in behind it. With the Jackals, we could cover a lot of rough terrain fast. And we needed to – the distances involved were so great, and our numbers so few in relation to the amount of ground we had to cover.

Finding a safe route for the turbine's journey to the dam was anything but straightforward. The Para PF did most of the work, and we chipped in as and when we could. Having studied the aerial reconnaissance photographs, the hardest part of the job, apart from the obvious need to avoid known Taliban threat points, was to make sure the super-heavy dam turbine vehicles steered clear of any stretches of soft ground; avoided VPs [vulnerable points, or ambush-friendly choke points], watercourses, including ditches and streams, and any of Afghanistan's generally ancient and rickety bridges.

The 611 highway stretches south-east from Kajaki FOB, skirting the Helmand River. One of the most dangerous routes in Afghanistan, the 611 is actually a dirt track, which the Taliban mine with IEDs at every opportunity. After about four kilometres, Route 611 turns south, contouring a bend in the river, then continues due south, skirting the green zone to the east. This part of the Kajaki green zone, with its dense complex of vegetation and housing compounds, is where the Taliban most like to lurk and strike. There are a couple of ANP checkpoints on Route 611's southern leg, but the biggest asset our forces have in terms of countering the Taliban is the roughly circular area of high ground that starts about one kilometre due south of the FOB. The hills there spread out east, west and south, dominating both the 611 highway and the most dangerous part of the Kajaki green zone. Three remote British observation posts [OPs] established on the hills help maintain overwatch on the local Taliban forces, and give the fire support groups stationed there an excellent field of fire when it comes to whacking them.

The other place the Taliban hang out in force is north of the Kajaki FOB, on the other side of the Helmand River in the closely grouped settlements of Mazdurak: Barakju, Risaji and Khvolehabad. Another

OP on the high ground there, named Essex ridge, dominates and seeks to suppress that particular rats' nest as needs be.

At the end of August 2008, the huge operation to move the 220-tonne turbine the 180 kilometres from Kandahar up to the dam got underway. Both sides understood the massive symbolic importance of the op. Several hundred extra insurgents were reported crossing from Pakistan to reinforce Taliban war bands trying to stop the turbine reaching Kajaki. Against them, ISAF and the ANA fielded a 5,000-strong convoy protection team.

For the first 90-kilometres leg of its journey from Kandahar, US and Canadian troops protected the 200-vehicle convoy. But for the second leg, which led along a remote, back-country track codenamed Route Harriet and deliberately chosen to deceive the enemy, more than 3,000 British troops, including large numbers of men from the Parachute Regiment, took over convoy protection duties. In the Jackal group, our job at this point was to guard the junction of Route 611 and Highway One.

The Taliban fell heavily for the deception plan: Route Harriet led through the Ghorak pass, near Route 611 and the village of Kajaki Sofla. With British help, the Afghan National Army's 3/205 'Hero' Brigade cleared the surprised Taliban units out of the village, allowing the convoy safe and uninterrupted passage along the final few kilometres to the dam.

Escorted by Harrier close support aircraft and AAC Apache helicopter gunships, the turbine – and the 90-tonne crane that was needed to install it – made it to Kajaki intact on 2 September. In the course of the twelve-day operation, coalition forces estimated they'd killed more than 200 Taliban fighters.

It was one thing getting the turbine to the dam. But now it had arrived, the Taliban were determined to prevent the private Chinese contractors from installing it. They maintained a relentless pace of attacks on the dam and on the single supply route leading up to it. With no guarantee of safety, no company, not even the Chinese, who don't normally balk at danger, would agree to drive in the 900 tonnes of concrete and aggregate needed to finish the job. And so, after all the time and effort involved in getting it up to Kajaki, the new turbine is still sitting there, carefully protected from the weather and the enemy, waiting for better days.

CHAPTER TWENTY-TWO

With the Kajaki turbine operation at an end, Brigade now tasked 1 and 2 Troops to continue patrolling Highway One. Our new job was to stop the Taliban hijacking supply convoys, stealing the supplies and shooting the drivers. While we got on with that, 3 and 4 Troops would remain in position at Garmsir with the US Marines, blocking insurgent activity to the south of the town.

There's nothing I like more than an open-ended, roving brief. But route security patrolling was a bit of a bone task, i.e. repetitive and boring. It was also a big ask: the bit of Highway One for which we were now responsible was more than 150 kilometres in length. And there was an edge of danger, if not of the kind we preferred: aware that we were beginning to patrol it, the Taliban had started laying strings of IEDs along the main supply route in an effort to blow us up.

After a couple of weeks snuffling around looking for insurgents, we needed a replen [replenishment] of food, water and fuel. With re-supply still one of our main problems in theatre, and heavy-lift helicopters still not available in sufficient numbers, we were warned off for a parachute drop from a C-130 Hercules transport aircraft.

On the appointed day, we set to preparing a drop zone. Darkness began to fall: when the light starts to go in southern Afghanistan, it goes really fast. That pleased Toddy. With ginger hair and pale skin that was prone to burning, LCoH Anthony Todd disliked being in the sun and did everything he could to stay out of it. If I could, I therefore gave him jobs that needed doing in the middle of the night. We secured an area of flat land a few kilometres north of the highway, then Toddy went round it placing firefly infra-red [IR] markers ready for the C-130 Hercules scheduled to come in at 2300 hours.

The Herc was going to make one pass, and one pass only, dropping six pallets of supplies. In the case of most air drops, the loadmaster and his team on the back ramp of the C-130 try to get all the pallets off the back of the aircraft as quickly as possible: that way, the supplies fall in a relatively small area, which means it's easier to find them, and also means we can usually get to and protect the stuff before any looters or enemy forces try to nick it. Most Afghan people are dirt poor, so poor they do things like rush in and scrabble to pick up spent cartridge shells when we've finished a practice shoot at Bastion. They either sell the brass on, or turn it into teapots, ashtrays and ornaments. We had to stop them doing that after the Taliban used the cover of brass collecting to lay an IED on one of the firing ranges. The blast killed a British soldier. But the poverty in Afghanistan isn't going away any time soon: sometimes, you can see women crouched in the dust at a road junction, picking up grains of wheat or rice that have fallen off the back of a truck as it makes the turn.

We sat waiting for the Hercules to arrive. We had our engines off so as not to advertise our presence to hostile ears, and so that we could hear the aircraft coming in. It's so quiet in Afghanistan at night you can hear for miles – much farther than you can in most parts of the UK. In the distance, we heard the faint thrum of the C-130's engines. Toddy started the fireflies winking so the pilot could see the drop zone. The drone of the aircraft's engines increased to a loud rumble, then a roar, then the C-130 came overhead and we heard the whoosh as the pallets started winging out the back end. Parachutes blossomed in the darkness, massive, dark-grey mushroom caps floating to earth as we watched through the NVGs.

We were parked off at what we thought was a safe distance. But then I heard the same kind of noise a doodlebug makes, when you hear it on the old newsreels of Nazi V-1 rockets striking London in the Second World War. Nasty – and much, much too close to our position for comfort. I thought, 'Uh-oh – the pilot's either missed the drop zone entirely, or the parachute's failed to open. Now we're in for it.' I was right on both counts: the Herc had slightly overshot, and one of the chutes had failed to deploy. We had a large wooden pallet with a tonne of stores lashed to it whistling towards us through the darkness at the speed of gravity.

The stores bomb sounded louder and louder. I began to think it was going to land on our heads. I thought about moving, but when you're playing Russian roulette with a giant heavy pallet, then one patch of sand is as dangerous as the next. If we did start up the engines and move, there was just as much chance we'd wear the pallet. Best to stay put and pray it didn't rain boxes of tinned corned beef. In fact, come to think of it, I hate corned beef: if I was going to get killed in a stores drop, I much preferred to die in a hail of chicken tikka masala. As a precaution, we took cover inside the vehicles, but left the hatches open to keep an eye on developments.

The pallet was so close above I could hear the failed parachute harnessed to it flapping uselessly. You can die in any number of ridiculous and futile ways. But getting killed by your own stores drop? Next thing, there was an almighty, ear-splitting explosion about 200 metres from where we were parked. Thank fuck, the pallet had missed us. Then an overpowering smell of tomato and basil hit my nose. I thought: 'Tomato and basil? What the fuck?' I was sure I must be dreaming. Then someone said: 'Can anyone else smell pasta sauce?'

'Can I ever,' Toddy said. 'It fucking reeks of the stuff.' Then I realized: one of the ration meals was tomato and basil spaghetti. It came in plastic boil-in-the-bag sachets. A vast load of it must have been on the pallet; and at least half the bags must have burst on contact with the earth. I got on the radio to BJ: 'Zero Alpha, this is Whiskey One: one of the parachutes has malfunctioned. The pallet's lying off about 200 metres to our north. The load has spilled – we're going to take a look at it now. Confirm no one's been hurt.'

We drove up to where the pallet had creamed in. I jumped down off the vehicle and walked up to the mound of ruined stores. It stank. There was spaghetti with tomato and basil sauce everywhere. I turned to the other lads. 'The bad news is, tomato and basil pasta's off the menu. The even worse news is we have to get in amongst that mess and fish out the batteries and other stores we need. And when I say "we", what I actually mean is "you". One more thing: the only way you're going to find the stuff we need is by using your hands.'

There was a lot of moaning and groaning, but the lads got stuck into the mess. They salvaged fifty-odd bars of flapjack smothered in tomato and basil sauce – and, to my great relief, the much-needed radio batteries. We couldn't leave them lying around for the enemy to find: they'd be on the end of an IED before you could say 'that looks like a command wire'. Finding our own batteries attached to enemy explosive devices happened much, much more often than it should have done.

Once we'd recovered and stored the undamaged supplies, we collected up all the used parachutes and pallets, dumped them on top of the basil and tomato pyramid and doused the whole lot in diesel fuel. I stood back and looked at the pile. How to light it? 'I know,' I thought, 'I'll set fire to it with a phosphorus grenade.' I pulled the pin, chucked the grenade, turned and started to run.

The grenade exploded early. The bonfire went up with a loud whump, spraying more sauce to all sides. With no spare kit to change into, we had to climb back into the wagons and drive on, reeking of tomato and basil. All we needed was the Parmesan.

After two weeks of suppressing insurgent activity on the designated sector of Highway One, 1 and 2 Troops came back into Bastion with the Jackals, and Major Will Davies took over from BJ as D Squadron's OC. I'd known Will Davies since he'd been a 12-year-old boy running round Combermere barracks with his sister. Major Davies had no recollection of me – why should he? But back in those happy days it was his father, Colonel Davies, who'd promoted me to LCoH.

With Will Davies now in command, I stood in as the Squadron Corporal Major [Warrant Officer Class Two] for SCM Danny Hitchings while he was away on R&R [rest and recreation]. With other units taking over responsibility for Highway One, we formed a mix-and-match squadron with a roving reconnaissance brief. By now we'd got used to the Jackals, and SHQ Troop, 1 and 2 Troops moved south to the Garmsir/Marjah/Nad Ali Area of Operations. Our job was to deny the Taliban freedom of movement from Pakistan into Helmand province, and generally suppress their activities as before. We took over from a US force at FOB Dwyer, which lay just outside the town. The outgoing US Marine Corps presence there had been more than 2,000 strong. The total British force, which included a unit of RHA 105mm guns, numbered about 150. That difference in strength is typical of the two armies. We might be seriously lacking in numbers, but at least we had plenty of room in the FOB. A unit of ANA troops joined us a day or two later. My experience of the ANA to date had shown me that they varied greatly in terms of combat efficiency: some were very good and some were very bad; most were somewhere in the middle. We were very happy to discover that the unit we were now working with had been trained by the Royal Marines, and as a result they were excellent soldiers. Which just goes to prove that, despite what all the cynics have to say about native Afghan forces, it can be done.

Even though the vast majority of the ANA at FOB Dwyer were non-Pashto tribesmen who, in order to minimize the risk of Taliban reprisals against their families, came from elsewhere in Afghanistan, a fair number of them wore cotton balaclavas or scarves out on patrol to conceal their identities.

Once we'd dumped our kit and settled into the FOB, the first priority was to familiarize ourselves with our new area of operations.

That done, we'd then push round in a pincer movement to observe the POL, or pattern of life in the Marjah green zone. I'd lead three vehicles of the six in SHQ troop; the other section of three would operate in parallel a couple of kilometres to the south. Intelligence suggested that while there were a number of normal, law-abiding citizens farming fruit and vegetables or trading legal goods and services, much of the sprawling settlement was yet another Taliban-infested stronghold: people were openly brandishing RPG-7s, AK47s and PKMs, intimidating the local citizens, and selling opium products in plain sight on the streets.

Bang in the middle of Helmand's biggest opium poppy belt, the main built-up area of Marjah is a roughly rectangular 19x10-kilometre grid of compounds connected by straight lanes that cut north–south and east–west, with a mosaic of fields and orchards stuck in between. Marjah struck me as a mud-built, crapped-up version of Milton Keynes, only with drugs, guns and a very bad attitude. And a lot more waterways, the whole zone being criss-crossed with dozens of canals, dykes and irrigation ditches. The Int brief also suggested that the entire zone was brim full of enemy-held compounds, most of whose male, fighting-age occupants were more or less involved in the narcotics trade. Studying Marjah now, I thought the spooks had it dead right: the town was a big, walled and moated fortress: very difficult to penetrate in the first place; seething with heavily armed militant insurgents; chock-full of vulnerable points where any fool could set a brilliant ambush; and extremely difficult to hold if we did ever get inside and defeat the enemy.

Like just about every other population centre of any size in Helmand province, Marjah's existence depends on the River Helmand, which breaks up into meandering streams that create two separate green zones on its eastern and western banks. South of the town, all the different branches of the river rejoin.

A main route – in reality a series of roughly parallel dirt tracks – leads south and east from the town towards Pakistan, taking opium and hashish in one direction and bringing enemy fighters, goods, weapons, ammo, money and supplies back the other way. FOB Dwyer sits just off this route, having been located there especially to keep an eye on the local traffic. Nothing like looking for trouble.

We patrolled forward from the FOB, initially without meeting any opposition. It might have been a good plan on paper, but as we drew near the town we saw that we hadn't reckoned on the problem of Marjah's irrigation system. The US engineers who'd dug the neat grid of irrigation channels might have meant well back in the 1960s, but what they'd also created was a series of defensive moats that now served the Taliban's purpose brilliantly well. The network was exactly what you didn't want when it came to flushing out an enemy. Since those distant US-friendly days, local attitudes to Western input had changed just a bit: the Taliban kept cutting off the water supply to the irrigation channels – they didn't like anyone doing business unless they were taking a cut, but they did like to fuck things up in general. Where it wasn't a ditch, a stream or an irrigation channel, the terrain was slightly undulating and sandy, with loads of greenery, walls, compounds and all the rest providing plenty of cover for the enemy.

Pushing on regardless with my half of SHQ Troop, I managed to find a bridge that looked as if it would take the weight of a Jackal, allowing us to cross and join up with the other two troops. We trundled safely over to the other side, reaching a wide gap in Marjah's perimeter wall that acted as a gateway into the town; or, putting it a slightly different way, into the medieval hell-hole that now lay before us. I ordered my half of SHQ Troop to pull up so that we could get eyes on the locals. While we settled in to observe at that location, 1 and 2 Troops hooked further east and south as planned, to act as the other jaw of the vice. The idea was to squeeze the bit of green zone we now bracketed and see what popped out. But there were so many waterways and they were so difficult to negotiate that, try as they might, 1 and 2 Troops couldn't get into the desired position. As we pushed forward, I saw them parked up about a kilometre to the south-east. We might not be able to do exactly as we'd planned, but forward reconnaissance is all about having to work with the ground truth and making the best of it.

We'd not long arrived at our own agreed location when an Afghan man approached the patrol. He was youngish, in his early twenties. My driver LCoH Jason Ashford, whose parents came from my own stomping ground, Llanrumney, Cardiff, put his rifle on him and told him to stop at a safe distance. Without being asked, the newcomer lifted his dishdasha. We had to check for suicide bombs, he knew the drill: but his promptness told me he'd either been in contact with ISAF forces before, or someone had briefed him on how to behave when he did meet them.

'I am from the ANA,' he announced loudly when we'd let him draw near. That was strange in itself – the fact that you're an ANA man is not the kind of information you want to be bandying about in a place like Marjah. He showed me an ID card ostensibly proving he was in the Afghan Army, but the cards and even the uniforms are easy to come by: like just about everything else in Afghanistan, they can be bought for the right price.

I was suspicious of the newcomer, but I beckoned him across. Afghans like to talk. With virtually no modern systems like radio and TV, a good chinwag is the main form of entertainment. If you can persuade an Afghan man to sit down with you and have a brew of tea, the amount of information he will give you can often be quite amazing. But this character seemed jumpy – he stood with his body half-turned away from me, as if ready to make a run for it at a moment's notice.

'If you're with the ANA,' I said, 'then you're taking a chance talking to us, aren't you?'

He smiled. 'No, it is OK – I am not from this place.' His English was suspiciously good – almost perfect. He was making a show of being friendly, but in reality I could see his small, shiny brown eyes darting everywhere. He was sussing us out: trying to identify the commander – in this case, me – assessing our weaponry, our general state of readiness and so on. 'There is no trouble here,' he told me, with a sweep of the hand. 'But in Marjah,' he pointed through the gateway to hell, 'there are many, many bad Taliban. They walk around with machine guns and RPGs openly, they rule the town.' With that, our new friend turned, walked smartly away and disappeared back into the nearest patch of undergrowth. I thought, 'Five gets you ten he's a dicker. As soon as he's made his report, it will kick off.'

I was just thinking about warning the rest of the squadron when a goat herder whose flock had been milling around us suddenly gathered all his animals together and drove them away. Interesting. As the goat shepherd disappeared from view, all the other civilians who'd been bumbling about near us also started to disappear. 'Heads up,' I told the lads, 'any moment now, there's going to be a spot of bother.' A series of mechanical clacks told me the boys were cocking and locking their weapons.

Two minutes later, I heard the whoosh of an RPG-7 launch. A rocket flew out from a small outhouse less than 200 metres away to the north-east, fizzed a metre or so above my head and exploded on the earth embankment directly to our rear. A long burst of AK47 fire followed immediately from the same spot, then another rocket grenade. Glancing over the sights of the GPMG, I saw an insurgent carrying an RPG-7 launcher run to a new firing position. Thumbing the safety off, I took aim at the spot where he'd gone to ground and opened fire.

More rounds and rockets were coming in from the range of compounds to the north. Having dissed it earlier, I really, really wanted my Scimitar turret back – especially the long bit on the front that fired 30mm cannon shells. The rest of the troop were firing back for all they were worth, peppering the enemy with the grenade machine gun, the .50 cal and the GPMGs. I popped some white smoke to make our vehicles harder to spot. We fired a few more well-aimed bursts at the enemy, with the result that they broke off and ran away. Three Jackals firing as one can put down a fearsome amount of fire, as the Taliban had just found out. Although we could see some of the enemy legging it, we couldn't just go on firing into a populated area indiscriminately. I decided we'd better extract, too. I radioed the other two call signs that we were going to pop smoke and then bug out. We were roughly in line abreast. I was in the right-hand vehicle. I flicked the launcher switches and fired off the grenades, but what I hadn't realized was that LCoH Cox's Jackal was almost exactly 50 metres ahead of me. My phosphorus grenades landed right on top of his vehicle, set it alight and caused far more damage than any Taliban with an RPG had done that day. I drove past him, laughing as he frantically tried to brush off pieces of burning phosphorus. We found it funny – somehow Damian didn't.

The intelligence reports suggesting a strong and aggressive Taliban presence in the Marjah green zone had been perfectly accurate. And while we'd beaten off their initial attack, if the enemy came back to have another crack at us with a couple of hundred men, our mini half-troop of twelve could find itself in bad trouble.

We popped another smoke, reversed out and checked there were no injuries. 'Leaguering up' or establishing a temporary camp in a safe location, we stopped to consider our options and report to Brigade. Brigade told us to maintain a presence in the local area and watch for developments.

A few days later LCoH Ashford was transferred into 2 Troop as a stand-in driver for Lieutenant Mauricio Gris (what a handle – it got shortened to 'Mau'). While we'd been beating off one Taliban attack, the other two troops had been involved in a separate fire fight. A flat tyre on one of the vehicles had forced the column to stop. They adopted an all-round defensive formation, but that hadn't discouraged the enemy: like us, they'd come under a hail of small-arms fire and volleys of RPG-7 rocket grenades. And like us, they'd returned the attention with interest.

In the course of the battle, Ash took a bullet through his Osprey body armour. It deflected and flew out the other side without harming him: the lucky, lucky bastard. But the troop had a hard time fighting its way out of the scrap: with no chance to repair the flat tyre, they had to hook the Jackal up and tow it out under fire. From then on, we knew that any time we fancied a spot of trigger time, all we had to do was stick our noses into the Marjah green zone.

As trained and professional soldiers, we had no problem facing the enemy in open combat. But as time and Operation Herrick 8 went on, it became obvious that the Taliban were growing more and more reluctant to stand and fight. Our weapons and sights were improving all the time. Ageing and relatively inaccurate, their primary weapons systems, the RPG-7, the PKM, the RPK, the DShK and the AK47 were becoming increasingly ineffective. As a result, they were resorting to ever lower and more cowardly tactics: forcing young children to act as suicide bombers; wiring donkeys up as booby traps; laying IEDs. Anything but take us on man-to-man.

We moved further north to probe and patrol the area around the town of Nad Ali. Nothing happened in and around the settlement itself, but as we tried to go back south again, the Taliban sprang a nasty surprise: spotting the fact that we were in an area that was hemmed in by irrigation channels, they opened the surrounding sluice gates. From my vantage point in the commander's seat, I watched as the area around us began to flood. 'Fuck,' I thought, 'we've got get out of here before we're stranded: they'll surround us and chop us up.' But how? Water was spilling over the edges of the embankments ahead and to either side of us, turning the ground we needed to take into an instant marsh. Already, it was climbing up the wheels. Quick on their feet as always, the Taliban had observed the Jackals getting stuck in the mud elsewhere, and realized that one of the vehicle's lesser strengths is its ability to deal with water. The Scimitars would have eaten up the boggy ground, but unless we could find a way out through the ever-worsening flood they'd just unleashed on us fast, they'd have us trapped.

'Drive on,' I told the rest of the troop. 'Foot to the floor: all we can do is attack it and try to get out.' We raced out of the rising flood, great sprays of water flying out to either side of the road wheels. All the time, I was praying that none of the vehicles would break down. With the seething water lapping at the sides of the Jackal, we made it out to dry ground and safety with moments to spare.

CHAPTER TWENTY-THREE

Our next task was to patrol the area south-west of Garmsir in an effort to interrupt the flow of drugs, weapons, money and insurgents between that area and Pakistan: similar mission, different patrol box. Sixty kilometres or so south-west of Helmand's provincial capital, Lashkar Gah, Garmsir sprawls along the east bank of the Helmand River. Not unlike Marjah, the green zone to the south of the town is criss-crossed by a complex of canals that help irrigate the agricultural land. The Helmand River bulges out here in a curious hook shape when you study the town on the map or satellite reconnaissance photographs, which is why ISAF forces call this part of Garmsir district the Snake's Head.

Dozens of different dirt tracks connect southern Helmand to Pakistan, which surrounds it to the east and south. A very large number of them lead to Garmsir, which acts as a kind of funnel for weapons, drugs and Taliban fighters heading north into the rest of Afghanistan, and for all kinds of stuff going the other way. The operation had several objectives that by now were becoming ever more familiar: to confront the Taliban head on and clear them out of the area; to secure, hold, and build confidence once our forces had the upper hand; to deny the enemy safe havens from which to regroup; to interrupt and ultimately cut off the supply lines from Pakistan; and to convince neutral locals both that it was safe to go about their lawful business, and that they could have faith in the Afghan government.

In common with Sangin, Musa Qal'ah and Now Zad, Garmsir's strategic importance to the Taliban led them to defend it tooth and nail. Imposing a presence in the town and surrounding district was something ISAF forces had been trying to do since first arriving in the country: what they'd got for their trouble was a long series of vicious fire fights, and we were the latest unit in an ever-growing line. As part of the effort to quell and defeat the Taliban, ISAF forces had built a number of military strongholds in the local area. With Camp Dwyer, these included FOB Delhi, hard by the Garmsir District Centre at the junction of the main east–west road bisecting the town and next to the bridge spanning the Helmand River. A string of smaller, satellite Patrol Bases [PBs] had been established around Garmsir, like pearls on a necklace only much, much less pretty. The Americans had named each segment of the military perimeter road connecting the PBs after US baseball teams: Route Cowboys, Route Red Sox and so on. 2 Troop, HCR, moved into PB2, about halfway along Route Cowboys facing the Taliban-infested green zone to the east. Banned from the military road, civilians used a separate track on the western side of the intervening irrigation ditch.

We suffered random sniping and the occasional attempted RPG strike in and around the PBs. But there were no pitched battles or extended fire fights – nothing to mention in despatches. It was Eid, the big celebration at the end of the Moslem holy month of Ramadan. As part of that, some of us were invited to a meal with a delegation of local elders. The food was basic, but since much of it was the fresh fruit we badly needed, really enjoyable. I sat next to the commander of the ANA unit based at PB2. He said he was on our side, which was lucky, because the guy looked like the biggest pirate who'd ever lived: he had a big black hairy beard, masses of greasy curls springing out from under his battered, olive forage cap, and loads of gunshot scars he'd collected from fighting the Russians, the Taliban, and every other bugger who ever crossed him in the course of a lifetime spent at war. Every so often, he'd try and show me another of the many, many scars he had on his body, just to add a bit of spice to the conversation. I kept nodding politely as he explained how he'd come by each one. I also kept a close eye on the long, wicked Russian bayonet he kept unsheathed at his side the whole time we were talking.

When I got into my sleeping bag later, I couldn't get off: my brain was buzzing – I began to wonder if someone had slipped something into my tea. When I did finally drop off, I had a strange dream: in it, one of the Jackal commanders in my troop, LCoH Paul Harris – the very same Harry 73 I'd promised to look after – was blown up and killed in his vehicle. I woke with a start: the dream had been so real, it felt as if it had actually happened. It stuck with me. It also made me feel – once again – that I'd promised Harry 27 way, way too much when I'd said that I'd look out for his son.

The next morning, I had to give the troop orders before we went out on patrol. Feeling badly rested and grumpy, I snapped at the boys to make sure the Vallon mine detectors were working correctly. With the dream still at the front of my thoughts, instead of driving slowly along the route as we normally did, I decided we should barma the whole five kilometres between the Patrol Bases we were scheduled to patrol. I was also very particular in reminding the patrol about what 'actions on' to take in the case of mine or IED strikes; about correct barmaring procedures; and about ambushes and casualty evacuation drills. The dream haunted me. I wasn't going to tell Harry 73, but it had left me feeling extremely anxious for his safety.

I detailed off a four-man barma team. Moving on foot, the team's job, as always, was to detect and mark explosive devices planted in the ground ahead of the troop. We'd be heading south from PB2 and making for PB3. I was in the second vehicle in the convoy. Harry 73 was in the lead Jackal. The clearance team walking ahead consisted of Trooper Ibbotson, Lance Corporal Eddie Bateman, and the barma team commander, L/Sgt Si Kingston, Royal Engineers, our resident expert on explosive devices. Last in the line-up was a replacement soldier whose name I did not know.

There are any number of different types of IED, but they fall into one of three main categories. The first one is the basic pressure-plate, or victim-operated device, where the weight of a vehicle – or a soldier – triggers a cache of buried explosives; the second type is the wireless remotely triggered device, which can sometimes be electronically jammed; and the last one, the command wire IED. But you can have a mixture of all three. Almost all of them need batteries to make them work. The third, command wire type is especially dangerous because it's impossible to jam – and it's a selective weapon: the enemy can allow one or more vehicles to pass over a given device before detonating it.

A pre-buried device can be left in the ground for months or even years before the Taliban, spotting one of our units heading into the area, come in and take the opportunity to trigger it.

If they don't have time to bury the IED a few weeks in advance, then once they've refilled it, the Taliban water the concealment hole. If water is in short supply they urinate on the ground. The blazing Afghan sun quickly bakes the watered surface to the same hard consistency and appearance as the surrounding earth, meaning there is little or no remaining surface sign to detect. Like the Americans, we've started using unmanned aerial vehicles [UAVs] to spot enemy IED teams in the act of planting bombs. Unlike the Americans, we don't have a large supply of UAVs, and too many of our spotter drones make so much noise the Taliban can hear them coming from miles away – especially in the dead quiet of an Afghan night. Needless to say, as soon as they do hear them, they scarper. Since my first tour of Afghanistan, the British Army had bought some American Predator UAVs: they fly so high you can't hear them, and they're controlled by someone thousands of miles away in an office in Nevada. Not only that, they can be armed with missiles and used to strike the bomb teams remotely. The Predator is an awesome machine. We need more of them.

We began moving south along Route Cowboys, which sounds as if it might be glamorous but was just the same old dusty, rutted track with an irrigation ditch to its right. Kingston and Bateman were swee-ping with the Vallons, their detectors describing interlocking arcs of sweep; the new man and Ibbotson were on the flanks with wooden sticks, checking for telltale signs of command wires that detonate IEDs.

We'd only been going for about twenty minutes when the new boy walked past a short length of electrical cable sticking up out of the ground. It was exactly the kind of indicator he'd been trained to spot and indicate. Then Eddie Bateman, who was next door, saw a tiny piece of white plastic half-buried in the ground at his feet. Thinking it was rubbish, Bateman kicked away the covering earth. More dirty white plastic appeared in the ground. Seeing that, Bateman decided it might not be a very good idea to kick at it again. His heart-rate had just trebled. He'd just realized he was staring at the top of a plastic barrel. The kind the Taliban favoured for packing with high-explosive. His voice a little higher than its normal pitch, Bateman shouted to Si Kingston: 'Si – I think we have something here.'

Kingston moved across to look. His heart-rate, too, now trebled. 'Fuck!' he said. 'Get back – that's an IED!' The column had halted. Everyone fell back from the IED except Si Kingston and Bateman. Sweeping around the barrel with their Vallons, they found more elec-trical cable. It led to a battery pack. In the ground just beyond that lay the IED's pressure plate. Kingston went dead still. He had stopped less than a foot from the plate.

We set up a cordon around the area and made sure the electronic countermeasures [ECM] kit was working in case the device had a remote radio trigger. At the same time we established an ERV, or emergency rendezvous point, where we could regroup, put out all-round defence, deploy snipers and wait for the EOD Sappers to come in and make the suspect device safe. But we had to be careful not to choose an ERV location that was too predictable. The Taliban watch us all the time. If they detect a pattern to the way in which we respond to a given situation, then they'll seek to exploit that predictability on another occasion. And as we've said, EOD officers are a prime target:

the Taliban know it takes a very long time and a very large amount of money to train personnel in bomb disposal; and they know there are relatively few bomb disposal officers available. In a combat zone, therefore, it's essential to keep changing operating procedures in order to keep the enemy guessing. Once we'd set up the ERV and established our perimeter, we sent a team into the local compounds, warning the locals not to come near the site.

Kingston, who'd spent much of his Army career detecting explosive devices, called for support from the Counter-Improvised Explosive Device Task Force [C-IED TF]. The biggest worry I had was that the IED we'd found might be part of daisy chain: an interconnected series of IEDs spread over a wide area. Daisy chains are especially dangerous: one or more of the IEDs is often booby-trapped, exploding the whole chain if any are moved or a cable is cut.

While we watched, the IEDD [Improvised Explisive Device Disposal] team slowly uncovered the device. As they unearthed and examined it, they told us that the barrel was packed with 20 kilos of HME, or home-made explosive: in this case, that old Taliban favourite, ammonium nitrate fertilizer, mixed with a couple of other ingredients like nails. They followed a length of buried wire to the detonation device that had been hidden in the ground more than 10 metres away. We'd been lucky: if the Taliban had been lying in wait with a command wire and triggered the bomb, then all four men in the barma team would have been blown to bits. And it probably wouldn't have done Harry 73 and the other two men in the lead Jackal all that much good, either.

Thinking it was going to be the last patrol of the tour, I now told Harry 73 about the dream. He said: 'I wish you'd told me that before we started this patrol.'

'Don't be soft,' I retorted. 'It would only have made you worried.' I thought the near-miss had neutralized the force of my bad dream. But events were to prove otherwise.

CHAPTER TWENTY-FOUR

We were now very near the end of our six-month tour of duty. I'd been a bit optimistic in thinking the Route Cowboys patrol where we'd come so close to annihilation was our last hurrah – Brigade still had a couple of jobs that needed sorting. They now tasked 1 Troop to move north from Garmsir along the eastern bank of the Helmand River, rendezvous with and then help protect a convoy of civilian trucks carrying grain from Lashkar Gah to Garmsir. For the first time in two years, the mayor of Garmsir had bought a large consignment of grain from the mayor of Lashkar Gah. That might not sound very important when you live in a country like the UK, where millions of tonnes of grain and other goods get moved around the country on a daily basis. But at the time, its political and economic significance in that area of Helmand province was huge. Among other things, it was a sign the locals thought that large-scale trade might once again be possible.

The idea then became to prove that the Afghans could organize, manage and protect the convoy themselves, with the help of the Afghan National Police, and strictly without our help. An ANP detachment from Lashkar Gah would escort the convoy halfway to Garmsir, at which point a second unit from Garmsir itself would RV with the first unit and take over. The fact that the ANP was in charge of the operation was viewed as a very big deal – their reputation needed all the help it could get.

Three other Jackals were now attached to 1 Troop. I'd be working with my old troop commander Tom Long, who had been promoted to captain. It felt good to be working with Tom again – he was a friend and I respected his professionalism. Our brief stated we should only intervene as a last resort.

The next thing I discovered was that the Garmsir grain-shifting team could only come up with five, 10-tonne jingly trucks – half the number they actually needed to move the consignment in one go. They'd have to make two trips, with the obvious increase in risk of a Taliban attack on the second. But the shortage of vehicles was their problem, not ours. Our job was to act as close but invisible escort to the first convoy, which we were informed had duly set out from Lashkar Gah at four-thirty in the morning. But when we reached the agreed rendezvous point half an hour later, there were no trucks, and no sign of any trucks. Still, I knew there was only one point where they could cross the Helmand River – at the bridge that now lay a short distance to the east. For more than an hour, we waited there for the trucks to arrive. Nothing happened. We were just about to give up and pull back to FOB Delhi for further instructions, when a large lumbering shape loomed up out of the gathering dawn: a jingly truck. A second truck rumbled into view, followed by the rest of the convoy. We positively identified the trucks as being the ones we were supposed to shadow. The Afghans in general are absolutely terrible at getting anywhere on time, but, great stuff, at last we were making progress.

One of the ANP vehicles riding shotgun with the convoy drove up to our position. The commander climbed out and asked to speak with me. He was waving his arms about, clearly in a bit of a state. 'We need your help. One of the trucks has got stuck in the river. That is why we are late. You must help us to pull it out.' I wanted to help, but just about the only firm instruction we'd had on this job was precisely not to help out under any but the most extreme circumstances: which is to say, if the entire convoy came under heavy enemy fire and was in danger of being wiped out.

The hands-off approach wasn't just for political purposes. If any ISAF forces were seen to be helping the locals, then all the grain would be viewed as contaminated: no one would want it, and the whole operation would have been for nothing. I tried to explain this to the agitated ANP officer, but he shook his head. 'We can't do it ourselves: we do not have the necessary vehicles. Only you can help us get the truck out, you must help us, please.'

We drove across and looked at the truck in question. It had come off the beaten track and skidded into an area of soft ground leading down to the river. My immediate guess was that the driver had fallen asleep at the wheel. But it didn't look too badly bogged in. And there were no groups of heavily armed hostiles in sight. In fact, it was still so early in the morning that there was no one else in sight.

'Fuck it,' I said finally. 'Let's do it.'

We fixed a tow rope to the front of the stranded truck, took up the strain and started to pull. The truck popped straight up out of the river bed and onto the bank; we unhooked and retired to a discreet distance as quickly as possible. With the convoy now back in business, we positioned our Jackals out to all four sides and at a distance of 2 kilometres. I took station two klicks ahead. In this way, we shepherded the grain trucks to the easterly outskirts of Garmsir.

The reaction in Garmsir was amazing. You'd have thought the local citizens had just won a lottery jackpot. I'd never seen so many people in one place in Helmand province, and I'd certainly never seen so many of them looking so happy. A local elder came up to us: 'The Taliban have always put a tax on the grain, but now we have it without the tax and we did it ourselves. Our grain house has been empty for two years, but now our people can buy it from there and trade it.' OK mate – result!

I was just basking in a warm glow of job satisfaction when I heard sounds of a major disturbance from the northern end of town. As we closed cautiously on the location to investigate, the shouting and screaming grew louder. We stopped at the edge of a large, angry crowd. It had gathered around an ANP man lying motionless on the ground in a pool of blood, along with small bits of his body and torn clothing. There was a strong smell of explosive in the air. The interpreter asked a few of the locals what had happened: 'They're saying there has just been a suicide bombing.' I found it hard to believe the next bit. The crowd said the Taliban had convinced a 10-year-old boy to strap on a suicide vest packed with explosives. They'd then persuaded his 5-year-old brother, who was standing nearby, to detonate it remotely. To convince him to go through with it, the insurgents had told the younger child: 'When your brother walks up to the man, you will help him to die. That is a good thing. Allah wants it: you are helping your brother – he will go to live in heaven and have a better life.'

The resulting explosion killed both the elder boy and the second-in-command of the ANP team that had just helped bring in the grain convoy. What did the Taliban think they were achieving by such cowardly and horrible acts? Maybe they thought they were making a statement along the lines of: 'Don't think you can work with the foreigners. They can't keep you safe from us. We know the trucks have just arrived with the grain, and this is what we think of it. We can strike with impunity.' If so, then the action backfired: the cynicism, gutlessness and horror of what they had done left the whole community shocked and disgusted. To me, the act also smacked of desperation. If the enemy had to resort to using small children to fight their battles for them, what did that say about them?

The suicide bombing had an immediate impact: as soon as the ANP unit guarding the trucks got to hear about it on their mobile phones, they drove away to a man, leaving the grain convoy unguarded. So now, at the last moment, there was all this grain standing at the edge of the town with no one looking after it. Asking for trouble. We still weren't supposed to guard the grain directly; our orders were to keep an Afghan face on the op. To get around the problem, I called the nearest ANA detachment at FOB Delhi and asked them if they would escort the trucks the last kilometre or two in to the warehouse. Luckily, the ANA agreed to help. Rolling up in a fleet of pick-ups, they escorted the cargo safely to the store.

Two days later, while we stayed behind in FOB Delhi, 2 Troop took over duty on the second grain convoy. We were all very keen for that to happen, in order to show that the Taliban hadn't succeeded in intimidating anyone with their vile suicide tactics. Just outside Garmsir, the troop met the ANP detachment, who didn't want to be seen talking to ISAF for the usual and obvious reasons, then shadowed them all the way up to Lashkar Gah. Having picked up the second convoy of jingly trucks, they started back on the return journey. But one or another of the jingly trucks kept breaking down, repeatedly holding up the convoy. All of which meant the grain and its various escorts spent more than twenty-four hours on the 50-kilometre trip, under constant threat of ambush and IED and with no sleep for any of the drivers.

Like most of the drivers, a REME soldier at the wheel of the third Jackal had been driving without a break for hours. But it wasn't his driving that caused the accident: nearing Garmsir on the return leg, the edge of the track gave way under the front nearside wheel of his wagon, which began sliding sideways into the canal. The other two members of the vehicle's crew weren't wearing seat-belts: they jumped clear as the Jackal slithered down the embankment. The driver, who had his seat belt on, struggled desperately to undo it. As the Jackal hit the bottom of the slope, it overturned and landed upside down in the canal. He suffered serious injuries and is still partially disabled. But the good thing was that he lived, a solider went back home to his family and can tell the tale.

Leaving the overturned Jackal to the rescue team, the rest of the grain convoy pushed on to the warehouse in Garmsir.

CHAPTER TWENTY-FIVE

It wasn't up to us to act as counter-narcotics agents: if we stamped out the trade and deprived people of income, then some of them were going to pick up a weapon and fight us to earn the money they'd lost. But given that Helmand province is a giant opium factory, and that much of the money fuels the insurgency, if we could catch the Taliban directly involved in drugs activity, then they were a legitimate and desirable target.

We knew that the Taliban were smuggling weapons and ammunition across the Pakistani border, we just didn't know the exact route. So, on a bright sunny day (like every other day), I gathered the troop in the briefing room. 'Right boys,' I said, 'let's go and find out where these little twats are coming from with their explosives.'

Jokingly, CoH Ben Woollaston said, 'That's easy – Pakistan.'

Little did Ben know it, but that was exactly where I wanted to go. My plan was to head south along the Helmand River, staying on the western side and looking for crossing points. On the way, we'd interdict any enemy vehicles we came across. Then, when we got to the point known as the 'Fish Hook', about 100 kilometres from the Pakistani border where the river changed direction from north–south to east–west, we'd stop and reassess. There was just one tiny flaw in my plan: Battle Group wouldn't let us go that close to the Pakistan border.

We set off south through the green zone. The Jackals were all fitted with secure satellite radios which meant we were in constant touch with HQ. We took advantage of the dead ground, only breaking cover when we needed to look at a village or other point of interest, but even though we moved as stealthily as we could, the telltale smoke signals from the villages marked our progress.

It was make or break time. I got on the radio and told FOB Delhi I was moving to grid PR478900 – 160 kilometres from camp. The watch-keeper replied, 'Roger call sign 1, send update when you get in location. Out.'

We moved on cautiously but at speed. We had intelligence that an area close to the Fish Hook known as the Castle was a Taliban depot – the only problem was locating it. As we drove south over a steep hill we had a perfect view of the village beneath us. The Castle was on the northern side. It wouldn't have looked out of place in a film about the Crusaders. My interest quickened. There was a number of newish 4x4s and jingly trucks parked in front of the ruined structure, and about fifty men who looked as if they'd just stepped off a film set for Osama Bin Laden's latest propaganda movie. Some of them were carrying weapons. As soon as they spotted us they began shouting and rushing about – and cocking their weapons. We'd uncovered a Taliban wasp's nest, and we were about to get stung. We immediately set about gathering as much information as we could, noting vehicle types, routes in and out, the dress and disposition of the men and a detailed description of the layout of the compounds forming the Taliban lair. Heavily outnumbered as we were, my main worry now was that we'd be outflanked or cut off to the rear and killed. Or, even worse, taken prisoner. I gave the order to swing back north and use the Jackals' speed to outrun the Taliban before they could set up any ambushes or lay IEDs in our path. But before we set off, I saved the GPS information so that we'd be able to follow the enemy routes again and lay our own ambushes when we came back.

We arrived back in FOB Dwyer where I reported to the Ops room. The squadron leader, Major Will Davies, was at his desk. He looked up. 'How was your day, Mick?'

'Er, OK sir. We went down towards the Pakistani border.'

'Really? Was it busy?' I submitted my patrol report and the photographs we'd taken. 'Yes,' he said when he'd studied them, 'I can see it was.'

The SCM, Danny Hitchings, had moved to Camp Bastion to oversee the preparations for our handover to the Queen's Dragoon Guards [QDG]. I was back to acting SCM and it was my turn on the desk as the watch-keeper at SHQ. My duty as a watch-keeper was to make instant decisions in response to radio comms from troops in the field. Manage things, in other words. That meant sitting on the ops desk at FOB Dwyer, when I really wanted to be out on the ground.

Captain Van Cutsen took over command of 1 Troop. Like myself, 'VC' had recently rejoined the Army after spending a few years in civilian life. Major Davies gave VC his orders: 'I want you to set up an ambush in this area south of the Fish Hook.' Our time hadn't been wasted, then.

VC led the six Jackals under his command to a remote spot some 20 kilometres south of Garmsir, but that was still in comms range with the desk. Here, the River Helmand cuts through a high desert plateau that runs all the way south to the Pakistani border. 'High' means just that – much of this arid wasteland lies at an altitude of more than 2,000 metres. The whole area was ribboned with known drugs and weapons routes that ran north to south from Garmsir, or south-west to north-east from the Pakistan border towards Lashkar Gah. For hundreds of years, caravans had used these routes to trade spices, silks and other precious goods between Afghanistan and the rest of Asia. Now, sadly, the main cargo moving up and down them is narcotics.

The Jackals were out stalking prey, and I heartily wished I was with them. With the opium harvest not long in, it was the prime time for the drug-runners shifting the resin south on the first stage of its journey to the world market. There was also a good chance of intercepting the money men travelling back up the other way with cash to feed the opium growers and the Taliban foot soldiers mixed up in the trade.

The idea was simple: we'd place the Jackals hull down out of sight at strategic points around the 'bread-basket', or ambush zone, and wait to see what turned up. To the right and east of the six lurking Jackals was a high ridge. Any suspect vehicle coming over the top of that ridge travelling south on the main route from Lashkar Gah was going to run right into the reactive OP. In case a bad guy spotted the trap early from the ridge, VC placed two of the Jackals in cut-off positions, one a couple of kilometres to the north, the other roughly the same distance to the south-west. Now, if a suspect vehicle broke and ran in any direction, one or more of the Jackals should still be able to catch it and scoop it up.

It was an early September afternoon and the Afghan weather was its usual blistering self – about 40°, or like standing near the mouth of a blast furnace. The Jackal has a nice comfy seat and brilliant suspension; when it's so hot, if there's nothing happening it can sometimes be hard not to nod off. Back on the ops desk, the radio crackled into life. I sat up: while they couldn't see an actual vehicle yet, the crew of the most easterly Jackal had spotted a dust plume snaking up from the top of the ridge. A powdery light-brown stain against the brilliant blue sky, it was coming from the direction of Lashkar Gah.

Staff Sergeant Nick Wright of the REME was the Jackal's commander. He raised his binos and studied the area. A white Toyota pickup came into view – the vehicle of choice for Afghan drug-runners. It was travelling at extreme speed for the rough terrain – another tick in the suspicious box. As it came down over the ridge, VC and Coxy spotted it. Travelling at about 90 kilometres per hour, the pick-up hurtled by, 200 metres to the south of their position. As it sped across their field of view, VC and Cox could see what looked like large grain sacks piled up on the vehicle's rear flat-bed. They radioed ahead to CoH Ben Woolaston and LCoH Todd in the western cut-off group: 'White Toyota headed your way at speed. Suspect bags in the back –

might be bomb-making fertilizer. Or drugs. Move to intercept.' Revving their engines, the boys needed no second telling: they floored it and set off in hot pursuit.

The Jackal's air-damped suspension means it can cover rough terrain at very high speed, while retaining the stability it needs to fire its onboard weapons systems accurately. The six-cylinder 5.9 litre Cummins engine gives it a top road speed of 130 kph, and it can shift along at up to 100 kph off-road depending on the terrain. Just about enough to overtake a top-of-the-range Toyota travelling flat out on the same surface, on a good day and with a following wind.

The radio chatter told me the boys were getting a bit excited. I understood why. Listening to the edge in their voices made me want to be out on the ground with my troop more than ever. Speeding due west, as it creamed over the edge of a blind ridge the pick-up narrowly avoided a head-on collision with Woolaston's Jackal. Spinning the steering wheel, the suspect driver swerved at the last moment, just managing to stop the Toyota from rolling. Despite the near-miss, he showed no sign of slowing down. Far from it. Piling on the revs, he veered due north. Great, we had a runner. Hot pursuit. I was shouting for updates on the radio. I sent someone off to go and fetch the Squadron Leader; he needed to know what was happening.

VC, Nick Wright and Coxy fell in behind the pick-up and gave chase. Sitting just off to the east of the fleeing vehicle, they kept station with him on a parallel track. Flat out, they followed the pick-up for 17 kilometres. We all knew the northerly direction was a ruse: at some point, the runner would have to swing back south. His only chance of escape was to cross the Pakistan border. Ben Woolaston told Pete Townsend in the southernmost Jackal to stop, lie up, and cut the suspect off if he turned towards the Chagai hills as expected.

Realizing the Jackals were faster than his Toyota over the rougher stretches of ground, the runner feinted west again, ran on for a couple of clicks and then turned due south. Bingo. He was now on a direct collision course with Pete Townsend and Mark Doran, lurking in wait a few kilometres ahead of him. VC called them up: 'He's heading straight towards your position! He's about 3 kilometres out.'

Townsend turned to his gunner: 'Mark, get your weapons ready.'

Then, without warning, the Toyota jinked behind a large dune and disappeared. For a moment, the pack in pursuit thought they'd lost him. From the calm of the ops desk, I realized the suspect had done what I'd have done; stopped and gone to ground in a fold of land. But as Nick Wright crested a slope, he spotted the Toyota's bonnet sticking out from the side of the dune. The second he realized Nick had seen him, the runner shot out of the hide and ran for the border again.

The other five Jackals kept up the chase, swarming around the Toyota like something out of the movie *Mad Max*. The runner might not know it yet, but they were funnelling him into a trap. The Pakistani border wasn't all that far away now. If he somehow gave Pete Townsend and Mark Doran the slip, he could make it into the Fish Hook where there was a lot more cover – and a lot more Taliban. The green zone there is one of their biggest strongholds. But crouched directly in his line of flight, Townsend and Doran weren't about to let that happen.

The suspect saw the waiting Jackal at the very last second. There was flat ground all around, but it was rough, with patches of sharp stones. That meant the track was the only safe route; coming off it risked a puncture or worse. The runner decided to go for broke; he charged for the small gap between the Jackal and the left-hand edge of the track, made it with a whisker to spare and shot clear out the other side. The Jackal's driver was Magpie Munday. He floored the gas pedal, swung in pursuit, and caught up with the runner. The Jackal had a GMG fitted on the rear pintle, but that was much too much gun for a mere Toyota pick-up – one burst risked blasting the driver to bits. In the commander's seat, Pete Townsend couldn't fire the Gimpy either: an area weapon, the machine gun's cone of fire would almost certainly have killed the man, and we had to bear in mind the fact that he was still only a suspect. The Toyota jinked right and left, but Magpie stuck with it. The runner was now within 5 kilometres of the Fish Hook –

the troop needed to do something drastic. Mark Doran called down: 'Pete – can I open fire on the vehicle? See if I can stop him?'

'Yes, try and take the vehicle out.'

Resting his SA-80 on the Jackal's rear wing, Mark fired at the speeding Toyota's front offside tyre. His first bullet missed. It slammed in through the driver's door, skimmed across the man's thighs and punched out through the opposite side. Doran's second round blew a massive hole in the tyre. It deflated, but even then the driver didn't stop. To help him see reason, Mark put another round in through the rear tyre. The Toyota nose-dived, skidded sideways and slewed to a stop.

The driver got out. All six Jackals closed around him in a ring. The man was unhurt but he was scared and in shock, shouting and waving his arms. 'Don't shoot!' he yelled in Pashto. 'I am just a driver, please don't shoot me.' His mobile phone started to ring. He delved into the pockets of his dishdasha and brought it out. Pete took it off him and handed it to the interpreter, who was so slow we all called him 'Lightning'.

Toddy, who was search-trained, started rummaging the vehicle. He didn't have to look very far: sixteen canvas sacks sat out in plain view on the flat-bed. Toddy stabbed one with his bayonet. A dark amber treacle oozed out, coating the blade and dripping down the side of the bag.

By now, several other members of the troop had gathered round the back of the Toyota. The others put out all-round defence. VC said: 'Opium tar.' He was right. The sacks were marked in Arabic with their point of origin and intended destination, and each bag was stamped with a gross weight: 40 kg. That made 640 kg of raw opium, more than half a tonne. The sacks had been tightly sealed, but they'd been thrown around so much in the course of the chase that some of them had split at the base. As they lifted the sacks out to photograph and weigh them, the opium tar began leaking out, a treacly, dark-brown goo that stank to the skies. Cut with cheap additives and sold as street-grade heroin, the haul had a value of at least £5 million. At this point in the supply chain, it was worth a lot less than that to the Taliban – perhaps $200,000. But if the point of the patrol was to stop the flow of Taliban-controlled narcotics and starve them of whatever funds we could, then 1 Troop had just had a good day.

When I thought about it a bit more, I realized they'd had a very good day: growing and harvesting opium is extremely labour intensive. The poppies don't need much in the way of care when they're growing; but you have to collect the milky sap from the plant at just the right moment, and it's one hell of a job. A field-hand has to go round each seed head with a special little cutting tool. This has three or four sharp steel blades set a few millimetres apart. In Afghanistan, the worker makes three or four upward cuts in the pod over a period of two or three days. The beads of white latex-like sap that seep out of the pod are then left to dry into sticky, dark brown 'poppy tears', before being scraped carefully into plastic tubs, again by hand. A one-acre field of opium poppies harvested in this way produces about 4 kilograms of raw, black-tar opium. So we'd just nabbed about 160 acres-worth of raw product. Dozens of farmers and field-hands had been paid to grow and harvest the drug. The farmer got about $130 per kilo of opium tar; the labourers got about ten bucks a day each. Result.

The 'terp had been listening in to the suspect's phone. He said: 'It's his boss, the drugs baron who employed him. He's saying, "Let my driver go and give me my opium back, or I will send men to kill you and all your family. They will also kill all the soldiers and all their families."'

For his part, the suspect kept repeating the same story: 'I am only a driver, he's only paying me $200 for the trip, please let me go and deliver the drugs or he will kill all my family at home.'

Back at SHQ, I was straining to make sense of the broken bits of radio conversation I could hear – the extreme range and the fluc-tuations in atmospheric conditions made reception extremely poor. I heard VC say: 'Tell him he should have thought of that before he agreed to run drugs. Tell him his only chance is to quieten down and tell us everything he knows.' Fucking right. The 'terp passed that on.

The driver crouched down and tried to make himself look as small as possible. It was an old ploy – when you're in the crap, try to make yourself look as insignificant and pathetic as you can. Then he started bleating again: 'He will kill all my family. Let me go! He will kill all my family.'

Mr Big was still ranting and ranging from the safety of his lair – the 'terp was holding the phone away from his ear as a torrent of threats and curses came down the line. 'And tell the boss-man to bring it on,' VC added. 'We'll be ready and waiting.'

Toddy switched his attentions to the driver's cab, while a couple of the others searched the detainee. Todd found a long package lying on the rear seat. After checking for booby traps, he carefully removed the plastic wrapping. Inside was a one-metre-long pressure plate encased in more waterproofing. Two wires led from the pressure plate to a green, cube-shaped battery pack. All they had to do was connect the units to an explosive charge, and the Taliban had a working IED. Not only was the suspect ferrying opium, he was also a bomb courier, getting paid to transport the components of an IED.

Captain VC reported in the new find. By now, the Squadron Leader, Major Will Davies was with me on the ops desk. 'Bring the suspect in,' he said, 'and bring all the evidence with him, including the vehicle.'

'Only one problem with that plan,' I thought. 'The camp has no holding facilities for prisoners.' I went outside and asked a few of the lads to convert FOB Dwyer's makeshift gym into an even more makeshift interview room and holding cell.

The troop arrived back in with the detainee. We were only allowed to hold him for seventy-two hours. Following the newly approved procedure, they'd cuffed his hands in front of him and placed a blindfold across his eyes – you are no longer permitted to hood people. With two of the pick-up's tyres shot to ribbons, it was undriveable: one of the Jackals was dragging it bodily on the end of a wire strop.

We hauled our man out of the vehicle, frog-marched him to the temporary holding facility and put two soldiers on guard to make sure he didn't escape. Once he'd been fed and watered, the 'tactical interviewer' – you're not allowed to call them interrogators any more – took charge of the detainee's mobile phone. It turned out to be very interesting: there were telephone numbers for numerous individuals in Pakistan and Afghanistan, a list of addresses in both countries, and in some ways most tellingly of all, the numbers of more than a dozen madrassas, or religious schools, in Pakistan. Some Pakistani madrassas pump their students' heads full of hatred for the West, fire them up as jihadi fighters or suicide bombers and send them over the border to attack us. More often than not, the hotheads actually end up helping to fuel the Taliban-controlled drugs trade.

Major Davies called it in to Brigade. They said: 'Keep him close. We're going to send a helicopter to pick him up.' By now, the shock of capture and detention had started to wear off the detainee. He started yelling: 'What has happened to my vehicle? I want my vehicle back – give it to me.' We told him the bad news: he wasn't going to get his vehicle back. In fact, we were going to take it out into the desert and destroy it: we were short of things for target practice. His Toyota pick-up was perfect.

We loaded some rusting but still mostly full propane gas canisters inside the Toyota, dragged it out to the end of the gun range, and then blazed away at it with 30mm APDS [armour-piercing discarding sabot] rounds. The gas canisters ignited, followed a millisecond later by the petrol tank, and then the whole vehicle went up in one of the loudest and most spectacular explosions I'd ever witnessed. Chunks of ex-Toyota pick-up rained down around us; with hindsight, we might have done better to stand further back. Some of the scattered lumps of vehicle burned for a bit before turning into blackened, smouldering lumps. Big boys toys. In the desert, you have to make your own fun.

We drove back and told the detainee the extra bit of bad news: when the helicopter that was coming for him arrived, one of our men would escort him to Lashkar Gah for further questioning. But there's many a slip, and one happened now: the helicopter arrived twenty minutes earlier than the appointed time. Added to that, the landing site was 600 metres away from the holding cell, and when the Chinook came in, the detainee wasn't prepped and ready to be moved. The Chinook's crew wouldn't stick around and wait while we sorted things out. They took off again thirty seconds later – just as we arrived at the HLS with the suspect in tow.

With forty-eight hours of the seventy-two legally available detention hours already spent, Brigade told us to move the detainee and the captured drugs evidence down to FOB Delhi. 'You want us to send 580kg of opium with him? You realize how much that is? The ANP have asked if they can have 60kg as evidence for when the guy comes to trial. Don't you think 60kg will be enough?'

There was a short pause: then Brigade said: 'That might just be enough.'

Shortly after the seventy-two-hour time limit was up, Brigade came back up on air: 'Where is the detainee you picked up?'

I said: 'Someone at your location already ordered us to hand that suspect over to the ANP in FOB Delhi. As far as I'm aware, they've still got him.'

Immediately, Brigade got onto FOB Delhi to ask if the detainee was still there. We heard the answer on the comms net: 'The ANP have lost him: they have no idea where he is, or where the 60kg of opium tar went either.'

The voice at Brigade went up a notch: 'But he's got links to all these high-ranking Taliban members. We think he might be a senior Taliban player – he can't just have disappeared.' It was too late. He had.

We tried to follow down the trail with the ANP, but our enquiries met with shrugs and blank faces: no one knew anything. This silence meant one of two things: either the police had taken him out into the desert and shot him for the drug-running, IED-transporting scumbag he undoubtedly was; or his boss had come good for him and he'd walked out of prison following payment of a hefty bribe.

In the meantime, we still had the 540 kilos of opium resin to deal with. I'd asked around, but nobody could make a decision about what to do with the stuff. So I decided to get on and burn it. I had a detail take the remaining sacks of opium to a patch of waste ground just outside the camp. I didn't want to risk taking it too far out into the wilderness: by this time, every Afghan for miles around knew we had the stash. If we wandered too far away from the FOB, there was a strong chance we'd get bounced by a large pack of drugs-and-money-hungry locals. We built a big bonfire out of old pallets, used tyres and the sacks of raw opium, and then splashed the whole lot with kerosene: we had loads of the helicopter fuel to spare. There was a breeze blowing from the south-east, perfect: that would blow the fumes away from the camp. Everything was looking good.

I walked up and set fire to the drugs. Flames flickered up from the edge of the pyre, and in no time at all it was blazing merrily. Our second bonfire that day. Dark fumes towered up into the air, but as planned, the breeze carried them away from our location and away from the FOB. I set off back to camp in the Jackal. As I did that, I suddenly felt the breeze die away. Slowing to a crawl, I twisted round in my seat. The column of oily grey smoke that had been blowing away to the west was now going vertically skyward. There was a moment or two of complete calm. Then I felt the flicker of a new wind on my face: one that was blowing from the opposite direction. Coming directly towards me – and towards the camp. The dark smoke from the bonfire bent and began to scuttle before the new breeze. A second or two later, dense, stinking opium smoke was swirling around the Jackal. I drove on, praying the wind would shift a second time. But no matter how fast I drove, the dense cloud stayed with me.

I parked up and watched as the fumes from the world's biggest reefer snaked their way across and into Forward Operating Base Dwyer. A minute or two later, I got out and wandered back into the makeshift operations room. The boss came to see me. He looked different, not quite his usual self. Pointing at the greasy grey fog swirling around outside, I said: 'Major, we're going to need a waiver from the CDT [Counter Drugs Team]. We've all breathed in so much opium, we'll fail the statutory drugs test at the end of the tour.' The slightly glazed smile on the boss's face broadened. He was quiet for a while; you wouldn't want to accuse him of looking dreamy. Then he said: 'Very well, Corporal Major – carry on.' Marvellous. Everybody was extremely happy that day. Turning FOB Dwyer into a giant hubba-bubba pipe was a definite highlight of my second Afghan tour.

CHAPTER TWENTY-SIX

October came in, and for the first time in daylight hours, the temperature in Helmand province cooled to the low thirties Celsius. Then, towards the end of the month, the advance party of C Squadron, The Queen's Dragoon Guards [QDG] arrived at Camp Bastion ready to take over from us when our tour ended. We picked the QDG guys up from Bastion and drove them down to FOB Dwyer. Dwyer is like every other British FOB in Helmand province, which is to say pretty grungy, and extremely limited when it comes to the basic comforts. The only thing that marked it out was its small runway, which the US Marines used for their Harrier close air support aircraft and Cobra gunships.

On 15 October, Major Davies asked me what framework patrol we were scheduled to carry out that day. 'We have to give the new QDG commanders a ground briefing on the Area of Operations; take them out on a familiarization patrol. If they could take a few photos of the known local vulnerable points [VPs] in the AO, then when the rest of the QDGs arrive, they'll be able to brief their lads. I've also got to attend an O Group [orders group] at FOB Delhi, in Garmsir town centre. If I join you for the first bit of the patrol, then maybe you could drop me off there later?' No problem. I gathered everyone into the briefing room and gave the whole troop the orders for the QDG ground familiarization and reconnaissance patrol.

Only too aware that the enemy would be watching our movements and looking for opportunities to attack, I decided on a decoy operation to outwit them. The bridge a short distance away from FOB Dwyer was one of the most dangerous local VPs: the Taliban had attacked our convoys and patrols at that choke point on several occasions. No one in D Squadron had been injured as yet, but it wasn't for lack of trying on the enemy's part. The two QDG men we now had with us were Sgt Paul Hill and a corporal I knew only as 'Mac'. They needed to see the VP up close, and learn how we avoided and dealt with attacks. My idea was to recce the river-crossing point as usual; dismount and do normal anti-IED barma drills, but then not actually cross the bridge. Instead, we'd feint north, then turn south-east, swing north again, take photographs of the secondary VP from a different direction and finally hook back south-west into FOB Delhi to drop off the boss.

So much for best-laid plans. When everyone was clear about the mission, we mounted up. Because we had three extra personnel with us in the shape of Major Davies, Sergeant Hill and Corporal Mac, we had to rejig the vehicle manning in the column of six Jackals. I led from the front because I knew the local turf better than anyone else. While I acted as driver, Major Davies occupied my normal place in the commander's seat behind the general purpose machine gun. Lance Corporal Junior Salmon took up position as our top-gunner on the GMG. Having all the command eggs in one Jackal was a very bad idea and ran counter to standing operating procedures – but needs must when the Squadron Leader needs a lift, and the QDG recon element need to find out what's what on the ground.

Sgt Hill took the commander's seat in the second Jackal immediately behind mine, with Trooper James Munday in the driver's seat and the vehicle's normal commander Paul Harris, aka Harry 73, perched up behind them on the .50 cal machine gun. We cut north as planned, set up a couple of 'hasty' VCPs or vehicle checkpoints when we got near the bridge, searched a few passing cars and trucks and then moved up to take pictures of the crossing point. That took us about forty minutes. We could see we were getting dicked by a couple of Taliban spotters: they were watching us from a hillside about 400 metres away. We were well within our rights to shoot them, and they were well within range of all our weapons. Instead, Corporal of Horse Ben Woollaston, who was in the rearmost Jackal, fired a couple of warning shots. The dickers gathered up their stuff and ran away.

We moved on south-east as planned, covered a few more kilometres of ground without incident and then swung north again as planned.

As we came down a shoulder of bare hill we saw an encampment of Bedouin, their tents straggling out in a rough crescent to the south. I told the QDG guys the nomads had been there for some weeks. Normally, when we passed by, the kids came out and waved to us. But on this occasion, the few children visible tucked their heads down, looked away and moved back inside. As combat indicators went, that one was very bad.

We were now moving east across a stretch of sandy, undulating ground about 600 metres away from the secondary vulnerable point. I drove past the ruined foundations of an old house, keeping to the right of it and sticking to the lower ground so the vehicle wouldn't be skylined.

Moving in a convoy on enemy turf, it's a very good idea as we've noted, if everyone stays in the 'Afghan Snake' – each following exactly in the tracks of the lead vehicle or person. It diminished the risk – unless you happen to be out in the lead. But at the same time, Sgt Hill in the Jackal immediately behind me needed to get better eyes onto the VP. Hilly now attempted to do just that: he swung left out of my tracks by no more than five metres, and climbed to the top of the low rise that lay almost directly ahead. The blast of a massive explosion echoed across the surrounding hills. I glanced back. A huge fireball topped with a mushroom cloud of black smoke hung in the sky above the spot where Hilly's Jackal had just been. For a moment, I thought we'd come under RPG attack. Then I heard Tpr Salmon shout: 'Harry's wagon's hit an IED!'

'Fuck!' I spun round in my seat. As I did that, my Jackal bogged into a patch of soft sand. I stood up to get a better view. A tall plume of smoke and dust was rising from the shattered remains of Sgt Hill's Jackal. Bits of the vehicle lay scattered to every side. Where were the three men who'd been crewing it? Then I spotted two bodies – one lying quite close to the vehicle, the other about 20 metres in front of it. The second man was moving, but I couldn't identify him. I thought: 'Fuck – is that Magpie Munday? Where's Hill? And where the fuck is Harry 73?'

Then I saw Harry: he was staggering about behind the shattered Jackal, trying to walk back up to it. Afraid that Harry would step onto a second device, everybody shouted: 'Harry! Stop! Stand still!' In deep shock, Harry 73 kept going.

The training cut in. The first thing we had to do was clear a safe zone around the vehicles. Then we had to get to the fallen men and do what we could to save them; call in the MERT and secure a helicopter landing site. And while all of that was going forward, we had to maintain vigilant all-round defence to deter any opportunistic Taliban attack.

Toddy jumped out, deployed his barma team and started clearing a safe route between his own and the stricken vehicle. As the team cleared the ground, Toddy and our combat medic, L/Sgt Robinson, moved in behind them, desperate to help the injured men. Watching, I had the same feeling of dread I'd had as a young Scorpion gunner in the Falklands War, when two motorcycle despatch riders immediately ahead of us had hit an Argy minefield. The explosion had blown both men off their bikes. Then, as now, we'd wanted to get them immediate help. But because of the risk of more mines, it had taken us five or six minutes to reach the injured despatch riders – by which time they'd already died from loss of blood.

With every second that ticked by, I was mentally urging the barma team to hurry up. Harry 73 was on his feet; the guy I later discovered to be Sgt Hill was moving. But the other man, James Munday, was lying very still. That almost certainly meant he was the most serious case, and as such the immediate priority. Robbo and Todd reached

Magpie Munday in just over a minute, but to me it felt much longer. They knelt down to start giving him emergency first aid.

By now I'd managed to extract my vehicle from the soft sand. Toddy had pulled up behind the bomb-blasted Jackal. I drove round, parked up in his tracks and took momentary stock. Major Davies was on the radio sending an urgent SITREP to the battle group. Nick Wright, the REME Staff Sergeant in command of the third Jackal, already had another team clearing a helicopter landing zone. Robbo was still down beside James Munday, working like a demon to save him.

As I moved towards them, Robbo stood up, looked at me and made a slicing motion across his throat with the edge of his hand. I stopped and stared back at him. No: that couldn't be true. Not James. Not Magpie Munday – the same man I'd told to stay in the Army because he had such a great future ahead of him. Not now, on what might well be our final patrol, and with only a few days before we were scheduled to fly home. I went up to James and knelt down beside him. He looked calm and untroubled, as if he were deep in a peaceful sleep. It was strange – not only did he look at peace, but I couldn't see any sign at all of an injury. I kept thinking, 'James isn't dead – just look at him. He can't be.'

I leaned forward and laid my fingers on the side of Magpie's neck. 'Come on, James,' I murmured, 'you're not going to die on us – not here in this crap-hole. Not now.' Determined to find a pulse, I moved my fingers across his neck and throat. But however hard I tried, I couldn't find the beat of moving blood that I wanted. A mixture of anger, shock and dismay rocked me. James was definitely dead and beyond help. As gently as I could, I tilted his head back. There was a small hole about the size and shape of a twenty-pence piece under his lower jaw. I couldn't understand what that was. I knelt there beside him for a long moment, shocked to the very heart.

While I was looking at James, Toddy had grabbed hold of Harry 73, put him back into the driver's seat of his Jackal and told him to stay there. But the younger Paul Harris had his own ideas: he grabbed a

Vallon and started trying to sweep around the column for IEDs. The Vallon he'd picked up was useless, the broken end of it hanging by a couple of strands. Harry hardly knew where he was or what he was doing. But crashing around the place waving a broken mine detector, he was a risk to himself and to others. As I watched, he dropped the Vallon, crawled over to James Munday and started trying to resuscitate him. 'Grab Paul,' I told Trooper Grover, 'stick him back in the Jackal and make sure he stays there until the MERT arrives.'

I shouted the casualty update across to Major Davies, confident he'd pass the details on to the battle group and the incoming MERT. Then I moved to join the team that had been attending to Sgt Hill. Hilly had a hole in his left leg that was leaking blood, and he said his neck hurt: but his pulse and respiration were normal. To staunch the flow of blood, Robbo applied antibacterial powder and a HemCon dressing, which helped seal the wound. Examining Sgt Hill more closely, Robbo realized that when he'd been fired forward by the blast, Hill had also broken his collarbone on the Jackal's roll bar. Applying a neck brace to protect the injured area, Robbo shot some morphine into him. But Hilly was far from complaining. 'Never mind all that,' he said: 'has anyone got a ciggy.'

Ben Woollaston took out a packet of cigarettes. He lit a cancer tube and handed it to Hilly: 'That's one you owe me,' he said. 'I'm writing it down in my notebook.'

Harry 73 was white and he had blood coming out of both ears. Robbo bandaged Harry's head and checked him over: he had severe bruising to his right hip-bone and pelvic area; but apart from those injuries, a spot of concussion and the shock, he seemed fine – lucky wasn't in it. He kept asking: 'Where's the other lads? Where's Magpie?' 'Don't worry,' I said, 'we're dealing with Magpie.'

I couldn't tell Harry that James was dead.

But Harry 73 wasn't finished. Pushing Trooper Grover off him, which took some doing, he clambered out of the Jackal, picked up a badly damaged TACSAT radio and started trying to call in air support.

A trained FAC, Harry couldn't understand why he wasn't getting any response from the set. I shouted: 'Grover – get hold of him and put him back in the Jackal. Sit on him if you have to.' When Harry 73 resisted Grover's attempts to lead him back to the Jackal, Grover half-carried him to the commander's seat, strapped him in and then sat on him as recommended.

CoH Cox secured the ground. With the clear and ever-present danger of attack and an emergency medical evacuation to cover, all gunners had permission to engage enemy targets at will. Under the gaze of the guns, we began moving the injured to the helicopter landing site. We had no body bags with us, so we covered James in a poncho liner. I knew James was dead, now; I'd accepted that. But a corner of my mind still wanted to give him comfort. As we lifted him onto the back decks of a Jackal, I murmured: 'We're lifting you now, James – we're going to get you back to Bastion. Then you'll be going back home.' It only seemed right to let Magpie know what was happening.

We strapped Sgt Hill to the special spine board we carried for back injuries, lifted him onto the Jackal with James and then, with Robbo on one side helping to keep him still, and Harry 73 strapped into the commander's seat, Ben Woolaston drove very, very carefully over to the HLS. We laid James Munday out on the ground ready for evacuation.

By now, Staff Sgt Nick Wright had cleared and secured the helicopter landing site. As the MERT Chinook circled in to land we took up all-round defence, fingers ready on the triggers: the Taliban were itching to down one of Task Force Helmand's scarce and invaluable Chinooks – but we weren't going to let them. The MERT came in with an escort of two Apache gunships. Ben Woolaston and Nick Wright picked Magpie Munday up and carried him onto the helicopter. When Sgt Hill and Harry 73 were safely on board with James, the helicopter wound up and lifted away.

Later, I tried to work out what had happened to Magpie. All I could think was that the sheer force of the explosion had shot one of the bolts securing the Jackal's floor plate up through his jaw and into his head. In which case, James had died instantly.

CHAPTER TWENTY-SEVEN

As the MERT thudded off towards Bastion, I asked Brigade what they wanted us to do with the damaged Jackal: could we strip the secret kit, stores and ammunition off the wagon and then just simply blow it up? The answer was no: Brigade wanted us to stay where we were, secure the area and wait for a Foden recovery truck and two WMIK Land Rovers to come out and tow the wreckage back to Camp Bastion.

Given that we only had five Jackals and fifteen men left in the troop, Major Davies asked for – and got – air cover while we waited for the recovery team to arrive. A pair of French Mirage fighter-bombers came on station. The problem we had when it came to air support was the fact that Harry 73 had been the troop's dedicated FAC. Except in cases of last-ditch life-or-death emergencies, only a properly trained Forward Air Controller can call in air power. But Harry was on his way back to Bastion.

We had a Royal Marines specialist providing intelligence feeds. He told us the Taliban were very excited: celebrating the 'success' of the IED strike. Then he recognized the voice of 'Khaled', a known local enemy commander: 'We have killed three British soldiers! Come, brothers, come and help us kill the others!'

We set up a ring of steel in a 500-metre diameter circle with the damaged vehicle in the middle and one of the undamaged Jackals next to it. We were on an undulating sandy plateau about 20 kilometres north of FOB Dwyer. Even on the most optimistic estimate the recovery vehicle – a vintage Foden six-wheeler that was coming from FOB Delhi 30 kilometres away – would take at least two hours to arrive. Plenty of time for a cuppa – as long as Khaled and his merry men didn't come to tea. The river valley and the local green zone lay to our immediate east. Ben Woollaston had parked his Jackal on top of a small hillock. From there, he looked down on a series of compounds bordering the nearby stream. I was on the circle's southern arc; Nick Wright was a couple of hundred metres to my right and east; Todd was covering the north side of the all-round defensive clock face, and Cox was watching the north-western arc.

The Bedouin camp we'd passed lay about 300 metres to the southeast, next to a bend in the river. Intelligence was still reporting a lot of enemy chatter. Aware that we were likely to be listening in, they kept saying: 'We are coming to kill you. We are coming to kill you.' Playground stuff – but if you are, then bring it on. Darkness began to fall. We kept asking for a rough ETA [estimated time of arrival] for the recovery truck, but no one back at Bastion could tell us – they'd lost comms with the recovery convoy. Marvellous.

At 1730, as the light was beginning to go, Ben Woollaston spotted a group of men directly below his position. They were stealing through the reeds towards the compounds. As they reached a gap, one man in the group snagged the hem of his dishdasha. The garment furled back: beneath it, Ben had definite sight of an AK47 assault rifle. The group was armed – and they were headed our way.

Khaled came up on air again: 'We will only attack if there is no air cover.' Maybe, like us, he was worried about the risk of civilian deaths and injuries, rather than saving his own skin. But I somehow doubt it.

We'd been due to lose our air cover at 1800 hours. But because of Khaled's loose comment about not attacking while it was present, call sign Anvil Three, the Forward Air Controller at FOB Dwyer, tasked the French call signs to remain on station overhead. The jets overflew the compounds and reported no enemy activity seen. Even though we knew an attack was imminent, the fact that it hadn't started yet meant that Anvil Three retasked the fighter-bombers to another location.

A lone male suddenly began walking towards our position. It might be dark, but the full moon beaming down gave our NVGs a brilliant light. The dicker was heading straight towards Cox's Jackal. Coxy transmitted: 'I've got one solo pax [person] coming south from the area of the VP towards my vehicle.' Then I heard him shout a verbal warning: 'Halt! Do not come any closer. Move away.' The interpreter shouted the same warning in Pashto. The snoop was now less than 100 metres from Cox's position. Ignoring the warnings completely, he kept right on walking. There was an outside chance he might be a scavenger looking for scrap – there are plenty of those in Afghanistan. But the focused way in which he was approaching made us all think the same thing: this was either a very determined dicker, or a suicide bomber. Already within 20 metres of Cox's Jackal, if he triggered a large suicide bomb then we were looking at death and serious injury.

'If he comes any closer,' I told Coxy, 'fire a warning shot to the side. And if he ignores that, take him out.'

Cox fired a round from his SA-80. The dicker veered south-east and then began to circle our southern perimeter. Some people don't know when to give up. When he'd seen enough, our man turned east and disappeared into one of the Bedouin tents.

I kept watching through the weird green aquarium light of the LUCIE thermal sights. A few minutes later, the dicker reappeared – only now he had a large group of Bedouin in tow: men, women and children, it looked like the whole encampment. Our Pied Piper led the group over a hill to the south. Afghans have a high opinion of the Bedouin: if they can, they will almost always try and move them out of harm's way. But when they do move the Bedu, you can pretty much bet that the bullets are about to fly.

I radioed Woollaston, the commander of call sign Three One: 'Ben, come back in – you're a little bit exposed where you are now.' Ben reversed his Jackal further back into the defensive ring. 'All call signs,' I transmitted, 'this is Mike One: that's obviously their reconnaissance done and dusted. They've moved the women and children out. Stand by.'

The reeds screening the nearby banks provided the enemy with perfect cover. I ordered the cordon to tighten further still. My pulse began to beat a little faster. If we were going to come under attack, then we needed to be in a tight circle: like the old Wild West wagon trains, and for the same reason. In that formation there was much less risk of a single vehicle getting picked off.

Five minutes went by and nothing happened. But we knew it was coming. Then, as if on signal, a salvo of RPG-7s speared in at us. I spotted three separate firing positions. Some of the rocket grenades were direct fire – aimed to hit the Jackals; the rest streaked up skyward to air burst directly overhead. I sent a contact report to Zero. The Rage call signs were now ordered back on station.

Muzzle-flashes winked from the reeds and the neighbouring compounds. Another RPG flew overhead. The boys were already sending back a wall of lead; no one had needed the order to return fire. Still in the driving seat of my own Jackal, and with the boss hogging the GPMG in the commander's seat beside me, I couldn't get my mitts on an area weapon. But the boss was enjoying every second, hammering away on the machine gun for all he was worth. I watched the long, curling flights of orange tracer sail in towards the enemy firing points.

Next to me, Ben Woollaston's Jackal was taking massive incoming: I could hear AK47 bullets pinging off his side armour. His face taut with concentration, Junior Salmon found the right range: he was lobbing grenades into the enemy compounds in good style. Then someone – either Cox's or Woollaston's gunner – hit three Taliban with a well-aimed burst of .50 cal. Their arms flew out to the sides and they fell in a heap. The Taliban have no MERT, they can't treat their wounded while a fire fight is still in progress. But even large numbers of injured often won't stop the Taliban; nine times out of ten they shrug off their losses and keep at you.

A stream of grenade machine-gun fire from Toddy's vehicle exploded in a stand of reeds, spraying lethal packets of red-hot shrapnel to every side. A red light began to flicker at the heart of the dry stalks. A new volley of RPGs arced out from the compounds, flashing past to either side. Beneath the crackle of the enemy assault rifles, I made out the distinctive, deep-throated thump of a 12.7mm DShK heavy machine gun. The Taliban had brought plenty of firepower to the party. But I reckoned we overmatched them: the combination of GMGs, .50 cals and 7.62mm machine guns was giving the enemy serious problems. The Heckler & Koch Mk 19 grenade machine gun was easily our best new weapon. Firing 40mm high-explosive fragmentation grenades at a rate of more than five per second, it gave us a whole new edge in battle.

Low of fuel, the French call signs now went off station. A pair of USAF F-18s took over. Warming to the fight, Toddy's gunner sent a new burst of GMG fire into the reeds. A bright tongue of orange flame flared into life. A moment later, the whole reed bed went up with a whump. A sharp smell like burning straw carried on the night air. Smoked out, a group of enemy fighters broke like grouse from the beaters, turned and started running away. Outlined against the flames, they made an easy target. We hosed them down with everything we had. The Taliban dropped boneless in their tracks.

After that, the enemy fire died away until there was silence. Suddenly, we saw the lights of the recovery vehicle. The Foden had a flashing orange beacon on its roof – there's nothing like coming in covertly. The WMIKs had to be out there somewhere in the darkness with them. We tried to warn the crews to stay clear, but we couldn't raise them. Wisely, seeing the fire fight up ahead, the QDG Regimental Sergeant Major leading the package decided to stop short.

I was just hoping that might be it for the night when Intelligence reported Khaled saying: 'They are stuck; we will attack them again soon.' Khaled was no fool: we were vulnerable; but if we had to recover the Jackal under fire, then we'd just have to remind the Taliban they weren't dealing with the Automobile Association.

With the lull in the fighting, the Foden tow-truck lumbered up out of the darkness like some metal dinosaur. Lowering a huge hook, it grabbed on to the wrecked Jackal's front end and started trying to drag it away. But the Jackal wasn't having any: as soon as it came under strain, its bodywork split in two. Bits of it thumped to the ground. 'Only one thing for it,' I said, watching the goings-on through the NVGs. 'We'll just have to get over there and lift those pieces onto the recovery truck by hand.'

Working with the Foden crew, our resident Sapper Nick Wright directed salvage operations. When all the wreckage was loaded, we started out back towards Camp Bastion in convoy, with the Foden nice and snug in the middle.

Looking back, I spotted the enemy. They were grouped in a wide arc to the north-east, tracking us in pick-ups at a range of between 400 metres and 2 kilometres. Khaled boasted: 'We have killed many of the enemy soldiers. We have defeated them: they are running back to their base like chickens.' The TIC [troops in contact] had officially closed. The vehicles shadowing us weren't local farmers out for a drive in the middle of the night, they were Taliban. But until they showed weapons or opened fire, we couldn't have at them.

We had to move off the beaten track: if we didn't, there was every chance the wolves on our tail would call ahead and get their mates to plant more IEDs in our path.

Four hours later, we reached FOB Dwyer. To say we were glad to get in was a major understatement: after the IED strike, the loss of a valued comrade, a three-hour fire fight and then the long trip home, everyone was exhausted. All I wanted to do was have a quick shower and get my head down. But the loss of James Munday weighed heavily on everyone's heart. We called the rest of D Squadron together. When they were all assembled, Major Davies told them that Magpie Munday had been killed. A wave of shock, disbelief and dismay spread through the room. When he'd finished speaking, Major Davies went to write up his patrol report.

As I sat there trying to write my own version the following morning, I kept thinking back to the time when I'd taken over the troop, and James had come to see me about leaving the Army. Thinking he had a great future in the Household Cavalry, I'd encouraged Magpie to stay in the regiment. If I hadn't done that, then he might not now have been lying dead in the camp morgue. I wasn't to know that and it was wrong to carry the blame. But it's something I have to live with – for ever.

CHAPTER TWENTY-EIGHT

James Munday's funeral took place on Tuesday, 28 October 2008, at St Peter and St Paul's Church, Coleshill. There in an unofficial capacity as a friend, I travelled up in a minibus with some other members of D Squadron who were anxious to pay their last respects. As we drove into the town, even 5 miles from the centre we saw that almost all the shops and other local businesses had put up Union flags to show their support.

When I'd served in Northern Ireland in the late 1970s, there had often been hardly a blink when a British soldier died in action. But in a testament to James Munday's popularity, and to the value that is now put on the lives of serving forces personnel, more than 1,000 mourners lined the route of his funeral procession: family and friends; veteran and serving soldiers; and many members of the public who'd never met James but wanted to express their solidarity with the family of a young man killed on the front line defending his country.

James's close family led the mourners: his mother and father, Caroline and Robert Munday; his brothers, Robert, Steven and Jack, and sister, Laura-Jayne Blackmore; and his grandmother and grandfather, Sheila and Colin Mann. I went straight to the church. The hearse drew up outside, a high-sided black wood and glass Victorian carriage drawn by two jet-black horses, their heads crowned with tall black plumes. Six of James's friends lifted his coffin from the back of the hearse and carried it to the graveside. We buried James with full military honours, including a rifle salute, the official Household Cavalry mourners gleaming in full dress uniform. People laid hundreds of wreaths and other floral tributes at the foot of the town's war memorial, which had been decked out especially in the colours of Liverpool FC, the football team whose fortunes James had followed passionately since he was a little boy.

Robert and Caroline Munday said: 'James was an adventurous, gracious and caring son, who excelled as a soldier and died doing a job he loved.

'James was a tremendous character, who lived life to the full. He was a talented and fearless skier, an enthusiastic horseman and was relishing the opportunity to help those in need on operational service.

'We are devastated by the loss of James, who will be sorely missed by his family, numerous friends and colleagues. We are so proud of what he achieved as our son and have been humbled by the many messages of condolences received.'

Among other things, I said: 'James showed all the best qualities that you would like to find in a person: honesty, thoughtfulness, resourcefulness, a good sense of humour, and he was never work-shy. He was a young soldier who, not surprisingly, was already earmarked for early promotion. I feel honoured to have known him and to have had him in my Troop. He will be massively missed by all who knew him in D Squadron and the Household Cavalry.'

Then Colin Mann, an ex-Coldstream Guardsman, read a poem that had been especially composed for the occasion. When the minister had spoken his last words and the coffin been laid in the ground, a file of Life Guards fired a volley of shots into the air.

By now, Harry 73 and Sgt Hill had been back in the UK for several weeks. Both had been through Selly Oak hospital in Birmingham, which treats many of the people injured in Afghanistan. Harry 73 was close to being his old self again. And although Sgt Paul Hill was using a wheelchair to get about, the fact that he was still alive and breathing after what had happened that day near the FOB was a great thing to see. It's pretty amazing how much damage the human body can not just survive, but actually beat, with a strong will and proper care.

Harry 27 came up to me. 'Thank you for looking after my lad, Taff. You only got him blown up.' We shook hands and laughed. I glanced across at James Munday's mother and sister and younger brother, standing no more than 5 metres away. Magpie's brother Jack was a little bit younger than James, but he looked so uncannily like him that they might almost have been twins.

Afterwards, at the wake, James Munday's mother drew me to one side. We stepped out into the cold air and closed the door behind us. 'James always said how glad he was to be in your troop. He said he always felt safe when he was with you.'

There was nothing I could say to that.

The weather in the weeks before the funeral had been fine: there'd been the odd showery day, but for autumn it had been sunny and reasonably warm, with no frost and no hint at all of snow. But the day of the funeral had dawned cold: and now, as Caroline and I stood talking about James and his love of skiing, the temperature suddenly plummeted. The sky above us darkened to the colour of lead, and big, white flakes began falling slowly in the still air. They settled on Mrs Munday's hair and shoulders, resting a moment before melting into droplets that gleamed, and then vanished before the next snowflake settled nearby. It felt odd, the snow coming suddenly like that, as we spoke of her son and the sport that he'd loved.

Then Caroline told me another strange thing: only the year before, she and James had seen a television item on the Armed Forces Memorial at Alrewas in Staffordshire. Placed on top of a mound that was formed like an Ancient British hill fort, the huge stone memorial honours the names of forces personnel killed on duty. Caroline said: 'The picture settled on the circular wall that has all the names of the dead carved on it. James turned to me. He said: "My name's going to be on that wall soon, Mum." I knew he was just teasing me, trying to get a reaction: he said things like that, sometimes. His sense of humour could be very different.'

Like most squaddies, I thought. And anyone else whose job carries with it the risk of death and injury.

'What did you say?'

'I said, "Don't be ridiculous, James. You're not going to die." But he was determined to get a rise out of me. He said: "When I'm laying face down in the sand, Mam, remember it was you who signed the consent form so I could join the Army in the first place because I was under age."'

I watched the snow for a moment, the white spots turning grey where they settled on the ground. 'Soldiers say a lot of things like that when they're going to war. Most of it's nonsense – you know that.'

Caroline held out a black-gloved hand to catch a falling flake or two. 'I know. But it was strange. Like the snow today, of all days. The first snow of winter.'

I left the wake and walked back to the graveyard. Now it was quiet and the crowds had gone, I wanted to pay James my own last respects. I stood looking down at the fresh mound of earth, thinking about Magpie Munday. It was impossible to escape feeling some responsibility for his death. There was no one standing near me, but I said: 'I wish I really could have looked after them all. I wish I could have kept James safe.' I hadn't wanted to go out on that last patrol in the first place.

Heartache is part of a soldier's life. Several hundred British forces personnel have been killed in Afghanistan since we deployed there. But the ones you know personally, the ones you've worked, lived and fought with, they become special, and James had been one of those. As I walked away from the graveside, Sizzler's words came back to me. 'Be careful what you wish for.'

Amen.

CHAPTER TWENTY-NINE

Afghan National Army base, Gereshk, Afghanistan: 9 January 2011.

We set off for the *shura* at eight-thirty in the morning. I usually like to lead from the front, but this time out Lance Corporal of Horse Ashford volunteered to take point, which as we've seen is almost always the most dangerous place to be in Afghanistan, whether on foot or in a vehicle. Ashford's gunner was Trooper 'Biscuit' Brown; his driver was Lance-corporal Kennedy; Lt Whiting, the squadron Intelligence Officer [IO], was hitching a ride in the back.

We were in a column of four Jackal armoured vehicles. As D Squadron, Household Cavalry's Squadron Corporal Major [SCM, or Warrant Officer, second class], I was three months into my third tour of Afghanistan. Commanding the last vehicle in the column, I was senior NCO of the Troop. My gunner manning the Browning .50 cal machine gun behind me, was Trooper 'Notters' Notley, and my driver was Lance-corporal 'Bren-gun' Brennan. We also had a civilian passenger in the back: 'Hash', our local Afghan interpreter. Obviously his name doesn't mean he spent the whole time smoking weed.

The tribal elder who'd requested the meeting lived in a village in an outlying sector of the Gereshk green zone. The only problem was that to get there meant travelling along Afghanistan's most dangerous road, Route 611. The meeting was scheduled for ten o'clock, and the village was only about 30 kilometres distant. But in Afghanistan, at war, we'd learned to leave plenty of time for the unforeseen.

This section of Route 611 links 'Lash' – Lashkar Gah, Helmand province's administrative centre – with Gereshk, where my unit, D Squadron, Household Cavalry was based. Gereshk stands at the junction of Route 611 and Highway One, Afghanistan's one and only hardtop east–west trunk road. On top of that, the town lies on the Helmand River, and has been a major Taliban drugs, weapons and contraband trading hub for years. For all of these reasons and more, Gereshk was of high strategic importance. When we got there, a new 30-kilometre stretch of the 611 leading north from Gereshk to Sangin was under construction, using Afghan labour recruited by means of the 'radio in a box' programme. RIAB uses a network of small, 300-watt radio transmitters and local Afghan broadcasters to reach local people directly.

To protect the local civilian contractors helping to build it, a series of outposts has been set up at intervals along the new stretch of Route 611, much like the old Roman mile forts on Hadrian's Wall. These posts are manned by a motley crew of hard nuts known as the militia. Militias are generally raised by locals to protect themselves, and some of the Route 611 fighters were local. But most of the militiamen at Gereshk were from the 'stans: those countries hard by Afghanistan whose names also end in 'stan': Turkmenistan, Uzbekistan, Kyrgyzstan and all the rest. Only a very few were from Pakistan, which tends to supply fighters to the enemy side. Mixed in with the 'stan' mob was a sprinkling of Chechnyans – but the job attracted just about any bugger who couldn't find regular employment, liked a scrap and could handle a weapon. The job in this case being to stop the Taliban from killing the road gangs and planting IEDs along Route 611 to kill us.

Paid a daily rate in hard currency, dressed in a rag-bag mix of uniform and civilian clothing, and armed with just about any weapon that took their fancy, the Route 611 militia were like something out of the movie *Mad Max*: fearsome and ruthless killers who made for a very bad enemy. They worked for a mullah whose brother the Taliban had very unwisely killed. Their manager was 'Mad Carl', a contract ex-squaddie from Newport, South Wales, about two miles from Trowbridge where I'd grown up. We'd probably battled as kids. Carl had suffered a stroke, leaving his left eye with a slight droop, which made the Mad Max mob fear him all the more. I'd been told that the US government picked up the tab for this mercenary force, and we all had the feeling that the minute Uncle Sam stopped paying them, there was every chance they'd turn their guns on us. While it lasted, I was glad they were on our side. Usually. But as always with irregular Afghan forces, they could easily get their loyalties mixed and needed careful watching.

At that time of the morning it was still cold. We had layers on, vests, sweaters, fleeces, anything to keep warm. But as we started to rumble east out of the world's worst-smelling town and along IED Alley, perched in the commander's seat of the rearmost Jackal I was still cold. Everyone knows how hot Afghanistan gets in summer, as in temperatures of up to and even beyond 50 degrees Centigrade. But in winter the cold, especially when the north-east wind drives the perishing air down off the Hindu Kush mountains, can be almost as bad. At any rate, it was fucking freezing.

The stench resulted from Gereshk's complete lack of sewerage. 'Infrastructure' is an unknown word in most parts of Afghanistan; it would be nice if there was any, especially in Gereshk, and especially when it came to disposing of human waste. In the meantime, the whole sorry burg smells very, very bad. Given the fact that we were billeted in with the Afghan National Army *kandak* [battalion] in their base next to the bazaar and smack in the middle of town, this was a bit of a problem.

As usual, the rock-hard militia reacted in different ways as we rolled past them. You definitely wouldn't want to play tiddlywinks with these guys – they're hard core. Many looked away or gave us the evil eye. Not very many looked friendly.

A few days earlier, a large Taliban force had rushed a makeshift outlying 611 militia post in what should have been overwhelming numbers. In the blistering fire fight that followed, the Taliban had fought their way to within 20 metres of and come very, very close to overrunning the position. Two militiamen were killed and several injured, but the mercenaries held firm, and after an hour or two of hard killing, they beat the insurgents back with serious losses.

Besides preparing the surface, I noticed that some of the road gangs starting work as we nudged out of town were installing thick metal grilles to stop the Taliban placing IEDs under the 611's bridges. To reduce the risk, the new stretch of road only had two of those, but the sight gave me a strong flashback to Northern Ireland, where the IRA had used the same tactic. I'd served there at the age of 18, which now seemed a long time ago. That's because it was a long time ago – 32 years, to be exact.

The sun warmed up, and we got warm with it, and then hot, and then we all wanted to strip off the layers we'd carefully put on to keep out the cold. But we couldn't, because we'd have had to stop, remove our body armour and combats, and that wasn't on in the middle of a live mission in a combat zone on a notoriously dangerous route. So we sat there boiling in the open-top Jackals.

Gradually, the gap between the militia posts began to increase, until finally we were out on our own in open country. We turned off the main track, and headed for the north–south sand dune ridge-line that paralleled the road. We then struck on west towards the *shura*. On this side of Gereshk the terrain was mainly sand: all types of sand. Hard sand and sand so soft that, if you trod in it, you sank in the talcum powder up to your knees; fine sand and grit; sand shaped in dunes and hummocks; sand hills and flat pans and wadis and sandy sinks. And it changed consistency all the time. After a few kilometres we turned north, ran on for another thirty minutes or so and then turned east; wheeled on some more and finally turned west about face towards the green zone and our real objective. The twists and turns had been a feint. The terrain changed and trees and shrubs began to appear, hugging the rich, fertile soil along the river; then walls and compounds and irrigation ditches and crops came up, the whole Afghan green zone in all of its deadly glory. From prior intelligence, we knew the area we were headed into was hostile, Taliban-infested and prime ambush country.

The tribal elder we were supposed to be meeting was a senior figure, so we had the OC, Major Rupert Lewis, with us to do the negotiating. Major Lewis was in the back of the second wagon, with CoH 'Shagger' Shaw commanding the vehicle and Trooper Mitchell, who was built like an ox, at the wheel. Lance-corporal Warren was top gunner. Major Lewis and I formed the core element of D Squadron's TAC, or tactical headquarters. Not long promoted Corporal of Horse, Paul Minter was commanding the third vehicle in line, with Lance-corporal Selby standing ready on the .50 cal, and Trooper Price doing the driving. Sgt Si Dodds, our team medic, was in the rumble seat.

We'd been taking it slowly and carefully, so it was gone nine o'clock by the time we came into an area of firm, low sand dunes about 5 kilometres from the target village. Directly ahead of us, the track split in a Y-shape junction whose arms pointed to the north and north-east. I gave the order to halt. This was my third six-month tour of Afghanistan in three years and I was halfway through it. The Taliban hadn't killed me yet, and I had no intention of allowing any scumbag terrorist fuckwit to do that now. And nor were they going to kill any of my men. Taking either of the tracks leading right and left was a mug's game. The Taliban knew we were coming – we'd been dicked en route. There was every chance they'd have mined both the obvious options.

Ash decided to go straight through the middle of the Y-junction, taking what any of us would have thought was the safest route. My vehicle started to lose traction in the soft sand. 'Put your foot down – keep the revs up,' I told Bren-gun. 'I don't want to get stuck.' Ash had gone about 20 metres forward. A deafening explosion split the air. His

Jackal catapulted skyward in a huge gout of smoke and flame. It bounced and rolled over sideways before settling back upright. A person flew out of the vehicle as it flipped before crashing back to earth. As he landed, Lt Whiting completed a near-perfect forward roll and then climbed to his feet.

With its additional armour and four men up, the Jackal weighed the best part of 6 tonnes. The blast had plucked the vehicle up and tossed it like a matchbox. Small bits of it rained back to earth, pattering like large metal raindrops in the soft sand. A towering cloud of ash, smoke and dust hung over the explosion site. One of the Jackal's road wheels rolled out of the grey-brown fog and shot off to one side. There was a roaring sound in my head and for a moment I thought the blast might have made me deaf.

I smacked the pressel switch on my chest-rig to activate the personal role radio [PRR]: 'Contact IED. Wait out.' Then I checked the GPS read-out and transmitted our exact location. As the dust began to settle, I saw that LCoH Ashford and his driver, 'Kenno' Kennedy, were lying motionless on the ground about 15 metres or so to the south. Directly ahead of me, Paul Minter's vehicle had bogged slightly into a patch of soft sand. That meant I couldn't get my own Jackal forward to help the injured men without coming out of the safe tracks. It was too risky to break out – where there was one IED there were usually more: the Taliban have started sewing them in fields, and sometimes the devices are connected in a spider's web so that one triggers another.

Realising that I wanted to move up, Minty told his driver to reverse. Price slammed the engine into gear and the Jackal's rear-end came within an inch of hitting us. He crunched into forward gear, took a new set of tracks that lay slightly to the right, pulled clear and stopped. I moved my Jackal on through and told Bren-gun to stop when we'd gone as far as we could. Minter's Jackal swung in and parked up behind mine. 'Out!' I shouted. 'Remember to stay in the tracks!' Everyone baled out. 'Grab the stretchers! And the Vallons! Start barmaring – let's get up to them.'

I heard someone screaming. I looked across and saw Lt Whiting standing stock still to one side, very near two other fallen men. The blast had flung the IO about 12 metres clear of the Jackal to the right side. He looked as if he was in mild shock, but he was OK. I knew he was OK because he was standing exactly in the spot where he'd landed and not moving. If he took even one single step to any side, he risked initiating a second device. That meant Lt Whiting was thinking, and if he was thinking and standing upright, then even though he was covered from head to toe in dust and debris, and looked like a kangaroo caught in the headlights, for the moment, at least we didn't need to worry about him.

The other three men who'd been in the Jackal with him had been less lucky. Trooper Brown had also been launched out of the Jackal to the right-hand side. Biscuit was yelling his head off, and in a moment I saw why: one of his feet was on the wrong way round, turned 180 degrees from the approved and desirable position. Lance-corporal Warren, the gunner from the second Jackal in line, came past me. Warren was sweeping the Vallon detector from side to side, clearing a path to the injured men. Tremendous. Less good was the fact that Warren kept getting double tones from the detector: more buried IEDs – loads of them. We were in the middle of a widespread and carefully planned explosive ambush. The Taliban had second-guessed us. Noting us avoiding the obvious routes elsewhere in the past, they'd laid the IEDs between the fork of the Y. Then I thought: 'Hang on – if they've laid this many devices, then the chances are they've mined both the routes out of the junction as well.'

We travelled in a big circle around the wrecked Jackal, following Warren as he found, marked and avoided more buried IEDs. As we came up level with it, we saw that the vehicle had been more or less reduced to its component parts – there were bits of the fucker lying everywhere. There was a giant, smoking crater under its rear, right end. In one way, it looked as if the crew *had* been lucky: the Jackal had clipped the extreme left-hand edge of the IED's pressure plate.

If they'd hit it dead centre, they might all have been dead.

We reached Ash Ashford. Mine clearance is painstaking and painfully slow work – by the time we got up to him, I was boiling with frustration. When men are lying injured and in pain, all your instincts are to run to them. But if you do that in a war zone, then you risk becoming part of the problem, not part of the solution.

Major Lewis shouted at me to stay back, but I couldn't – these were my soldiers, I had to get to them. I climbed along the side of the smouldering Jackal to get into the cleared zone.

Ash still had his body armour on, and his rifle was lying to one side. He was bleeding heavily from the mouth. Si Dodds appeared at my shoulder. We bent closer and saw that Ash had bitten right through his lower lip. I caught his shocked, staring gaze: 'Can you move, Ash?'

'I can't move, Boss – my back.' Ash was white with pain and looked in a really bad way. But as ever, he was smiling, even though there was plainly more to it than just a bitten lip. Once we'd checked him over, a stretcher party came up. We loaded Ash onto the stretcher as gently as we could, then the bearers carried him back and placed him across the seats in the front of my vehicle.

Warren barmared on to Kenno, who was lying a few metres further out to the side. Si Dodds and I moved up to him. Kennedy couldn't move his legs and one arm was bent up behind him at an angle so impossible it had to be broken. He said: 'I can't breathe.' Then he started to slip out of consciousness. I leaned forward and nipped his ear: 'Kenno! Stay awake!' I shouted. 'Don't go to sleep!' He groaned and his eyes rolled backwards up into his head. I tweaked his chin with my fingers. If they once slip away, then too often badly injured people don't make it back again. Dodds gave Kenno a good going over. Kenno snapped back to life. 'I can't feel my legs. My back's killing me. My shoulder's hurting.' I left Sgt Dodds to deal with Kennedy and moved on towards Trooper Brown.

Brown was still in agony. His right ankle had snapped, and his foot was still on the wrong way round. His left leg also looked broken, only further up, at the thigh; and his left kneecap was sticking way out to one side. But if he still had the strength to yell, then I reckoned Biscuit was going to survive.

Shaw had taken control of the air and called in the MERT: the Chinook was already on its way up from Camp Bastion. Luckily, Bastion was now no more than 30 kilometres away. A pair of Army Air Corps AH-64 Apache gunships that had been responding to a separate incident nearby now came up on station overhead. A welcome umbrella. But as yet, there had been no follow-up Taliban attack.

All the training was coming good, we'd rehearsed this exact scenario: one vehicle down, four men injured, three seriously. Everyone was doing his job: there were people manning the radios, others providing all-round security; the OC was down next to Trooper Kennedy with Si, they were doing what he could for him; the stretcher teams were working well. Only now the screams were real, and the blood and the broken bones were anything but fake. I suddenly remembered the MIST report – had anybody sent that? The MIST report gave the MERT team the concise information they needed about the injured, so the onboard medics could prepare the appropriate treatment. Yes, the MIST report had gone.

Biscuit was lying face down. He was still screaming. He needed a shot of morphine. I burrowed into his webbing and found the two auto-injection syringes all British soldiers are supposed to carry in theatre. The syringe had a red cap. I removed it, exposing the white end of the syringe. I stuck that up against Biscuit's buttock. 'This is going to hurt a bit, Biscuit,' I said, as I pushed down hard on the purple end. A pain shot into my thumb. I looked down. I'd pressed the wrong end of the syringe. The needle had punched straight into my thumb bone and stuck fast. I'd just injected myself with a large shot of morphine. What a twat. Brown said: 'That didn't hurt at all.'

'No, that's because I just fucking auto-injected myself,' I told him.

I pulled the needle out of my thumb bone, grabbed hold of the second syringe, pressed the correct end up against one of his arse-cheeks and whacked the plunger. The needle shot through the cloth of his combats and pumped morphine into him. This time, he screamed. I asked: 'Did that hurt?' I was trying to remember how long the drug took to start working. For some reason, I had it in my head as twenty minutes. But then I felt my right arm starting to go cold and numb. Two minutes? Whatever, it had already kicked in – I knew I had an interesting time ahead of me.

Brown said: 'My legs are hurting. My arm is hurting.' I took out a blue felt pen and wrote a big capital letter 'M' on his forehead followed by the time I'd administered the shot. I thought about doing the same to my own forehead, but then I'd only have looked even sillier. Si Dodds came up and checked him over. 'Let's get him onto a stretcher.' There were four more guys with us now. Then Lt Whiting suddenly showed up to help. Warren had reached the IO with a Vallon and released him from his temporary prison of sand. He looked a bit pale, but apart from that the lieutenant was obviously all right. He didn't look any taller for the experience, though.

The six of us got round Biscuit and started to lift him as carefully as we could; at the same time rolling him over onto the stretcher so that he was lying on his back. As soon as we touched him, Biscuit screamed louder still: it cut through you, you had to make an effort to block it out. Si said: 'We need to pull his foot straight. It can't stay like that.' Luckily, I'd trained on that particular injury. I got hold of Biscuit's foot and hauled back on it as gently but as firmly as I dared, at the same time twisting it to point in the right direction. Brown screamed again – the skin of his face had turned pale grey with pain. I managed to turn the foot so it was fixed on the normal way; but on his other leg, his kneecap was still skewed around to the side. It looked as if the kneecap had been torn off, but there was nothing we could do about that right now, We opened the doors of a second Jackal and laid Biscuit across the vehicle, using one door as a prop and then having a soldier sit in the opposite seat and hold up the stretcher's other end. The morphine hit his system, and Biscuit's screams turned to groans.

I moved back across to Trooper Kennedy. Doddsy was attending to him again. He said: 'We need to keep his head perfectly still. Get behind him and keep his head still and straight.' I moved round and cradled Kenno's head in my arms. Looking down, I saw bruising and bleeding on his right upper thigh. Si nodded. 'I think his right femur's broken. His right forearm is also broken: compound fracture, at least two places. And his right collar-bone is snapped in half. But it's his spine I'm really worried about – I think he might have broken it.' Si spoke the words quietly in my ear so Kenno didn't overhear. Kenno was still drifting in and out of consciousness, I didn't like the look of him one little bit. Every time he started to go, I nipped his ear-lobe to bring him back. 'Kenno – stay awake!' 'I'm sorry,' he said, 'it was my fault. I drove over the IED.' In his lucid moments, he kept saying he was sorry. I said: 'Don't be daft, mate – it was the Taliban's fault. Just think, you'll be back home in time for the Six Nations rugby.' We started to lose him again. I tweaked his ear and to my enormous relief he swam back up to the world. 'How's the crew?' he said. 'How are the rest of the guys?'

Major Lewis took over: 'They're fine, Kenno – all fine. Don't worry. The MERT's here, they're taking you all back to Bastion now.' But before we could carry Kenno down to the helicopter landing site, we needed a spinal board from the MERT. Minter had taken his crew and cleared an area of scrub the farmers were using to grow poppies. That meant the ground was less likely to be IED'd. Minty and his guys had also checked the area with the Vallons. The site was only about 300 metres away, but that was much, much too far to move a man with a serious back injury.

There was a cluster of compounds about 200 metres to the north of our positon. All the time, I was watching them, waiting for a follow-up attack. The Apaches were still giving us top cover – if the Taliban did try anything, they'd get a good going over from their 30mm cannons, and a roasting from our own guns.

The MERT Chinook thundered in and landed in a gigantic sand storm. As it came down, one of the medics was ready on the ramp with a spinal board. One of the lads grabbed it and hurried across. With Si supervising, six of us eased Kenno onto the board. Then we carried him gently down to the HLS and got him onto the Chinook. By now, the other injured men were already on the helicopter receiving attention. The massive twin counter-rotating blades started turning, lazily at first and then faster and faster until they were blurred discs spinning silver in the billowing khaki dust clouds. Then the pilot worked the collective; the rotors bit into the warm air; the giant bird lifted clear of the ground, hesitated for a second, then dipped its nose and thundered away.

With the injured in safe hands, the next thing was to clear up the mess. By now, it was late afternoon, so we had to hurry. The Jackal might be in bits, but its weapons systems, ammo, GPS, Bowman radio and any secret kit had to be gathered up and taken off the battlefield. The Taliban use anything and everything of ours they find. It took us a little while to locate the vehicle commander's GPMG. The blast had blown it more than 100 metres out to one side. To reach it, we once again had to sweep slowly and carefully for IEDs. We found yet more of them, spread over a wide area. We had to mark and dog-leg around them as before. Finally, we got to the missing weapon, picked it up and retraced our steps.

Next thing, we had to recover what was left of the wagon – that couldn't stay where it was, either. The enemy would love to examine its armour close up, get an idea of how to defeat it; and they'd most likely reuse what they could of it into the bargain. We called up FOB Price and whistled for a tow-truck. With no wheels left on it, the Jackal was in such bad shape we needed to load it on a flat-bed. One started out from FOB Price straight away. While that was en route, HQ decided the IED field we'd strayed into was so big and so dangerous, they'd send out a RESA [Royal Engineer Research Advisor] explosive ordnance disposal team to deal with it.

The RESA team got to us about an hour and a half later. Some specialist US EOD experts came with them. The engineers started to clear a 200-metre-wide lane for the flat-back. In no time at all, they'd discovered the pressure-plate of another IED. Digging carefully around it, they uncovered five old, but still live and lethal Russian 105mm artillery shells. Underneath the shells and wired to explode with them was a 20kg cache of HME – home-made explosive. A real monster. Underneath that again, the team spotted what looked like an anti-tamper device. That decided it: they weren't going to take any chances. They were going to 'bip', or blow the device in place. They set a charge, rolled out a length of det cord and we all retired to what we thought was a safe distance.

Knick-Knack appeared on the horizon at the wheel of the flat-back. I don't know his real name, but Knick-Knack was a Territorial Army part-timer and a double-glazer in civilian life. Posted out to Afghanistan for his sins, he was putting his HGV licence to very good use driving flat-backs and other large military vehicles. The rest of the boys in the recovery crew were Welsh, and had history with Ash. For the wrecking crew, Ashford's involvement made the recovery operation personal: they weren't hanging about.

When the flat-back was close but at a safe distance, the RESA team blew the charge. The IED's pressure plate flew up into the air, but some of the shells failed to explode. A couple of the American bomb disposal experts crept back up to the smoking crater. The explosives were on fire. It isn't easy to faze EOD guys, but they looked a little pale when they saw that. The was a strong chance that the whole thing would explode and reduce them to atoms. They set a new demolition charge, legged it back out with the clacker [initiator] and blew the IED for the second time. A god-almighty explosion spewed earth and sand and steel high up into the evening air. A pressure-wave of blast and heat surged out. I looked up. Someone said: 'Fuck! We're too close!' He was right: we were only about 30 metres from the seat of the explosion. Not far enough.

I heard this strange whirring noise from overhead. Faint at first, the whirring grew louder and louder. Everybody dropped back and took cover. The screeching banshee wail from above gradually deepened. Something thumped into the ground less than 20 metres away. I stared at it. One of the Russian shells. By pure good fortune, the unexploded projectile had landed in the small patch of ground between us and the RESA team. How it didn't hit and kill anyone, I'll never know.

After all the excitement, it was half past six in the evening. The RESA team finished securing the area. We winched the dead Jackal up onto the flat-back and then set off in convoy with it back to FOB Price. A convoy travels at the speed of its slowest unit, and the flat-back really crawled along under its heavy load. On the way, I asked for a SITREP on the casualties. We knew Ash had suffered a broken collar-bone. But now we found out that when he'd smashed into the Jackal's roll bar, one end of the severed bone had pierced the top of his right lung. No wonder he'd been in such bad shape.

Kennedy had broken his right femur, an arm, an ankle and two of his vertebrae. Sgt Dodds had been right. Kenno's spleen had also ruptured, leaving the medics no option but to remove it. He was heading back home to specialist care in the UK. But Ash had to stay in Bastion hospital, the change in air pressure that comes with flying was too dangerous for someone suffering from a punctured lung.

Brown had a broken ankle, but his foot was probably going to heal; his right kneecap had been dislocated, and not broken off. Biscuit, too, was staying in Bastion. The really great news was, the medics thought all three men would live to fight another day.

Toddy's troop dropped the flat-back off at FOB Price. The rest of us got back into Gereshk at 0130 the next morning. Another busy day at the office. And we were still less than half the way through the tour.

CHAPTER THIRTY

Talking about busy days at the office, this is what my normal working day is like. I was up and about before the rest of the men, who were sleeping in because they'd been out on a night patrol. I'd just filled my solar shower bag after doing a stint in the makeshift gym, and I was on my way back through the Ops room when the duty watchkeeper, Captain Gerry Wellesley, informed me: 'There's an ambush going on about 10k away.' It was only half past seven in the morning, but business was already booming. I stopped. 'OK – are any of our guys involved?'

'No – it's all the ANA and the Taliban.' We call that, 'Afghan good' – as in, the Afghans are busy killing one another, not us. Gerry said: 'Two of our call signs are already on their way to help.' That was good news, the rest of us didn't need to crash out unless the fire fight escalated – I could leave the lads to their well-earned lie-in. I started walking over to the shower cabin. Before I got there, another soldier hurried up to me: 'They're bringing in an ANA man – he's been shot in that contact and badly injured. They need a medic.' I went into the troop room and found Guardsman McNeil. 'You're needed – we've got an injured ANA man coming in. Are you good to go?' He picked up his stuff and fell in behind me.

A shanty town built on the hill to the *kandak's* immediate west overlooks the whole base, and from time to time an enemy sniper gets up there and takes a couple of pot-shots. We also got the odd hand grenade thrown over the walls. But this morning, on that front at least, it had been quiet.

I came back out blinking into the dazzling early sunlight to see a dusty old tan-coloured pick-up swinging in through the gate. The medic and I ran up to it and lowered the tail-gate. The ANA guy was lying in the back on a blanket. The blanket was soaked in blood and there was more blood on the flat metal bed of the truck. 'Let's get him off,' I said. We climbed in, lifted the man out and laid him on a stretcher. He screamed in agony as soon as we touched him. Mac cut away the legs of the injured man's combats. The back of his right thigh was missing – there was a huge gaping wound where the muscle had been. A Taliban AK47 bullet had shot that away, then travelled on and embedded itself in the other leg. You could see the bone, the blood and the yellow bits of fat inside the wound. The Afghans are some of the hardest people on the planet: after the initial burst of screaming, the ANA man had fallen silent. He was watching us work on him, clearly in extreme pain but impassive.

I whacked some morphine into him – this time making damned sure I shoved the purple end of the syringe up against his arse. We cleaned the wounds, put some HemCon dressings on to staunch the bleeding and bandaged the guy up as well as we could. We didn't try and extract the bullet. That was going to take a spot of specialist surgery. There was a vehicle leaving for FOB Price, and we managed to get the casualty on it. 'Breakfast', I thought once he was safely en route, 'must get some breakfast. Even if it's only a cup of tea. But first, I need to get cleaned up.' I headed in the direction of the shower again.

Hash, our Afghan interpreter stopped me before I got there. What was this, Groundhog Day? 'They're bringing in a body – a Taliban killed in the fire fight.' OK, so the shower would have to wait. When they bring in an enemy corpse we have to conduct intelligence checks to see if the individual has been involved in other incidents. I heard the roar of an engine and looked across to see a Ford Ranger coming in through the gates. There were two ANA men in the cab. They stamped on the brakes and the ancient wagon shuddered to a halt. I walked up. They'd thrown the dead man in the back like a piece of meat on the way to market – he lay crumpled and twisted up on himself where he'd landed.

A line of red-black bullet holes stitched up his left side; the left half of his chest had been shot away; AK47 rounds had shattered his left wrist and elbow; his eyes were staring wide and a couple of his arm bones were sticking out of the flesh. We were dealing with a dead man, they don't come any deader. The only thing that still looked undamaged was his beard, the full Taliban. It was long enough to grab with a fist and its colour matched the black of his dishdasha. We lifted him out of the vehicle and laid him on a stretcher. I shouted for our Royal Military Policewoman, Lance-corporal Rachel Cairney to come and do her stuff. Rachel conducted her intelligence checks of the corpse. I asked the medic to confirm exactly how the fighter had died: 'multiple gunshot wounds resulting in major organ failure.' I already sort of knew that, the guy's heart had been shot clean out of his chest. But I needed the form of words for the report, and that needed to get done straight away. By now it was about nine a.m. It was already beginning to feel like I'd been at work for a long time.

I tracked down a couple of ANA men and gave them formal charge of the body. They took a leg each and dragged the enemy fighter along the ground towards the morgue. It's safe to say they didn't show him too much respect. I was just thinking about having that shower when another guy came up to me: 'The ANA have just arrested two local nationals in a white Toyota pick-up. They found nineteen British Army illume mortar shells in the back of the vehicle.' 'Bugger it,' I muttered. 'OK, wheel them in.' I headed for my office. It was my job to 'tactically question' the two suspects. We needed to know how the suspect pair had got hold of so many illumination rounds; where they'd been taking them and what they intended doing with them once they got there. Illume rounds are basically slow-burning incendiaries, we use them at night to light up enemy positions. The Taliban like to pack them in with other explosives to beef up the explosive power of an IED. But Army illume rounds don't usually go astray – so how had our detainees come by these?

I found the two men plastic-cuffed in the room we used for 'tactical questioning'. They looked the part: ragged beards and black robes, a mean glint in the eye that betrayed a deep hatred of me, the British Army and anyone else who didn't share their exact beliefs. I quizzed them a bit and made a few notes – to my surprise, they gave me some useful information. When it was plain they weren't going to give me any more, I got Hash to tell them that later on that same day we'd be moving them on down the line to Camp Bastion for further questioning. Imagine how happy they looked. I glanced at the wall clock: quarter to eleven.

I didn't even think about taking a shower. Sure enough, I'd no sooner waved my two new friends a fond goodbye when we got heads-up that five known pro-Taliban 'elders' from the settlement of Spin Majid were demanding an immediate parley. Spin Majid was in Babaji district, to the south-west of us between Gereshk and Lashkar Gah. Until the British Army cleaned it out in 2009 with Operation Panther's Claw, Babaji had been one of the most dangerous areas of Helmand province. Now though, the village of Spin Majid had a working school, a clinic, and a small bazaar had opened for business.

The 'elders' told Hash they had a message from the Taliban: unless we released the body of the dead fighter into their custody that very same day, then the Taliban were going to go in and shoot the crap out of Spin Majid, and kill all the people in it down to the last child. I told Hash to tell them I'd be happy to meet. As soon as I'd done that, I got hold of Lance-corporal Cairney again: 'Grab your camera, Rachel, and all your other surveillance kit – we've got important visitors.' Cairney hurried off. I also informed our Intelligence NCO, LCoH Graham Green – 'GG' – of the elders' imminent arrival.

The five men turned up a few minutes later, which strongly suggested they'd been lurking nearby in the bazaar waiting for the invitation to come into camp. I could have been mistaken and I'd hate to play to the clichés, but as they strutted into my office, a glance at them said they were hard-core Taliban: like the guys I'd just dealt with, they had the team look: long black flowing beards; dark-green dishdashes and, just by way of variation, pure Daz white turbans. They had the hard-bitten, desert-hawk features of the local career warriors; and most tellingly of all, the hate-filled glares the Taliban dished out to us as standard fare. One of the five was a huge man, built like a grizzly bear – he sat in the corner of the ANA commander's office on one of the tribal rugs that carpeted the floor and glowered at me. The other four sat in a semi-crircle facing the commander's sofa. They'd been searched on the way in for weapons, which meant they were definitely unarmed, but even so I was glad I had the P226 Sig-Sauer pistol ready to hand on my thigh.

The ANA commander sat to the side on another rug, calmly drinking tea and eating a biscuit. All politeness, he asked my visitors if they wanted *chai*; they all said no, maybe they imagined we'd put something in it. They kept right on glaring. I thought: 'If you lot keep that up for much longer, then I'm going to shoot you.' But that would have seen me go straight to jail.

One of the five said: 'We want the body of our brother. You have to give us the body now.' I shook my head. 'Sorry, I can't do that. As you know, we hand the body of dead enemy combatants over to the Afghan National Army. Standard procedure. They then carry out their own investigations. When those are completed, we might be able to help.' If anything, the hatred in their eyes intensified. 'That's the way it always happens, gentlemen – there's nothing I can do about it.' The man to my right started shouting at me: 'Why are you in our country? We have our own law, sharia law, why are you here?' The middle guy pitched in: 'Why is ISAF in our country? Why don't you get the hell out?'

I suppose I could have replied: 'Because when the Taliban ruled Afghanistan, they allowed anti-Western terrorists to use the country as a safe haven from which to launch murderous attacks against civilian targets. Attacks in which thousands of innocent people were killed and badly injured.' Or I could have said: 'Because the Taliban are the major players in Afghanistan's heroin industry, and peddling drugs isn't a good way to behave.' But there would have been no point, so I kept my mouth shut.

Even so, I was thinking: 'There isn't usually a senior deputation like this to recover a dead Taliban fighter. So if I'm right, and these four are what the Americans call 'irreconcilable' Taliban, then who's the guy in the morgue? *Maybe he was their boss.*' If so, then that was a result. They ranted and raved at me for a few more minutes, all except the grizzly bear, who looked as if he wanted to kill me. Shaking with anger, the man who'd asked the last question jumped to his feet. They all stood up with him: 'Are you going to release the body?'

I looked at him. 'No, we're not. And you can leave, now – thank you for coming.' With a final glare, they stalked out. Good riddance. I raised my own gaze a little wearily to the clock again: it was gone two in the afternoon. Surely there was something missing from my day? What was that? Oh yes – shower.

Breakfast and lunch would have to wait, too, unless I could rustle up a sandwich: the men we'd caught with the mortar and the illume rounds were the next priority. I had to get them over to Bastion before anything else happened. I ordered up a driver and escort. We grabbed ourselves a vehicle and set off. Less than an hour later, I'd handed the suspects over to the unit concerned. But while the two men were undergoing further questioning, I had to go and explain why, when, where and by whom they'd been arrested; and then set that all down on the computer. By the time I got back to Gereshk it was coming up for nine p.m.

Another busy day at the office. I'd missed breakfast, dinner and tea. And I hadn't had a shower for a week. But then, tomorrow was another day.

Abbreviations

ACOG Advanced Combat Optical Gunsight

ANA Afghan National Army

ANP Afghan National Police

AO area of operations

APDS armour-piercing discarding sabot

Anvil One the main air tasking call sign

BDA battle damage assessment

CAS close air support

CASEVAC casualty evacuation

CoH Corporal of Horse

CVR-Ts combat vehicle reconnaissance – tracked

DC District Centre

dems demolition

det detonator

dickers the spotters who note and report our movements

ECM electronic countermeasures

EOD Explosive Ordnance Disposal (officer)

ERV emergency rendezvous point

FAC Forward Air Controller

Fireflies winking infra-red indicators that are invisible to the naked eye

FIST Fire Support

FLET forward line of enemy troops

FOB Forward Operating Base

FOO Forward Observation Officer

FSG Fire Support Group

GMG grenade machine gun

GPMG general purpose machine gun (or Gimpy)

GPS global positioning system

HCR Household Cavalry

HLS Helicopter landing site

IED improvised explosive device (booby-trap bomb)

Illume illumination rounds

Int Intelligence

ISAF the International Security and Assistance Force

ITU intensive treatment unit

JTAC Joint Terminal Air Controller (the person who calls in air support)

JHQ Joint Headquarters

KIA killed in action

LAD light aid detachment

LAVs light armoured vehicles

LCoH Lance Corporal of Horse

LEWT Light Electronic Warfare Team

LZ Landing zone

MERT Medical Emergency Response Team

MFCs mortar fire controllers

MOG manoeuvre outreach group

MSTAR man-portable Surveillance and Target Acquisition Radar

NVGs night vision goggles

OC Officer Commanding

O Group orders group

OP observation post

Pax personnel

PBs Patrol Bases

PF Pathfinders

PRR personal role radio

PRT Provincial Reconstruction Teams

PWRR Princess of Wales's Royal Regiment – the Tigers

QBOs quick battle orders

QDG The Queen's Dragoon Guards

QRF Quick Reaction Force

R&R rest and recreation

RESA Royal Engineer Search Advisor

RAP regimental aid post

RHA Royal Horse Artillery

RIP relief in place

RPG Rocket-propelled grenade

RRF Royal Regiment of Fusiliers

RSOI reception, staging, onward movement, and integration

SCM Squadron Corporal Major

SF Special Forces

SHQ Squadron Headquarters

SITREP situation report

stag sentry duty

T2s walking wounded

TAC Brigade tactical headquarters

TACSAT secure satellite radio

TIC troops in contact

TNTLS Tactical Navigation and Target Location System (the laser gun sight and raging system for the 30mm cannon and the onboard GPS)

UAVs unmanned aerial vehicles

UKTF United Kingdom Task Force headquarters

UXO unexploded ordnance

VCPs vehicle checkpoints

VPs vulnerable points, or ambush-friendly choke points

Acknowledgements

Many thanks to James's parents, Caroline and Rob, and the rest of James's lovely family for all the help and support they gave in allowing me to tell his story.

I'd also like to thank Shaun Fry for his contribution to the book – I still owe you a drink or three, Shaun!

This book couldn't have been written without Will Pearson – thanks for being on the end of a satellite phone!

As always, my biggest thanks go to Shelley, my wife, and my family for putting up with the grumpy old man ...